PART WILD

One Woman's Journey with a Creature
Caught Between the Worlds of Wolves and Dogs

Ceiridwen Terrill

SCRIBNER

New York   London   Toronto   Sydney   New Delhi

SCRIBNER
A Division of Simon & Schuster, Inc.
1230 Avenue of the Americas
New York, NY 10020

First Scribner hardcover edition October 2011

SCRIBNER and design are registered trademarks of The Gale Group, Inc.,
used under license by Simon & Schuster, Inc., the publisher of this work.

For information about special discounts for bulk purchases,
please contact Simon & Schuster Special Sales at 1-866-506-1949
or business@simonandschuster.com.

The Simon & Schuster Speakers Bureau can bring authors to your live event.
For more information or to book an event, contact the Simon & Schuster Speakers Bureau
at 1-866-248-3049 or visit our website at www.simonspeakers.com.

DESIGNED BY ERICH HOBBING

Manufactured in the United States of America

1   3   5   7   9   10   8   6   4   2

ISBN 978-1-4516-3481-5
ISBN 978-1-4516-3483-9 (ebook)

Some names and details have been changed.

For Inyo

You become responsible, forever, for what you have tamed.
—Antoine de Saint Exupéry, *The Little Prince*

Author's Note

I grew up loving dogs, from the free puppies in a cardboard box outside the 7-Eleven—my mother said no and broke my little-kid heart—to the Welsh corgi of my teenage years, my perfect mimic right down to the resentful glance over one shoulder as we slunk off to my room. Then by chance, at a particularly sad and frightening time in my life, I met an animal labeled "wolfdog" and decided that only a wolfdog could be the kind of companion I was looking for.

Wolfdog breeders believe that introducing a "wild streak" into the dog genome helps to reverse the damage caused by domestication, and produces an animal smarter, stronger, and more independent than a dog. To find out if they're right, I spent five years tracking down geneticists, wolf biologists, and dog trainers. To grasp the differences between wolves and dogs, I turned skulls over in my hands, peered at teeth, studied paw prints in the snow, and trained my telephoto lens on Half-Tail, a young female wolf of the Agate Creek Pack, as she howled to her pack mates. I found clues in genetics, in behavioral studies, and in theories about the origins of the dog. I hopped planes to Texas and Siberia, attended wolf conferences, visited a wildlife forensics lab, and drove dusty back roads to meet breeders and animal-rescue folks.

Right or not, wolfdog breeders wouldn't be in business without buyers drawn to the idea of bonding with a part-wild creature, as if surmounting the difficulties of that kind of relationship—as opposed to simply enjoying the easy one with dogs—will fill a great hole in their hearts. That's why I can't explain wolfdogs' genetics, behavior, or the difficulty of keeping them without revealing the reasons for my own longing and telling the story of my life with a wolfdog.

It's impossible to write about wolfdogs without writing about dogs, the canines designed to be our friends, and about wolves too, the wild creatures who neither need nor want a bond with humans. A book about wolfdogs has to contain it all—the personal desires whetted by myth, political battles in the borderlands where wild ways and human enterprise clash, and the complex and sometimes conflicting scientific studies that seek to expand our knowledge of all the creatures within the genus *Canis*.

Writing a book that combines the personal with science has meant becoming a little like a wolfdog myself: a *zweiweltenkind*—a child of two worlds.

PART WILD

CHAPTER ONE

April Fools

But ask now the beasts, and they shall teach thee.
—Job 12:7

Even in April, Tucson can be chilly in the middle of the night. Shivering in my Blue Space Monkey pajamas, I shifted into first and steered Hanna down Ajo Way toward Leda's housing development, streetlights casting a smoky pink hue over the desert. In the glare of my headlights, a coyote crossed the road. Bad sign in the Navajo tradition. "I'm not Navajo, so it doesn't count," I said, but kissed my fingers and then touched Hanna's dashboard three times just in case.

I'd ignored signs before and been sorry for it—Eddie's thick down-turned brows and sideways look when I went on a coffee date with a girlfriend, and just a few months after we'd started dating, the late-night appearances at my apartment to make sure I wasn't out with another man. "Sorry for waking you," he'd say, the shadow of his Indiana Jones hat large in the porch light. "It's just that I love you so much."

I'd only navigated Leda's subdivision during daylight hours, and now, at 1:30 in the morning, all the houses looked the same. I tried streets named after faraway Tennessee, Virginia, Iowa, and Ohio. "Better get over here," Leda had said on the phone. "They're coming." By the time I found her house and poked my head into the bathroom, one pup, a female, had already been born, and she sucked at a teat. Loop, Leda's wolfdog, lay on rags near a pile of towels and a heating pad, and Leda beckoned me to sit close and watch. Out came another pup, ash gray

1

like her sister. The pups wriggled and squeaked, their flat faces dashed with dark fur under each eye. Like domestic dog puppies, they wouldn't open their eyes for another two weeks, but those black smudges made them appear ready to battle the glare and surprise of the world.

Wolfdog puppies weigh a pound at birth, about the same as dog puppies. Born deaf and blind, and with an undeveloped sense of smell, they rely entirely on touch and taste. The first two pups found their mother's nipples by lifting their heads and moving them side to side. When a teat brushed their tiny black noses, they grabbed and sucked. Leda handed me a dark gray male pup just born, and showed me how to cut and tie the umbilical cord with dental floss. The knot would eventually dry and fall off, she said, placing the pup on a teat.

The fourth and last sac slid out and Loop moaned. This pup had been born fully enclosed. I pinched the amniotic sac with my fingernails, opening it first around the pup's face and then peeling away the rest of the membrane. It was another little female, but she wasn't breathing. Handing me a washcloth, Leda told me to dry the pup to stimulate crying, which was supposed to clear the fluid from her mouth and airway. She still didn't breathe. Leda showed me how to lay the pup flat on her belly in my palm, fingertips supporting her chin. Cupping my other hand over her back, I raised the pup over my head, and with a quick jerking motion, brought my hands toward the floor. The sudden movement cleared out the last of the fluid and allowed air to flow into her lungs. She cried as I stroked her belly and tied off the umbilical cord.

Although this last pup looked just like the others who went about their newborn business, feeding contentedly, she didn't behave like them. She strained against Leda and me as we held her, as if human skin burned to the touch. I placed her on a teat. She skidded down Loop's belly to the floor. I lifted her to another nipple. Again she slid off. The third time I placed my palm under her bum until she got a good grip. Her cries muted as she drank, her face disappearing into Loop's thick belly fur.

I have always loved the creature that struggles. I whispered, "I think she's the one."

CHAPTER TWO

Yearnings

The more I see of man, the more I like dogs.
—Madame de Staël

Two years before Loop gave birth and I chose that little pup for my own, I'd been living with Eddie in a small Texas town. He'd brought me a couple of mixed-breed puppies after the first bruises had shown. So of course I forgave him. He cried into my lap, saying how sorry he was. "I'm just passionate. I can't help it." The routine of feeding and brushing the pups I named Zoe and Jack became a refuge for me, and I was their protector when Eddie yelled at them, cursing their accidents in the house until they squealed and hid under my skirt. But Zoe and Jack were lost to me when I boarded a plane to get away from Eddie and return to my family in Oregon. Eddie called a friend of mine and left a one-liner on her voice mail: "Tell her that I *will* find her, and her dogs are dead."

I called a woman I knew in Eddie's town, but all she could tell me was that the dogs seemed to be gone. I paced the hallway up and down, up and down. *Eddie said they were dead. But maybe they weren't. Maybe he gave them away. What happened?* "What do you mean, *gone*?" I said.

"I'm sorry," the woman said. "I don't know any more."

Leaving my dogs meant failing them, and there was nothing I could do to make it right.

A year after I left Eddie, I enrolled in a graduate program in Tucson and promised myself that I would rescue a dog and keep it safe.

Knowing nothing of wolfdogs, I walked the fluorescent-lighted hallways of the Pima Animal Care Center, the ghosts of Zoe and Jack at my heels, and greeted rows of dogs, rubbing their ears through the wire. Then I heard a low moaning howl from a room at the end of the hall. The door, marked Employees Only, barred entrance to the ward where sick and aggressive and otherwise unadoptable dogs were kept. When no one was looking I wiggled the knob. The door swung open and I slipped inside. The howl had come from a slender-legged creature wearing a grizzle-gray coat, his neck collared by a white ruff, head too big for his skinny body. The card on his cage read "Cochise: male wolfdog hybrid." As a kid I'd read Jack London's *White Fang,* a novel about a wolfdog, but I'd never seen a real wolfdog before.

While the other shelter dogs pawed the chain link, desperate for human touch, Cochise lurked at the back of his cage, keeping as much distance from me as he could. I moved in for a closer look, but he stiffened, hackles pricked, tail high and quivering. I jumped back. His black nails ticked on the cement, a low growl in his throat. I saw the wolf in him, a certain wildness in his yellow eyes, his body hunched and ready to run. Yet when he watched the door, the expectation in his eyes gleamed. He waited for the one person who could touch him, who could lead him out of this place. Who was he, and why had he not come?

As I watched Cochise I felt an extra tenderness toward him, and something broken inside me righted itself. At Eddie's house I'd felt like a prisoner too. Inside the cracked and leaning walls of the adobe, I'd paced the warped pine floors where water pooled when it rained. He would glare if I talked on the phone, alert to any hint that I might be criticizing him. If I took a simple walk, he would yell, "You whore, you went to your other boyfriend's house, didn't you."

I'd been drifting, living out of my backpack and feeling like a failure when Eddie had appeared, a man with his own little construction business and a house he was fixing up to live in. He told me I was the perfect woman for him, pretty and smart. "You're meant to be with me," he'd said. I don't know why I believed him. It was lazy to stitch my life to his because he had the charm and confidence I wanted for myself. I knew how to be independent. At twenty-three I'd worked as a wilderness ranger for the Forest Service, doing six-day stints in the mountains of northern California, shooing black bears from my camp and drinking beer with pot growers who did *not* want to be turned in by no stinking ranger. I'd traveled alone for months in Central America. And yet there I was, a woman with no car, no job, and no friends in that faraway Texas town where voices warbled in the phone lines when the wind blew—wondering what I'd done to make Eddie shatter a coffee cup on the wall next to my head.

Early one morning, months after I'd moved in with Eddie, I called my mother in Oregon and whispered, "I need help," the folds of my nightgown stained with blood. I whispered so Eddie couldn't hear, but also because everything about me, even my voice, had grown tiny.

Now deep into a graduate program in Arizona, making friends again and living well on my own, I felt purposeful and determined. If the person Cochise waited for didn't come, I would get him out of there. I'd become the person he could trust. I stood in front of his cage only a minute more, then slipped out of the room and approached the front desk. "I want to adopt that wolfdog," I said.

The officer shook her head. The shelter's policy prohibited wolf-dog adoption because the animals were considered part wild. Cochise could only be returned to his rightful owner. The man had been contacted, but if he didn't come within seventy-two hours Cochise would be euthanized.

When I told her that I could give Cochise a good home, that I spent every weekend hiking and all summer backpacking in the mountains, the officer said Cochise had been in the pound before. He often roamed the neighborhood and had bitten two people, including a kid trying to pull her cat from his jaws. He would not be adopted out.

I was certain Cochise wandered and struck out because he was frightened. Whenever I knew Eddie would be gone for several hours, I wandered along the broken sidewalks of Tipton Street past Old Town Plaza, stepping aside as mothers hurried their children toward Our Lady of Sorrows, the bells announcing morning service. As I made my way down Market Street to the Brazos River, I hoped none of the shop owners had spotted me. The ones Eddie knew well would report whom I'd spoken to, how long I'd lingered. Ducking under the Brazos

River Bridge, I hiked the trail along the river, counting steps—one, two, three, four—until I reached the edge of town, where meadows rolled out of sight across the interstate. Sometimes I walked along that invisible line for an hour, daring myself to cross the highway and keep going. But my will always slackened, and I counted the steps back to town, *añiles del muerto,* sunflowers of the dead, bobbing their heads above beer cans and empty plastic oil containers. Pigeons scratched the tin roof of the abandoned grain mill where I climbed into the boughs of a sprawling cottonwood. My body cradled there, I touched the tree trunk three times with my fingertips and only then dared to look at the tooth marks on my shoulder. He said it was just rough sex, but it felt like rage to me, especially when he'd caress my neck, fitting his fingers perfectly into the prints he'd made there.

I left the pound without a dog and without Cochise. But the more I thought about adopting him, the fewer laps I made around my apartment, checking and rechecking doors and windows to be sure they were *really* locked and no one could get in. I was braver about taking the garbage out at night, less fearful that Eddie would step out of the shadows, smoking one of his Drum cigarettes: "I told you I'd find you. You're mine."

No, I was not. Cochise would be there. He would walk a circle of protection around me, and if Eddie tried to touch me, Cochise would make him run for his pickup. But there'd be no refuge from my wolf-dog. Cochise would launch his body at the cab, sending Eddie packing forever.

I called the pound the next day and got the automated service menu. Since I couldn't get a human on the horn, I drove to the shelter again, slipping into the quarantine room undetected. Cochise remembered me. His tail hung down and slightly away from his hocks, and his guard hairs lay smooth across his shoulders. Maybe he would understand dog language. I put my body into an upside-down V—palms on the floor, fanny in the air—mimicking a dog's play bow. He responded with a greeting bow of his own and then lay down with his chin on his paws, blinking at me. I imagined that in some way I'd reached him.

I approached the front desk again and received the same answers. No, the owner hasn't returned our calls, and no, you can't adopt him.

Two days later Cochise was gone. "His owner didn't claim him," the officer said. "I'm sorry. It's policy."

I should have pushed harder, demanded to speak to Cochise's owner, to know why he hadn't come. If my family hadn't claimed me, I might still have had Eddie yelling in my face, "You're lucky to be with me, you lost little nothing." My aunt, my cousin, my mother—these women came for me, said I belonged to them and made a way for me to go home. I'd read about La Loba, The Wolf Woman, a strong, healthy woman with a fierce, independent spirit.[1] I wanted to be fierce like that, to stand up for myself and protect the members of my pack. With Cochise gone, I was determined to rescue another wolfdog, to be the pack for the one who had none.

If I couldn't adopt a wolfdog from a shelter, I would find a rescue. I typed "wolfdog rescue" on Yahoo! and more than 28,000 hits popped up, not all for wolfdogs. Many of the listings weren't rescues or adoption agencies at all, but advertisements for exotic pets like bucket-fed, halter-trained zebra colts selling for $8,000: "Reasonable offers considered, or will trade for mid- to high-content intact male wolfdog." Another hit offered veiled chameleons and their cages for $199. There were ads for baby bearded dragons and capuchin monkeys, and animals I'd never heard of, like a cotton-topped tamarin, a small, long-tailed South American monkey, "diaper and leash trained, very loving. Wears baby clothes and sucks his thumb. Likes to lie around and watch TV with you."

Finally I hit on a sanctuary in North Carolina with wolfdogs for adoption. I called and spoke to Marisa, the owner, who asked if I had a place to keep such a large energetic animal. I told her that although my apartment had only a small fenced yard, I spent most of my time hiking and backpacking and would take my wolfdog everywhere.

"I have a real singer for you—his name is Alaska." He was a 150-pound timber wolf–malamute mix, she said, strong and loyal. His howl was the most beautiful sound I would ever hear. "He's very loving, but doesn't trust men," Marisa added. "They abused him."

Perfect, I thought.

In Texas with Eddie I'd dreamed of a Volkswagen camper van with a pop-top, propane stove, and refrigerator. *That van could save me,* I thought. I would sneak away in the middle of the night and drive and drive. After my escape, I'd traded in an old stamp collection and bought Hanna, a twenty-year-old sky-blue VW Westy. Loading her with natural history books and brochures about California's Inyo National Forest, I drove ten hours to the bristlecone pines I'd read about, trees that corkscrew out of the ground, their twisted grain making them better able to withstand a dry climate and unforgiving winds. That first night under the knotted limbs of two-thousand-year-old trees, I read about a young jay's first encounter with a monarch butterfly. Ignoring the dazzling orange and black wings that shout *poison!* the jay eats the butterfly, vomits, and learns the lesson, avoiding all monarchs in the future. I realized that although the reasons for human behavior, particularly my own, had so often eluded me, the natural world made sense. I vowed to be like the jay and avoid my own kind of poison.

Now I could go anywhere and take my wolfdog with me. When Marisa told me that Alaska would bond with me and protect me for the rest of his life, I knew he would have the fierceness of spirit I so wished for myself. We would spend days summiting peaks in the Sierras and the Cascades, descending into cool lake basins at dusk where we'd grow sleepy together around a campfire. I'd have a companion who could keep up with me in the wilderness, the wolf in him able to conquer steep terrain and surging river crossings. At home he would sleep on the bed, all 150 pounds of him sprawled across the mattress. I'd give him all the room he needed and a fridge stockpiled with beef bones. No more checking the doors and windows every ten minutes to be sure they were locked. Alaska would protect me, and I could quit running.

"Just by talking to you I sense you're perfect for this boy," Marisa said, explaining that she was Lakota and Cherokee, which enabled her to see into people and know their true intentions. "I have a spirit feeling that he's the right companion for you."

To guarantee Alaska's adoption, Marisa told me to send a $300 deposit right away. I express-mailed a check that afternoon and told friends about Alaska, the wolfdog companion I would soon fly out from North Carolina. I called Marisa to tell her I had transport for Alaska on United Airlines.

"I have to get the adoption papers together," she said. "Just haven't had time. This place is a zoo and three of my volunteers quit. Don't worry. Alaska is your baby. You'll have him by Christmas."

I waited a week and called again. Marisa told me to be patient, that she would send pictures of Alaska along with the adoption papers. Another week passed. When nothing arrived, I phoned again, and after leaving several messages finally reached her. "We have a slight problem," she said, and explained that Alaska's owner had left him at the rescue three years earlier with the understanding that he was to be kenneled there until she could come back for him. After three years with only sporadic payment for kenneling, Marisa figured Alaska's owner had disappeared for good, so she put him up for adoption to place him in a good home and recoup her costs. But now, out of nowhere, the woman had returned and paid her boarding bill with interest.

"But you didn't say anything about this!" My voice cracked. With the phone cradled against my ear, I paced the apartment, checking the windows to make sure they were locked. I turned clockwise in a circle and then unwound myself. I'd fallen in love with an animal I'd never even met. Alaska was mine and then he wasn't. Why hadn't Marisa told me about his history?

"I'm so sorry," Marisa said. "I really thought she was out of the picture."

When I asked if I could get my deposit back to put toward the adoption fee for another wolfdog, she said, "That's considered a donation to our sanctuary here, and we really appreciate it."

CHAPTER THREE

Voodoo

*No animal should ever jump up on the dining-room
furniture unless absolutely certain that he can hold his own
in the conversation.*

—Fran Lebowitz

Just when I'd decided to forget about wolfdogs, go back to the pound
and rescue a regular dog like a normal person, Heather, a grad school
classmate, called. "We're going to see some wolves," she said. "That'll
cheer you up." She explained that her friend Leda owned wolves and
planned to breed them for a spring litter. I'd wanted to rescue an adult
wolfdog, not buy a puppy, but Heather didn't give me a chance to
decline. "Pick you up in ten," she said.

When her car pulled into the driveway, I locked the door to my
apartment and wiggled the knob to make sure the door was secure.
Before I could step off the doormat, I had to turn in a circle clockwise
and then unwind myself. It was the only way I could feel safe. But I
couldn't let Heather see. How could I tell her that if I didn't do these
circles just right, according to the ritual I'd made up for myself, Eddie
might be waiting for me when I got back? I hadn't told Heather or
anyone about Eddie or his promise to find me no matter where I ran.
A few nights earlier, I'd come home and found a dozen red roses on
my doorstep. The card read Happy Anniversary Sweetheart. Eddie had
found me.

"Hang on a second," I said, and turned my body clockwise toward
her car, completing half the circle. Heather didn't seem to notice, nod-

ding her head to a U2 song on the radio. "Forgot something," I called. "Be right back." I unlocked the door and finished the circle. This was the same circle I'd made in front of the post office box I'd rented in Texas when I'd applied to graduate schools in secret. I checked the box daily, shoving my arm in to the elbow to make sure I hadn't missed a letter wedged at the back. One day I circled right, circled left, inserted the key—and there were three acceptance letters and only one rejection. My magic had worked. Now in the kitchen of my Tucson student apartment, I unwound myself and stepped back outside, careful not to make any clockwise gestures or I'd have to start over. As I climbed into Heather's car, I told myself that Eddie would not be there when I returned. I'd made sure of that.

Heather drove us to a Tucson suburb where the houses sat close together, shrubs pushing through the cracks of thin fences separating each yard. We parked in front of a split-level on a cul-de-sac, and Leda met us at the door, a woman in her early forties wrapped in an orange terry-cloth robe, her cropped blond hair wet and slicked back. She beckoned us through a sliding glass door into the backyard, her bare feet slapping the dirt as she led us to the wolves. From a roofed chain-link kennel, one of the creatures howled. "Meet Voodoo," Leda said, and told us that he was a pure wolf, mostly Mackenzie Valley, a subspecies of gray wolf.[1]

The hair on my arms pricked from the sound. I'd never seen anything like Voodoo. His spine and legs were long, and his tail hung to the ground. His yellow eyes blazed as he studied me. From behind Voodoo, another wolfy-looking creature gave me the once-over and put its nose in the air. Leda introduced us to Loop, a female mix of gray wolf and Siberian husky. Loop was shorter and stockier than Voodoo, and her dark amber eyes contrasted with his gold ones. Both animals had huge paws, their nails clicking on the concrete floor as they paced the length of their kennel, two strides down—their movements liquid and purposeful—two strides back.

As she unwound the loops of chain securing the kennel gate, Leda saw my baffled look at the monster-size padlock. "Wolves and wolf-dogs are clever," she said. "Smarter than regular dogs. Hell, they're smarter than most people." Wolves, she said, had to see something done only one time to know how to do it themselves. "If they watch you unlatch a gate, they'll do it the second your back is turned." She wedged a hip through the opening and Voodoo stood on his hind legs and pawed the air while Loop rubbed her head on Leda's robe. A breeze rolled tufts of fur around my ankles as Leda handed me a leash. We walked the animals into the house where they were allowed social time with people.

Loop paced the living room, jumped on the couch and off again, picked up a sock and trotted into the bathroom. "Forgot to close that door," Leda said when Loop reappeared with a roll of toilet paper. Meanwhile, Voodoo had trotted upstairs and lifted his leg on a rack of magazines. "Damn it, Voodoo! Get down here." He glanced at Leda calmly, turned his back, and disappeared into a bedroom, returning with a pair of her underpants.

Leda shook her head. "You have to be tough with them. Show them you're alpha." Voodoo dropped Leda's panties at the top of the stairwell and flowed down the stairs like quicksilver. From another room, I heard sounds of gunfire and men shouting. "That's my boyfriend, Rich," Leda said, nodding to a tall, bearded man who appeared in the doorway. Rich kneeled on the floor in front of Voodoo and looked him in the eyes, cooing "Good boy. You're such a handsome boy." Voodoo curled his upper lip, exposing teeth evolved to skewer prey and rip hide and muscle.

"Stop that, Rich," Leda said. "You're confusing him by being lower to the ground. You're supposed to be the dominant one. And for God's sakes, don't stare him in the eyes. He might bite your face off."

Rich scrunched his lips as if his shoes were too tight and retreated the way he'd come. The sound of gunfire resumed. "He's such a little boy," Leda said, sighing, "still playing video games. If I don't make his lunch, he'll forget to eat. But what a computer genius—I can't resist him."

Leda served us iced tea while we sat on the couch to look through a stack of photo albums featuring all the wolves and wolfdogs she'd owned over the years. She pointed to a picture of a large white wolf named Kid and identified him as an Ellesmere Arctic, a wolf of Ellesmere Island, the northernmost island in the Arctic Archipelago.[2] She told us that she'd trained Kid for search and rescue work, although he'd never done it professionally. "He liked the training sessions," she said, "but I doubt he would have worked off lead if he wasn't interested in the game." She also showed us pictures of Voodoo's parents and one of his siblings, a female named Grendel, whom she described as bad-tempered and stubborn, nothing like Voodoo or their parents.

Leda explained that people typically crossed wolves with Siberian huskies, Alaskan malamutes, and German shepherds. "You can see the husky in Loop," she said, pointing to Loop's tail, which sometimes curved over her back. "The tails of pure wolves never curl."

Voodoo sidled up to Leda with a lowered body posture and tried to lick her mouth. "He'd never let anybody hurt me," she said, stroking his head. "Wolves know who belongs in their pack and who doesn't." She told us she felt safe with Voodoo around, that if an intruder broke into the house, Voodoo would never let him out. She described his massive jaw strength, 1,500 pounds per square inch, twice as much as a German shepherd's. "I'd come home and scrape a dead burglar off the floor."

We sipped our tea and watched Loop and Voodoo circle the coffee table and climb up and down the stairs. Voodoo peed on a potted rubber plant. "That's it," Leda said. "Enough visiting. Out." She walked Voodoo to the kennel, then returned to wipe up the urine with a wad of paper towels. As she mopped the floor, she told us she was going to let Loop and Voodoo breed. Dogs can have puppies when they're still practically puppies themselves, Leda told us, but wolves usually don't mature sexually until they're something like twenty-two months old.[3] Voodoo was about to turn three, and two-year-old Loop would soon come into her first heat. "I'm dying to see the pups these guys throw," she said. "Both of them are so good-natured I know the pups will come out gorgeous and sweet-tempered."

She went on to tell us that because Voodoo was pure wolf and Loop was 75% wolf, their puppies would be 87.5% wolf. She called this calculation the "pedigree method," and explained the basic arithmetic, simply averaging the percentage of wolf heritage in the parents. Loop's puppies would be what Leda referred to as "high-content wolfdogs." "They'll be a handful," she said, "but worth the effort."

Much later I would learn that this "pedigree method" and the "wolf content" derived from it are unreliable in predicting the amount of wolfiness in a litter of wolfdog puppies. Depending on their ancestry, even puppies within the same litter may vary widely in appearance, temperament, and behavior. Still, breeders like to advertise a percentage of "wolf content" in the puppies they sell, with a premium on "high-content" animals.

When I told Leda about my failed rescue of Cochise, describing him as a wolf hybrid, she corrected me, saying that the term "hybrid" was wrong. "Dogs and wolves are the same species," she said. "A dog is just the dumbed-down version." For Leda, domestication had ruined a perfectly good animal—the wolf—which had degenerated from a kind of super canine to a dopey and dependent dog. To reverse the damage, the logical thing to do was to breed the wolf back in.[4] I wondered but didn't ask: *Why, if wolves and dogs were the same species, did they behave so differently?*

Though most European scientists consider the domestic dog a separate species, in 1993, the Smithsonian Institute and the American Society of Mammalogists reclassified the domestic dog from a distinct species, *Canis familiaris*—the familiar canine—to *Canis lupus familiaris*, adding *lupus* or "wolf" to the name and making Fido a subspecies of gray wolf. The reclassification of the dog has enjoyed increasing popularity as a result, in part, of studies that show that mitochondrial DNA (genetic material inherited from the mother), is strikingly similar, almost identical in wolves and dogs. Of course, mitochondrial DNA is only part of the genetic picture. Nuclear gene information, when it becomes available, will provide a more complete ancestral profile.[5]

But morphologists, who study the structure of animals, would say that dogs and wolves are different. While northern breeds like the husky and the malamute may look wolfy on the outside, the differences in skull shape and dimension are significant, and so are the differences in body structure, eyes, paws, teeth, coat, and ears.

Evolutionists would argue that while dogs and wolves share a common ancestor, as do wolves and coyotes, that doesn't mean Fido is necessarily the *direct* descendant of the wolf, and certainly not of the *modern* wolf. As a scientist who studies animal behavior, ethologist

Ádám Miklósi points out that while genetic data shows that the gray wolf is the nearest *living* relative of the dog, it is not likely a *direct* ancestor.[6] Instead, the wolf and the dog probably share a common ancestor, making them what biologist and dog behaviorist Jan Koler-Matznick calls "sister species."[7] Geneticist Bridgett vonHoldt explained it to me this way: "The most recent common ancestor of the modern-day wolf and modern-day dog was neither a wolf nor a dog. I think the problem is that when we think about evolutionary history and call this ancient animal a 'wolf,' we automatically think of a modern-day wolf. People tend to forget how evolution works."

Various scientific specialties have different ways of distinguishing a species but they don't provide much support for Fido's reassignment. On the other hand, the good old BSC (biological species concept)— the one most of us were taught in high school—may apply a little *too* well. My sophomore biology teacher Mrs. Rudfelt gave the example of a jackass mating with a mare to produce the sterile mule. These animals were of two different species, she said, because if they mated, their offspring would be sterile. Wolves and dogs can interbreed and produce fertile offspring, so they must be the same species, right? The problem is, coyotes and wolves, whose lineages diverged 1.8–2.5 million years ago, can do it too. In fact, *all* species within the genus *Canis* can interbreed and produce fertile offspring.[8] Scientists sometimes refer to the whole lot as *Canis soupus*. But joking aside, since not even American scientists would lump all members of the genus *Canis* into a single species, or suggest, for example, that the coyote is a subspecies of gray wolf, why do they make a special case for the dog and the wolf?

Carolus Linnaeus, the eighteenth-century Swedish botanist who devised the Latin naming system for plants and animals, would be amazed that American scientists are tampering with his designation *Canis familiaris* some 250 years later. He would have agreed with modern ecologists who point out that dogs and wolves don't occupy the same niche. Wolves live in the wild. Dogs live with people. End of discussion. In 1758, when he named the dog the "familiar canine," the canine people are friends with, Linnaeus used as a species-defining distinction the dog's quality of being domestic—its ability to befriend and serve people. Biologists and dog trainers Ray and Lorna Coppinger are blunt about it: "A dog is not a wolf, no matter what you call it." And although they may not want to admit it, wolfdog owners like Leda, and later me, often rely on the doggy part of their animals to help the wolfy part settle into a domestic environment.

Sitting in Leda's living room that afternoon, I knew nothing about the reclassification debate and very little about the differences between wolves and dogs. Voodoo and Loop, both born and raised in captivity, were very friendly but didn't seem very domestic or doglike to me. They didn't care what we were doing. They were busy exploring every nook and cranny of the house. But the truth is, I liked them despite their bad house manners.

"Dogs are human perversions of the wolf," Leda said, ice cubes cracking as they melted in her glass. She wrinkled her nose in disdain. "They're developmentally retarded. They grovel and love you even if you beat them. A wolf would never put up with that. You'd be dead."

I wanted to be like a wolf and fight back when someone tried to hurt me. At the clinic in Texas a nurse had said, "You have bruises on your inner thighs. Dark purple marks." She held up a mirror between my legs. "It looks like someone bit you. Anything you want to say about that?"

Nodding toward Loop who was pulling books off the shelf and shredding pages, Leda said, "They're friendly, but they still have a wild streak." She scooped up the books and told us a story about the time she'd heard scratching on the asphalt shingles and thought all the mourning doves in Tucson had descended on her roof. When she went outside to see what the fuss was about, she discovered that Loop had chewed her way out of the kennel, climbed an old wood pile next to the house, and from the peak of the roof howled down to Leda.

"You can't control them," Leda said, "and I love that."

Leda wasn't the only one attracted to the idea of a wild streak. When friends asked why I wanted a wolfdog, I would say that only a wolfdog had the strength and endurance to keep up with me on wilderness backpacking trips. But there was more to it than that. Their wildness would make them aloof and wary, I thought. Unlike dogs, and unlike me, they couldn't be charmed by some sweet-talking stranger. Their trust would have to be earned with patience and hard work, but in return I'd have a wolfdog's loyalty and protection.

Leda poured more tea. "Heather told me about that wolfdog you tried to adopt from North Carolina. I don't think he ever existed. That woman just took your money." Adopting a wolfdog on the Internet was a bad idea, she said, and I'd be better off getting a wolfdog puppy to bond with. "If you socialize them when they're young, they'll defend you to the death. And you should really meet the parents to know what you're getting into. What you see is what you get."

At the time I wondered why Leda emphasized the importance of meeting the parents when she'd just finished telling me that Voodoo's sister Grendel was ornery and *nothing* like her parents. I would come to realize that contradictory assertions like this were common among wolfdog owners.

Loop stretched and yawned and trotted toward the kitchen. Through the entryway I could see her counter-surfing for scraps, her black nose sucking scents like a mini-vac along the lip of the counter.

"You can have one of their puppies if you want," Leda said. "I plan to sell them for a few hundred dollars, but I'll give you one for the cost of its first shots."

How could I, in good conscience, accept a wolfdog puppy? I'd committed myself to the idea of rescue—if not a wolfdog from a sanctuary, then a dog from the pound. But maybe Leda was right and a wolfdog bonded to me at birth would be unconditionally loyal.

"It takes a special person to raise a cub," Leda said, rising to shoo Loop from the kitchen where she'd just peed on a pile of clean laundry.

My resolve was wearing thin, but I had to think. I couldn't be rash. What was I getting myself into, raising a wolfdog puppy? On the other hand, I'd never trusted anything that came too easily.

"Wolves and wolfdogs are hard to rear," she said. "But I'm around, so you'll have help."

As Leda mopped up the urine and reloaded the washing machine, she told me that unlike female dogs, which can breed semiannually, female wolves and "high-content" wolfdogs come into estrus only once each year. Male dogs are able to mate year-round, whereas male wolves produce sperm seasonally, with peak levels between December and March.

Wild wolves time their reproductive activities to make certain pups are born in the springtime when the weather is mild and there's plenty of food. Cubs need the ensuing summer months to gain strength before winter. In the far north, breeding time may come as late as April, so when the pups are born after a sixty-three-day gestation period, it may be early June already. In more temperate climates—and in places like Arizona, which are even warmer—wolves may mate in the latter part of January or early February, and give birth to five or six pups, a common litter size. That's what Leda was counting on.

"If Loop and Voodoo mate in February, we should have pups in April," she said. "And you'll have a wolfdog before you know it."

"Okay," I said, "I want one."

CHAPTER FOUR

Voodoo Child

*The day came when the risk to remain tight in the bud was
more painful than the risk it took to blossom.*

—Anaïs Nin

While I counted the weeks until April, Eddie sent more roses to my
Tucson apartment and left phone messages at home and at school. I
ignored these overtures, but when the messages became threatening I
filed a restraining order against him and checked and rechecked the
windows of my apartment, slamming the door against the slightest
shadow or crunch of quick feet in gravel. Eddie counter-filed, claiming
I'd made false accusations against him and was harassing him. A Texas
judge ordered me to appear in court, meaning travel to that state and a
face-to-face encounter with Eddie. My lawyer friend held a teleconfer-
ence with the judge and convinced him to rescind the order to appear.
The judge said that unless we both wanted to go to jail, there would be
no contact between Eddie and me.

No problem.

And then I met Ryan. When I first laid eyes on him, he was flipping
burgers at a friend's barbecue and laughing so hard his jaw seemed to
unhinge. I thought he must be crackbrained. When we talked he had
a bad case of the jimjams, unable to stand still for a minute or look me
in the eye, his glance skimming my face and flitting away. Terribly shy,
I decided, but not cracked at all and very smart. As I got to know this
lean, muscular rock climber with black hair trimmed in an Ivy League,

21

thickly-lashed blue eyes, and tattoos on each arm—an illustration from a Pablo Neruda poem and a praying mantis—I couldn't help being attracted. After all, he was the opposite of Eddie—gentle and outdoorsy, and he didn't have to roll a cigarette the minute we stepped into the woods. "Meet me at my crib at eight o'clock," he said one night, surprising me with a pair of climbing shoes and a matching purple harness. I picked him up the next morning and we drove the Mount Lemmon Highway, Hanna sputtering up the winding road to a jut of rocks called Green Slabs. At the base of a climb known as Monkey Business, I strapped on my harness and learned to tie a figure eight with one end of the climbing rope, following the smooth line twice for a double knot. Ryan taught me the climber's first rule: Never stand on the rope. Every time you did—shortening the life span of that cord and possibly a climber—you owed your partner a beer.

"You're on belay," he said, my signal to start up the rock face because he had both hands on the rope and would catch me if I fell.

"Climbing," I said, using the proper etiquette before starting out.

"Climb on."

When I'd scaled up fifteen feet, my leg stabbed the rock like a sewing-machine needle. Ryan called it the Elvis Leg. "Rock it to the left," he called up to me. "Put some weight on that foot. I've got you."

My fingers, crimped on a tiny ledge of rock, began to go numb from mid joint to tip. Then my toe slipped and I lost my footing, kneecaps slamming into a crag. Ryan held his grip on the rope. "See? I've got you," he said, and I fell in love with him that instant, dangling from a rope over a wide sweep of ocotillo limbs, the whole city of Tucson shimmering below.

After rappelling off Monkey Business, we slid off our tight climbing shoes and lay side by side on a warm slab of granite, gazing at the wall we'd just climbed. For the many times I'd stepped on the rope I owed Ryan at least two six-packs.

"Do you have a boyfriend?" he asked, reaching for my hand.

I didn't.

"Do you want one?"

*　*　*

I wore my climbing bruises like merit badges—knees red as cherry tomatoes and full of heat—and called my mother to tell her the news: I was in love with a good man this time, and I was getting a special kind of dog, a wolfdog.

She ignored the love part of my announcement. I'd made this declaration before and she'd had to rescue me. Perhaps the thought of going through another salvage operation made her tired, so she skipped the congratulations.

"Why don't you get yourself a nice big dog to take on your nature walks?" she said.

"I don't take *nature* walks, I trek in the wilderness. No dog can handle that kind of terrain and mileage."

"But wolves are wild animals. I don't even know if it's legal to keep one."

"She's a wolfdog," I said, "and she's not wild. Besides, I don't plan to advertise the fact that she's part wolf."

Leda had advised me against it. To everyone, including the veterinarian, Inyo would be introduced as a husky mix. She would need all her shots, and the ongoing debate over the use of the rabies vaccine in wolves and wolfdogs might cause a vet to refuse to give it to her.[1] And as a wolfdog, if she ever bit someone, Leda warned, she would likely be destroyed—even if she was vaccinated. In Tucson, wolfdogs, though legal to own, were considered wild, and when picked up by animal control they were often euthanized. Leda also cautioned that neighbors, fearing for their pets and children, might hassle me for keeping a wolfdog and call the authorities. "Everyone fears the big, bad wolf," she said.

I told my mother that wolfdogs made wonderful companions, and that, according to Leda, they provided better protection than some domestic dogs.

She sighed, knowing she couldn't talk me out of it.

Ryan never tried. We'd been sitting at his kitchen table drinking coffee when he'd suddenly said, "I deal with depression," and winced as if waiting for me to run for my life. When I didn't bolt, he told me medication kept the depression under control so there was really nothing to worry about. I had my problems too—who didn't?—and I could help Ryan, I thought, when Prozac couldn't do all the work. I smiled and told him it was okay, and his shoulders relaxed. After that, he wasn't about to question any decision I might make. He said he was excited to meet my new pup.

At three days old, the tiny wolfdog I named Inyo began to find her legs. She and her siblings wobbled, then crawled blindly forward along the linoleum of Leda's bathroom. They thumped against the baseboards, collapsed, and pulled themselves up again. If they happened upon our outstretched hands, we petted them eagerly, but each one turned away. We were warm, but not quite right, and they continued searching with their tongues for the familiar smell and touch of their mother.

During my daily visits to Leda's house I handled Inyo as much as possible so she would know my smell. Leda explained that wolfdog puppies should be handled by their future owners when they're just a few days old and bond with them exclusively at four weeks. "If you don't socialize them early," she said, "they'll be too skittish, and you'll never get a decent companion out of them." Inyo's eyes would open when she was about ten days old, and then she would have two weeks more to be with her siblings and mother before going home with me.

Some wolf and wolfdog owners believe that puppies should be removed from their mother when they're a few days old to increase their chances of bonding to a person rather than to a wolf or wolfdog parent. But Leda didn't believe in taking them from their mother so early that they would require bottle-feeding. "It's unnatural," she said. "Loop will let us handle the pups while she nurses them, so we're sharing the bonding experience. Those pups will see us as members of their pack and won't be shy of people." Leda also told me that the puppies needed the antibodies from Loop's milk to build immunity against disease. "I don't care what kind of formula you give them—nothing's better than the mother's milk. I've heard too many horror stories about wolfdogs blinded with cataracts because some dumb-ass decided to play mommy and bottle-feed. If you want to nurse and bottle-feed," she said, "then have your own baby."

While her siblings bumped their noses against the porcelain pedestal of the toilet and withdrew to the fluff and warmth of Loop's belly, Inyo ventured beyond the bathroom, all elbows and squeaks when lifted and put back on the heating pad. Each time I visited, her teeth were sharper as she champed on my thumbs and fussed. I lay on the couch in the living room and held her to my chest, stroking her back and ears and rubbing the fur on her neck. She nibbled my chin and licked my nose, then tried to climb over the back of the sofa. She was gaining her balance and pushing more ground behind her. At twelve days old, with eyes wide open, she went hell-for-leather to explore the living room by herself.

When I took Ryan to Leda's for a visit, Inyo nibbled his chin and climbed onto his shoulder like a cat. He caught her before she took a dive off the back of the sofa. He liked her energy, he said. She couldn't sit still any more than he could. Whenever I visited Inyo, Ryan wanted to go, and we spent whole afternoons playing with puppies.

As Inyo learned to walk, her mother practiced her jumping skills. Leda put Loop in the backyard kennel to give her a break from the pups, and less than five minutes later she heard shouting next door. Loop had figured out how to escape the kennel and scale the seven-foot fence to the neighbor's yard, where she attacked his dog. The neighbor, attempting to break up the tangle of fur and teeth, was bitten when he dove into the ruckus, but he couldn't be sure if Loop or his own dog had done the biting. "I don't know what I'm going to do," Leda said. "I'll probably get evicted again."

Again?

Leda insisted that Loop wasn't vicious, had never done anything like that before, and was simply being protective of her pups. Territorial behavior was natural for wolves and "high-content" wolfdogs. "Now you get why I tell people Loop is a husky mix," she said. "If I had admitted that she was part wolf, Loop might be dead now."[2]

Loop's jaws had sheered the dog's hamstring and nearly torn its throat out. Leda placated the neighbor with plates of Hot Pockets and paid all the vet bills. Fortunately, the neighbor's dog lived and Loop's "husky-mix" identity went unchallenged.

While that mess got sorted out, Leda sold two of the other puppies for $350 each. When one female puppy besides Inyo remained and the phone quit ringing, Leda said, "Why don't you take two? You'll have to get a second wolfdog anyway." She explained that Inyo would need another wolfdog for a companion so she wouldn't get lonely. A regular dog would bore her.

After witnessing the damage Loop could do, I declined the offer. Inyo would be plenty, and it was time to take my Voodoo child home.

CHAPTER FIVE

Homecoming

"But I don't want to go among mad people," Alice remarked.
"Oh, you can't help that," said the Cat; "We're all mad
here."

—Lewis Carroll, *Alice's Adventures in Wonderland*

I eased Inyo into the dog crate I'd bought at PETCO and loaded her onto Hanna's backseat. "Call if you need anything," Leda said, and waved us off. Away from her mother and siblings for the first time, Inyo howled and whimpered. I glanced in the rearview mirror and sang "You Are My Sunshine." I would get her out of that crate just as soon as we got home. She didn't like being cooped up, and I didn't blame her. I didn't like it either. Eddie had told me he had to keep me close or I might disappear, shaming him in front of everyone. Although I had not heard from Eddie, and never would again, every night I dreamed that I was trapped inside the adobe, all the windows and doors locked from the outside. Even the nights Ryan stayed over, I sometimes woke shouting and smacked my head on the bookshelf as I grabbed for the light switch. Ryan always stroked my hair until I could fall asleep again.

I shifted into third and Hanna putted up Speedway. Inyo stopped howling, and I twisted around in my seat to see her looking back at me with cloudy blue eyes that would turn amber or yellow in her tenth week. She pressed her nose to the wire to inhale the world she was entering for the first time. Good girl. That's it, girl. Almost there. In that moment I knew I would put all of myself into this tiny creature.

27

When I was ten my mother told me, "Men will always leave you. They die on you or treat you like shit, then walk out your door." The one who died was my father. I was five. The one who walked out was Ray. I don't remember how many times he left before it was forever. My mother says three or four times in the six years they were together, but it felt like he was always going. When they fought I would lie on my bed and count the tiny cracks in the ceiling—one, two, three—and tell myself that by the time I finished they'd be done yelling because I'd made them stop. If they didn't, it meant that I'd missed a crack and would have to start over. But sometimes my mother's voice reached me before I could finish: "Get in the car!" That was the signal that Ray had packed his Samsonite and gunned his Toyota Corolla up Jack Street. My mother just wouldn't let him go. We'd have to chase him down.

I didn't want Ray to go either, even though he made a permanent depression in the living-room couch while watching football, and when I came home from school, he'd say, "Kid, you're cruisin' for a bruisin'." Other times he played the pull-the-finger fart game and taught me to do chin-ups on his biceps. He wanted me to be a strong girl, he said, able to defend myself from bullies.

On the nights he took off, we sometimes found him in the Sentry Market parking lot spooning Häagen-Dazs chocolate chocolate chip from the carton, and my mother could coax him home. If Ray's mood had improved, he might even share the rest of his ice cream with me. Although he said there was nothing between my ears but a hard wind blowing, when he was in one of his good moods he would tell me he didn't really mean it, that I was clever for my age, and strong, and he wouldn't sell me at the little girls' market after all. I tried to figure out what I'd done to make Ray say I was smart, to make him put his suitcase back in the closet. Then he was gone for good, my mother had the couch reupholstered, and I gave up on families.

Now in my twenties, I wanted to belong to a pack and thought Inyo and I could be a pack of two.

I took my hand off the gearshift at a red light and Hanna popped out of first with a *bang!* and a lurch, another one of Hanna the Vanna's quirks. She would be the adventure wagon for Inyo and me—and

28

maybe Ryan too, if things worked out. I kissed my fingers and touched Hanna's dashboard three times. I was the jay again, and this time I wouldn't forget.

I parked in the driveway and carried the dog crate into the kitchen, but when I opened the door, Inyo wouldn't come out. She plastered her body to the rear of the crate and growled. Easy, girl. Easy. I cooed to her and then cradled her belly in my palm and tried to scoot her forward. She sank her milk teeth into the soft flesh between my forefinger and thumb. I hollered with surprise and pain, and rolled the four-week-old girl-pup onto her back the way Leda had told me to. "You have to be alpha," she'd said. Sometime between her fifteenth and twenty-eighth week, Inyo would lose those milk teeth, what biologists refer to as "deciduous teeth" for their quality of falling out or shedding, and I pushed away the thought of the permanent teeth that would replace them.

Inyo fussed and kicked, but I kept my hand firmly on her belly until she relaxed, then let her up. In a second she bounded out of the crate and unraveled the stitching in my sock. I clamped my hand over her muzzle and uttered a low growl. "No bite," I said. She reared backward, crossing her paws over my forearm, and tried to twist out of my hand. "You're an ornery chunk." I did another alpha roll, putting her on her back the way the Monks of New Skete described in *How to Be Your Dog's Best Friend*. With one hand on Inyo's belly and the other on her throat, I held her until she settled. When I let go, she knitted her wolfy brow but seemed to understand, at least for the moment, that my body parts were off-limits. Instead, she bit the chair leg. I slipped a toy squirrel between her jaws, and she bit down on the Squeeze Me sticker. The *tchirring* kept her rapt for two minutes until she eviscerated the plush toy and dug out the squeaker. Then she abandoned the fur pile for dead and tugged on the couch skirt.

Years later I would learn that adult wolves are very gentle with their pups. At the most active times of their day, dawn and twilight, wolf pups tear around the den site, chewing, shaking, and shredding whatever they like, even biting and tugging on their parents' ears and tails. Adult wolves do *not* roll pups over to discipline them, or pin them down and growl aggressively until they submit.

By three weeks of age wild wolf pups eat meat regurgitated by adult wolves. The pups provoke regurgitation by "licking up," nudging an adult's mouth and chin. The closest I had come to regurgitating for Inyo was when I gnashed a piece of cooked chicken or steak, and then spit it out for her. Now she was ready for something more substantial. I dug through the refrigerator for a knucklebone and boiled it for her. As the pot hissed and the hunk of bone knocked against the sides of the saucepan, the air smelled of iron and boiling fat. Inyo wiggled her black nose, curious at the scent. Then, suddenly fearful, she darted from the kitchen to hide under the bed. When the bone cooled I plunked it down in her blue ceramic bowl. "Inyo girl!" I called to her in a singsong voice, and she crept from under the bed toward the kitchen, lunging and growling at the thing in the bowl, prancing around to see whether the animal might try to bite her. Then she bounded into the living room and hid behind the couch, peering out, jabbing her nose skyward to sniff the air. After a few moments, she crept back toward her bowl, alert for cues of danger. In the kitchen doorway she glanced at me and then back at the bone. Seeing that it hadn't moved or attempted escape, she pounced, mouthing it until she got a grip and then slinking into the living room to gnaw in private.

Even though Leda had said that a wolfdog's adult behavior is shaped solely by the way the animal is raised, I knew that genetics mattered—though at the time I didn't grasp how much—and that when shaping canine personality and behavior, *every* experience counted. At three weeks of age, when a domestic dog's eyes and ears become alert to the happenings of the world, a window to the dog's psyche is thrown open until the animal is three or four months old. During that time, experiences positive and negative will influence the dog's adult personality and behavior. Determined to take advantage of any window that might open for Inyo, I introduced her to new people so she wouldn't be shy around strangers, taking her for short car trips to Trader Joe's for groceries and bike rides around the neighborhood in the handlebar basket of my cruiser. Safely tucked inside my shirt (one of the few places she remained still), Inyo took in Speedway traffic with its motorcycles and buses, honks and shouts. We entered and exited buildings, rode elevators and escalators, and walked along noisy streets to and from school.

Just as I tried to do everything perfectly with Inyo, I'd decided that if I was going to have a serious boyfriend, then everything had to be right with him too. He needed more self-confidence, I thought, but it certainly didn't help that he had a larger-than-life version of himself in his twin brother, Reece, whose imposing height and big bones made him look like he'd been suckled on beef and milk. Reece had been treated like the more competent child in the family, whereas Ryan had been the butt of jokes about his absentmindedness—his tendency to lose his keys and to wear mismatched socks. As an adult Reece had earned a doctorate and published a book, landing himself a professorship. Even though Ryan had completed a master of fine arts and worked as a line cook while earning his teaching certificate, he saw himself as a failure compared to his brother. I loved his ingenuity in the backcountry, his poetry and wit, and most of all his gentleness. The one thing that bothered me was his habit of blowing off a work shift when an opportunity to climb came up. But I figured that now, having just earned his teaching certificate, he'd take an interest in his work. Besides, how many boyfriends would write me a poem on a Fry's grocery bag and tape it to the front door of my apartment?

> C. makes a difference because she loves me and
> has made me a healthy soul.
> She makes a difference because she talks to animals
> she doesn't even know.
> She knows what good wine is
> but doesn't mind drinking the cheap stuff.

To make sure that our relationship was the healthiest it could be, I'd instituted weekly check-ins. Ryan and I were each to write down anything bothering us. Then we would air out problems on a Wednesday afternoon at Bentley's, a coffee shop on East Speedway—never in bed and never at either one of our apartments. Check-ins would ensure that we never quarreled like my mom and Ray and never developed resentments that might make Ryan boil over and abandon me. But usually I was the only one to have something to say on those Wednesdays. Often Ryan hadn't even written his check-in letter. I badgered him—how were we supposed to make this relationship the best it could be if he didn't share his feelings?

CHAPTER SIX

Tug-of-War

"And now," cried Max, "let the wild rumpus start!"
—Maurice Sendak, *Where the Wild Things Are*

I took Inyo everywhere—that is, until Tucson became so hot I had to wear oven mitts to hold Hanna's steering wheel. At seven weeks old, Inyo was too big for her crate so I blocked the kitchen doorway with a baby gate borrowed from my neighbor. A small kitchen with a linoleum floor seemed like the safest room to leave a wolfdog puppy unsupervised for a short time.

After a fifteen-minute trip to the bank, I came back to find Inyo crouched in a heap of potting soil, her nose speckled with white balls of perlite. She'd shredded the philodendron I kept in the kitchen corner. How could I have been so careless? Philodendron can be deadly to dogs, making their throats swell until they're unable to swallow. Surrounded by tattered leaves and dirt, I sank to the floor and watched Inyo for the slightest hint of distress, any sign that I should load her into the van and race to the vet. With soil between her toes she pounced on the perlite balls as if they were bugs, delighted and not the least bit sick. I swept up the mess while Inyo chased the broom.

The next time I had to run an errand, I kept Inyo in the kitchen with only her toys to chew. When I came home I felt like a forensic scientist at a crime scene. Inyo had peeled the linoleum back in one corner of the kitchen and chewed the corners off the cupboard doors to get under the sink. If her smaller, temporary teeth could take apart a cupboard door, what would her permanent set do?

A bottle of Goo Gone had been gnawed in half and the kitchen reeked of Windex and Murphy Oil Soap. The bottle of Murphy's lay on the floor, yellow oil burbling through a puncture in the plastic. Estimated time of death—five minutes ago. But Inyo was not in the kitchen. The baby gate was still up, so where was she? I stepped over the gate, a good twenty-nine inches tall, and followed a trail of Ajax powder and furniture wipes into the living room.

Inyo was as precocious as a pure-wolf pup whose locomotor skills mature much faster than those of dogs. Psychologists Harry and Martha Frank compared the development of malamute pups to wolf cubs and found that at nineteen days old the wolves were so coordinated and curious that they easily scaled the nearly eighteen-inch walls of their pens to explore the world. The malamutes at thirty-two days old couldn't climb over a six-inch barrier and rarely bothered trying. In the Franks' description, they "waddled around the barriers like so many fuzzy, animated soccer balls." If I'd had that little piece of information at the time, I wouldn't have been so surprised to find my living room looking like a frat house, with long ribbons of toilet paper draping the furniture.

I heard rustling from the bathroom and kicked aside half-chewed rolls of toilet paper, the green Ajax canister, and pairs of my dirty underwear and T-shirts Inyo had pulled from the hamper. Sucking in a deep breath, I peered around the bathroom door. All I could see was a grayish-blond butt and a bushy tail so long it nearly touched the floor. Inyo hadn't heard me come in. She was deep into her mission of ripping a Kotex pad. Tubes of toothpaste and bars of oatmeal soap were strewn on the floor, and she'd shredded my loofah sponge into mini-loofahs. When I approached, she didn't drop the pad, but looked up at me, a gurgle in her throat. *Mine, mine!*

And Leda had told me I needed two of these little creatures?

When I reached to take the pad away, Inyo's grumbling got louder. "No growl!" I said. She dropped the Kotex, punctured the back of my hand, and bounded for the bedroom.

After I cleaned up, throwing all the busted bottles in the trash and salvaging rolls of toilet paper that weren't soaked in saliva, I gathered what was left of the cleaning supplies to stow on top of the refrigerator.

Inyo trotted after me into the kitchen, playfully nipping at my ankles. *Fun! More fun!*

A few days later she declared a knock-down-drag-out with the kitchen table. She tipped it over, along with a stack of cassettes holding the interviews I'd done for my master's thesis, and dragged the tablecloth into the living room where she unspooled each tape ribbon. How could I have been so careless, leaving things within her reach? I hand-wound what tape I could, rotating the spokes on each cassette with my finger. Having already transcribed most of what I needed, I threw the tapes in a box and hefted them onto the closet shelf.

In the mornings, I crouched down in greeting with a wedge of apple, her favorite fruit, in my teeth. She would bound up to me, tail wagging, and lick the apple from my mouth. Before the hot, dry winds whistled through the saguaros we would chase each other around the paloverde tree in the yard. Inyo pranced in the dust, play-bowed, and sprang on my toes. I shrieked and jumped away when her milk teeth stabbed my flesh. Sometimes I'd curl into a ball, hide my face, and whine while she nosed and pawed, trying to dig me out. *You! Come out, no crying!* When she tired of these games, I could pick her up and snuggle her in the crook of my arm. I relished the moments she was too exhausted to fuss. Only then could I pet her the way I would a dog. Sometimes she would even roll over on her back at my feet, what Leda had described as a submissive gesture. "She's acknowledging you as alpha," she said one day on the phone. "Good job. Whatever you're doing is working."

CHAPTER SEVEN

Circus Circus

Keep your eyes wide open before marriage, and half-shut afterwards.

—Benjamin Franklin

Ryan asked me to marry him. Well, sort of. One warm evening in mid-May we sat on the floor of my living room, Inyo gnawing Ryan's toes, and wrote our personal goals on index cards. I thought that if most of our aspirations matched, it was a sign we were compatible. Mine was a bullet-point list. His was a messy cluster that ran over the edges of his card. But we both wanted marriage, animals, and a home of our own. Ryan wrote: "Would she marry me?" We hadn't been together long, but I'd be leaving Tucson with Inyo to start a Ph.D. program and a graduate teaching assistant position in Nevada that fall, and if I wanted him to uproot himself and come with me, he wanted to be married.

At twenty-eight I already felt old and thought this might be my last chance. I preferred to be engaged and live together for at least a year, but I pushed the door shut on the mousy voice that said to wait. I did want to marry Ryan, didn't I? Now or a year from now, what was the difference? My mother said that if I wanted her to plan the wedding in my home city of Portland, we'd better get it over with that summer because she was moving to the Southwest. That erased the last of my doubts. She took charge of the wedding, scheduled for August. Ryan began applying for teaching jobs in Reno where we'd be moving before the wedding, and I reserved a U-Haul truck for the second week of June. Along with ten-week-old Inyo, a stuffed U-Haul, and Hanna the

Vanna, we'd be on the road with Ryan's parrot, Lupe, a Sun Conure whose screech was as loud as his orange and green feathers.

Packing was easy. Inyo had reduced my clothing inventory to two pairs of jeans, one pair of quick-dry hiking shorts, and three T-shirts. I had two pairs of shoes left, my flip-flops and my hiking boots, minus the laces she'd chewed to saliva-soaked nubbins. Although I kept my shoes in the closet, the door was thin and she'd splintered it with her teeth to reach the musty leather. All my sweaters had snags and large holes. I put them in a box to use as rags. To my mother's disappointment, I'd never really cared much about clothing or shoes or makeup anyway. I wanted to be natural. As a teenager I'd allowed my eyebrows to grow together and refused to shave my legs. "You're such a pretty girl," my mother would say, sighing. "Why do you go out of your way to make yourself so unattractive?"

"I like the feeling of the wind in my hair," I'd announced, and rubbed my furry shins. Now, although I wanted a home of my own and did occasionally shave my legs, the only material possessions I cared about were books and personal journals. But I couldn't seem to get across to Inyo the difference between what was mine and what was hers, no matter how many times I said "No!" and swapped out one of my books for a marrowbone. Once we settled into a new living situation, I planned to get a better handle on how to keep my things out of her mouth.

Her early fear of the knucklebone had been replaced by a desire to explore whatever was new. Inyo was getting to know the world through her mouth—licking the hand of a homeless woman, gnawing a skate punk's board. She was a go-with-the-flow creature, a free spirit I was learning from. Inyo's craving for the unfamiliar was a welcome change from my need for predictability, the compulsion I felt to control everything in my life with check-in letters and clockwise circles, unwinding myself when no one was looking. For our long-distance trek I made a bumper sticker for Hanna patterned after those that read DOG is GOD Spelled Backward. Mine simply read GODFLOW.

On the morning of the move, the Sonoran Desert pulsed with heat, and my nose sunburned by seven o'clock. Inyo gnawed a rawhide chew while Ryan and I finished loading the U-Haul and tuned our Cobra Walkie Talkies so we could coordinate rest stops. Parrots are sensitive to heat, so Lupe with his clipped wings could ride perched on Ryan's shoulder in the air-conditioned cab of the truck. I'd have lobbied for a turn to drive the U-Haul, but that parrot had recently developed a peculiar attraction and tried to hump the top of my head.

Driving Hanna at a steady forty-five miles an hour, with Inyo riding shotgun, I grabbed fistfuls of ice from the cooler and floated the cubes in her water dish. Mirages appeared along Highway 93 toward Las Vegas, making distant trailer homes and outbuildings quiver, double, and blur. I pulled over occasionally to let the engine cool and to give Inyo a chance to run around and pee in the sagebrush. We made it as far as Indian Springs by midafternoon, passing Auntie Moes Trading Post and edging the Nevada Test and Training Range. I'd never spent time in Nevada. It looked like a sandbox. South of Beatty, a billboard for the Kingdom Gentlemen's Club showed a blond in a leopard-print bikini advertising FULL MENU. FULL LIQUOR. FULL NUDITY. By the time we passed the Shady Lady Ranch, a brothel, and then the Nevada State Prison, where signs along the highway advised against picking up hitchhikers, I was willing to risk overheating to cross Death Valley into California and skip the rest of southern Nevada. If we cruised the eastern edge of the state, we could take Highway 395 all the way to Reno.

Late in the afternoon we managed to putt our way through Death Valley before skirting the southern end of the Inyo Mountains. I waved to the bristlecone pines and wished we could detour there, but we had to push on. We stopped for turkey melts at Jack's Restaurant, where I discovered that Inyo had chewed up my copy of *How to Keep Your Volkswagen Alive,* the bible of VW maintenance. I gathered the tattered pages and stowed them in the glove compartment. We let Hanna sit, listening to her engine clack and thump as it cooled.

Watching Inyo romp through the sagebrush calmed my mind. She roamed among the clumps of yellow flowering rabbitbrush, blending so completely into the landscape that I occasionally lost sight of her, a quality that led to one of her many nicknames, Camo Inyo. Her grace awed me as she soared easily across wide ditches. I loved her sheer will.

I'd begun to notice changes in her body when we played chase and wrestled. At almost forty pounds now, Inyo was growing fast. At birth she'd had a flat face. Now her snout pushed outward as an adult wolf's would, and the dark circles around her eyes had faded. The top layer of her coat, made up of oily guard hairs that repelled water, was darkening to a pepper color. Her paws looked like clown feet on her skinny body, and she was developing the long, arched toes capable of spreading for traction.

Skulking around the stiff branches of desert scrub, Inyo cocked an ear to the dirt, then leaped into the air, front legs tucked to her chest, nose pointed to the ground. She pinned a pocket mouse and knocked it back like a shot of whiskey. Lupe, perched on Ryan's shoulder, turned his head to watch, squawking when he saw Inyo pounce on a second mouse that had been nibbling a mesquite bean. That one got away.

When it was time to drive on, I turned the key in the ignition—nothing. Not even a click. Hanna had seriously overheated this time. Was it the starter or the solenoid? Sprawled on the seventies brown plaid upholstery, I thumbed through the manual's loose and slobbered pages. A yellow VW pulled up behind us and a group of young hippies poured out, dreadlocks swinging. "Hey, nice wolf," one of the guys said. "My friend had a wolfdog, but they couldn't keep her home." He told me that the animal was in and out of the pound a lot. "It got expensive," he said, "and when Cheyenne gutted the neighbor's cat they had to move."

Oh my God, I thought. No cats. We can't live anywhere near cats.

They offered to help us push-start Hanna. One guy wore a skirt, which he hiked to his knees to help shove while Lupe screamed encouragement, flapping his bright orange and green wing feathers. The scent of patchouli and pot trailing behind them, the guys pushed Hanna until she rolled at a good speed, and I popped the clutch. She jerked and sputtered, and the engine turned over.

I'd already had one breakdown of my own on the trip. In a fit of exhaustion I told Ryan he shouldn't follow me to Reno, that this was all a mistake, we were moving too fast. He ought to turn that U-Haul around and go back to Tucson while Inyo and I continued to Reno alone. If he and I still liked each other after some time apart we'd get married the following year. It would be a good test of our relationship.

"You're overtired," he said. "Drink some water."

I took a lukewarm slug from our Nalgene bottle and we drove on.

We arrived in the Biggest Little City in the World by midnight, and on a tip made our way north on Virginia Street toward the parking lot of the Circus Circus casino. Brake lights flashed ahead as a policeman wearing a Reno Gang Unit jacket waved his light stick to direct cars into the other lane while his partner hog-tied a man with zip cord. Someone set off a bottle rocket, making Inyo pace the back of the van. "Easy, girl," I said. Women holding martini glasses danced in tight jeans to a cover band doing Buddy Holly's "That'll Be the Day." A man on the sidewalk yelled "God bless America" and vomited into the gutter. As we rolled by the Shamrock Inn Motel with its neon sign flashing NO Vacancy, frat boys tipped back Jell-O shots on the balcony. Metro Pawn was open in case someone wanted to buy a last-minute wedding ring, and three couples were lined up to get hitched in the Chapel of the Bells. Midnight heat and exhaust from the line of cars made the red letters of the Circus Circus sign look like flames. In the parking lot, luminous as a football stadium, Prowler and Aristocrat RVs had lined up for the night in the pink glow of the halides. We parked Hanna and the U-Haul next to a Big Tex trailer, and Inyo and I squatted to pee in the shrubs along Sixth Street, below the casino's giant neon clown. I padlocked the U-Haul while Ryan folded down Hanna's bed, and we climbed in, throwing T-shirts over our eyes to keep out the light. Lamps buzzed and Lupe burbled contentedly from inside his travel cage. Inyo chewed my toes through the blanket. My teeth itched, and a quick glance in the rearview mirror had shown highway grit in every pore of my face. First thing in the morning, I'd find a bathroom and discreetly take a sponge bath.

At dawn Inyo woke me by gnawing my toes. I took her out for a pee and set her up with breakfast before going in search of a bathroom. With a toothbrush in my back pocket I hadn't walked more than fifty feet into the Silver Legacy when I glanced back and couldn't see the door. As the theme music from *Wheel of Fortune* blasted in surround sound and the chinking of coins split my ears, I realized there were no windows or clocks, no way to orient myself. Siren lights mounted on quarter slot machines lit up one aisle. A marquee heralded the return of Kenny Rogers, and I wondered if the man had nightmares about being asked to sing "The Gambler" for the millionth time.

A cocktail waitress whose name tag said "Chastity" approached me wearing a leopard-print vest over a black leotard that exposed her butt cheeks. She had heavy-metal hair teased up high. "What do you want to drink?"

"What do you have?"

She rolled her eyes and bit her bottom lip. "Anything you want, honey," she said, "as long as you're betting." She listed a few drinks: kamikaze, head shrinker, beauty on the beach. I wrinkled my nose. "No thanks. I'm all set." I just wanted a cup of coffee and a newspaper so I could look for rentals.

Chastity pointed me in the general direction of the bathroom and turned to take the orders of a group of well-dressed middle-aged men playing Dragon Pai Gow Poker. They all ordered Glenlivet. I looked past the rows of video games like Time Crisis to a string of restaurants. At least there were plenty of places to eat—a steak house, a deli, a buffet—and Ryan and I could get breakfast for $1.99, with scraps of bacon and egg left over for Inyo and Lupe. Since we'd been on the road, Inyo hadn't touched her kibble. In fact, she hadn't shown much of an appetite except when she'd rooted through our sack of groceries the day before and gorged on a pound of Ryan's jerky. When I'd opened Hanna's sliding door and caught her in the act, she'd crawled to the back of the van with strings of dried turkey hanging out the side of her mouth. As she crouched on the foldout bed, gobbling the jerky, I studied her ears, once floppy, now standing tall, each one a thicket of fur inside. She was growing fast and extremely clever.

Ryan and I made several calls on rentals that morning, each one a dead end. We'd counted on students vacating the Reno rentals for the summer, leaving us plenty of options, but we hadn't factored in landlords opposed to pets. When we received the same stern response, "No dogs," I started having serious doubts about Reno. Maybe we should forget the whole thing and go back to Tucson. I could work in an espresso bar and reapply to other schools for the following year.

Ryan, more optimistic, persuaded me to stick it out for a few more days. "Cheer up, Huevos Rancheros," he said. "We'll find a place." We tried different newspapers, called every housing ad posted at the university. After three hot days, Hanna began to smell sour, and by the fourth day, I knew downtown Reno too well. If we had a medical emergency, we could walk across the street to Saint Mary's. For gas we had the Shell station around the corner. I knew the few dark places around the parking lot where Inyo and I could squat in the middle of the night. I could brush my teeth in the Silver Legacy and Circus Circus without getting lost, and if I wanted to, I could catch Def Leppard and Hall and Oates in concert. I knew to avoid the street corners where the toothless meth addicts hung out, and if we ran out of money, I could take my jewelry to EZ-Cash Super Pawn for a few bucks.

For dinner the fourth night Ryan and I ate at the Pub N' Sub, a corner tavern near the university. I stowed Ryan's leftover chicken wings in the cooler and latched it, weighting the lid down with a stack of his books. Albert Camus's *The Myth of Sisyphus* and Friedrich Nietzsche's *Beyond Good and Evil* would guard our food from Inyo—though I'd recently become disenchanted with Nietzsche, who'd written that if a woman receives the same education as a man it will render her "incapable of her first and last profession, giving birth to strong children." During the night Inyo opened the cooler and ate sixteen extra-spicy chicken wings, including the bones. (Ryan liked hot food and often made it clear to a skeptical waiter by saying "I want to see God.") The next morning, the blankets were covered in diarrhea and to my delight so was Nietzsche. I stuffed the blankets into a large black plastic bag and left Hanna's side door open to air her out while we went in search of a Laundromat.

Spicy chicken in means spicy chicken out, and Inyo groaned all day. "Your dog is a four-legged tornado," Ryan said, waving a hand in front of his nose.

The afternoon of our fifth day we saw an ad for a duplex apartment next to Idlewild Park, "pets on approval," just two miles from school. On the phone Bill, the landlord, hesitated when I mentioned we had two pets, but said we sounded like a nice couple and he'd be willing to meet what I emphasized as our "medium-size dog" and "small parrot." Ryan and I took sponge baths in the university bathroom, ran Inyo in the nearby park so she'd be mellow and not eat Bill's sofa, and stuffed our pockets with dried mango and hunks of cheddar cheese to keep Lupe from screeching.

Bill and his wife, Susan, met us in the driveway. The first thing out of Bill's mouth was "That's some 'medium-size' dog. She looks like she's gonna be big. Look at those paws, Susan. What kind of dog is that anyway? She looks like a wolf."

"Husky mix."

"Mixed with what?"

I shrugged. "She's really gentle."

As if she could sense how anxious I was to please Bill and get us a place to live, Inyo sidled up and licked his hands.

"She doesn't dig, does she?" Bill asked, patting Inyo on the head. As if on cue Inyo pawed his knee. "You know, Susan just planted a nice flower bed back there, petunias and marigolds, and we don't want it ruined."

I didn't know whether she would dig or not. "She doesn't dig," I said.

Bill softened and scratched behind Inyo's ears, seeming to forget about those paws and what they might portend.

"And how about barking?"

"No barking. She howls softly every now and then, but it's really pretty and she doesn't do it very often."

When Bill invited us inside to view the place, the guilt I'd felt about lying vanished. Bill and Susan were obviously a retired couple trying to make some extra money. The "duplex" was really a converted garage connected to the main house where they lived. The whole place had a 1950s L.A. look, with its green stepping-stones inset in red gravel and wrought iron gates painted blinding white. But the carpet and drapes, fake wood paneling, and fenced yard made it possible for me to imagine we'd be living in a real place. The rent was reasonable, and we were desperate. "We'll take it," I said.

"Now hold on." Bill held up his hand and told us he had two other applicants interested, and he was doing credit checks.

I ran through a mental checklist: I'd replaced the doors in my Tucson apartment and laid down a new sheet of linoleum where Inyo had shredded the flooring, so my previous landlord would give me a good report. I was square with student loans and had always paid my credit card bill on time. We should be okay. Ryan and I filled out the application and forked over the money for a credit check. Bill told us he'd have an answer the next day. We sputtered off in Hanna, me babbling on about how I was going to decorate the place, Ryan silent.

He said little the rest of the day, occasionally muttering that it was hot and he was hungry. The next morning, with Lupe on his shoulder, he walked to Java Jungle to peruse the new rental ads in the paper.

"I don't know why you keep looking," I said. "I'm sure we've got that duplex."

"Yeah, well, just in case."

Now it was Ryan's turn to despair. He announced that if we didn't get into that carpeted garage, he wanted to march back to Tucson. Reno was no place to live, he said. It was a place to pass through and keep going. As if in agreement, Lupe turned around on his Polly's Portable Bird Stand and squawked. But when I called Bill from the student center, he invited us over to "chat." Maybe Eleanor Roosevelt had been right: "When you get to the end of your rope—tie a knot in it and hang on."

When we pulled into the driveway, I rolled out the van's awning and tied Inyo's lead to the rearview mirror. Lupe was a cashew junkie, so I filled Ryan's pockets with roasted cashew pieces, and with Lupe on his shoulder we followed Bill's wife, Susan, to the back porch where she offered us iced tea and cold grapes, another one of Lupe's favorites. Maybe I'd ask Lupe to hang upside down and dangle by one foot. A parrot trick couldn't hurt our chances for the rental.

Ryan gulped his tea and grabbed a handful of grapes, forgetting to offer one to Lupe, who pinched Ryan's ear with his hooked bill and screamed. Bill clapped his hands and chuckled. "Weren't expecting that, were you," he said to Ryan. Ryan grinned, but I knew from experience that a nip from Lupe's beak really hurt.

"Step up," I ordered, and put my index finger out for Lupe to climb on. He cocked his head, the color of a tequila sunrise, and clacked his beak. I put him on my shoulder and gave him a grape, praying that he wouldn't start humping my head.

Bill looked from me to Ryan. "Well." His voice deepened and steadied like a father's when he talked to his son about having protected sex. I saw Ryan sink in his chair. Bill's gaze turned back to me and he smacked his lips. "Looks like you wear the pants in the family."

Ryan sank lower and his leg bounced. I reached under the table and put my hand on his knee.

"Your credit is good," Bill said to me. Then he looked at Ryan. "Son, your credit is in the toilet. You've got some real challenges. Real challenges."

Ryan opened his eyes wide and gazed at the corrugated fiberglass roof over our heads, blinking those long dark lashes. To add a little levity, I said, "Lupe, turn around," and Lupe made a circle on my shoulder, soft tail feathers brushing my cheek. I gave him another grape and he burbled happily. No humping so far.

But what the hell was Bill talking about? I remembered Ryan's near-empty refrigerator, a box of Cap'n Crunch and half gallon of milk on the top shelf, and the serial job losses. I recalled the night we'd been driving Vato, Ryan's blue Chevy Chevette that barely ran and had a hole in the gas tank that filled the interior with fumes. A Tucson cop pulled us over for a busted taillight, and it turned out Vato was uninsured. The cop fined Ryan $1,000 and towed the car. After that mess I'd assumed Ryan had learned his lesson about evading responsibility. Besides, he had an advanced degree, had worked hard for his teaching certificate, and had made a big move with me to Reno, which took guts, especially when I'd had cold feet and told him to go back to Tucson. Bill was probably referring to the typical lapse in credit card payments.

When Ryan still didn't say anything, I blurted out, "You know he's grown up a lot." Ryan twisted his mouth and glared at me, but I was riffing and we needed a home. "We've all got life lessons to learn," I said. "Ryan has a great teaching job here." He didn't, but whatever.

"I like you two, and I want to give you a chance," Bill said, and looked at Ryan. "I used to be a little wild and reckless myself. But now you're getting married, and I trust this young lady has got you all squared away."

Ryan sulked. Bill peered at him over the rim of his eyeglasses. "Cheer up, son. I talked to your last landlord. He said you're a nice kid and you pay your rent on time. But he did say you were the typical college boy—messy. And I can't have mess in my house."

As I signed the rental contract, I felt like I'd be living next door to my dad while I raised my son. Inyo howled from her tie-out next to Hanna.

"That's not so bad," Bill said. "It's kinda pretty, as long as she doesn't do it too much. We've got neighbors, you know."

For an added touch, Lupe shat on my shoulder.

CHAPTER EIGHT

On the Trail

A wolf, it is said, can hear a cloud pass overhead.
—unknown author

Inyo had outgrown her first quick-release collar and reduced her leather leash to frothy strips. So much for going natural. She'd also chewed the toes out of the dress shoes we'd bought Ryan to celebrate his first teaching job. "What the hell, man?" he'd said, showing me the ruined shoes that now looked like tattered sandals. I soothed him with the promise of replacements and as soon as we'd settled into our carpeted garage and unpacked most of our boxes, took Inyo to PetSmart for a new collar and lead.

We stepped through the sliding glass doors and headed straight for the fashion aisle, to row after row of bungee, retractable, and hands-free leashes, and the flimsy though handsome leather leads. There were spiked and studded dog collars and others with pink rhinestones suitable for poodles or go-go dancers. I chose a tan quick-release collar ornamented with blue stitching, and a matching six-foot nylon lead. For our more casual walks, I also bought a sixteen-foot Flexi lead so Inyo could move about more freely, sniffing bushes and fence posts other dogs had scent-marked.

While we waited our turn in line at the register, Inyo poked her muzzle into one of the low bins and grabbed a stuffed hedgehog. It's a conspiracy putting those enticing chew toys, biscuits, and pig ears low to the ground. While the unsuspecting dog owner stands around thumbing her money and thinking about what's next on the to-do list, her dog's schnoz is in the treat bin. The baritone *wonk-wonk* of the hedgehog squeaker finally caught my attention, but too late. The $14 toy had already gone into death throes in a flurry of stuffing.

"You'll have to buy that," the clerk said.

Inyo always strained at the leash as if she could never see enough of the world and we'd better hurry. Everything I'd ever read about training huskies said the owner had better be prepared to exercise patience because the husky was bred to pull. Training a husky-wolf mix could only mean I'd have to strive for the patience of a Buddha. Be consistent, I told myself. Dawn, noon, and midnight, in sickness and in health, sleet or scorching sun, Inyo and I would train. Late for school? Too bad. Hungry? Eat later. Talking long distance with a friend I hadn't seen in three years? Call her back. Tired and want to go to bed? I could sleep when Inyo was trained.

To stop her pulling, I would plant my feet suddenly or give a quick, but gentle tug on the leash before continuing forward. Tug-release. Tug-release. Deep breath, and do it again. "Heel," I said, and slapped my thigh, stepping forward with my left leg. Tug-release. Tug-release.

Walk. Halt. Sit. Walk. Halt. Sit. The books said that eventually the dog would learn to quit pulling because its desire to go forward would be frustrated. But Inyo didn't respond the way the books said. She would glance over her shoulder at me, her expression almost quizzical. Why had we stopped? What was the matter? Then she'd sit and chew her leash. I thought I detected an almost compassionate look in her eyes, as if she'd figured out that I was a stupid wolf and she'd have to be the patient one.

Despite losing an expensive pair of oxfords and several neckties to Inyo, Ryan often wrestled with her, hollering, "Send it, Inyo!" delighted when she tore around our apartment, her now four-month-old body so athletic she could leap over the queen-size bed without leaving so much as a wrinkle in the bedspread. Her bursts of wildness appealed to Ryan, who also had a wild streak that sent him climbing up steep rock faces rated "R" for Risky, and "X" for Extreme—meaning if you fall you're dead.

Although I liked the heady feeling at the top of a multipitch climb just before rappelling off a desert cliff, I preferred the beginner routes because heights put a zap on my head. I still got the Elvis Leg during ascents, and often froze against the rock face, afraid to reach for the next hold and too stubborn to downclimb and admit defeat. Instead I'd cling to the rock and cry. I began to realize that the real reason I wanted to rock climb was that it had brought Ryan and me together. I clung to the symbolism of a climbing partner, the person you trust to hold the lifeline between you and oblivion. If I admitted that I preferred to carry a fifty-pound pack through a hundred miles of Wyoming's Wind River Mountains or to trudge up Mount Hood with an ice axe and crampons because I could keep the ground under my feet, that meant I was a chicken—letting fear bully me—but worst of all, it meant I was the wrong woman for Ryan. Even with the wedding just three weeks away, he could still change his mind. It never occurred to me that I might be having my own doubts about him.

While Ryan trained Lupe to fetch plastic balls with silver bells jingling inside them, chattering on about teaching his conure to play chess, I took care of last-minute travel plans. We'd drive to my mother's house in Portland, and after the wedding, she and my stepdad (a Vietnam vet my mother said she married because having lost a leg he couldn't run away) would parrot-sit while Ryan and I spent a week backpacking with Inyo through Oregon's Mount Jefferson Wilderness.

I fitted Inyo with a dog pack in rust red. The contrast with her dark gray guard hairs and blondish undercoat would make Camo Inyo more easily visible on the landscape. She'd heft a few peanut butter dog cookies and a collapsible bowl in the deep, zippered pockets of the nylon saddlebags, giving her a chance to get accustomed to wearing a pack without carrying much added weight. Ryan and I would divvy up her lamb-and-rice kibble for the five-day trek, as well as some Greenies, tins of high-protein wet food, and her latest favorites: dried papaya spears and Happy Hips chicken strips.

With a locking D-ring carabiner, I'd attach Inyo's leash to the shoulder strap on my pack so she couldn't run off—my biggest fear. There was no one in the wilderness to catch her by the collar, and if she got lost I knew she wouldn't survive. Inyo had successfully killed three squirrels and several mice with a mouse-pounce, but she wouldn't know how to hunt bigger game or how to stay out of danger, skills a wild wolf learns from its birth pack. When wolf parents wean their pups, the family leaves the den and moves to a rendezvous site, a semi-open area with access to water and ample prey. Pups stay at the rendezvous site from about mid-June until September or October when they're old enough to tag along behind their parents and learn to hunt large prey by watching. Although Inyo wouldn't learn a thing about hunting from me, I'd keep her close at all times, and at night I'd secure her to a sturdy tree in camp using a lightweight chain so she couldn't chew through her lead and wander off.

Although she was only four months old, her sinewy body communicated readiness for the backcountry. She'd been able to free solo part of a Class 5 climb known as Manic Depressive—the route dicey when least expected, leaving a climber with thin placements for hands and feet and the prospect of a painful fall. Inyo managed to balance herself on Depressive's steep inclines that I didn't feel comfortable or poised enough to scale without a fixed rope. Her paw pads allowed her to smear, to angle her sticky soles to maximize friction against the rock face. She didn't need special climbing shoes, a harness, or rope to protect her traverse and ascent. Where I froze on the rock, Inyo would climb past me, moving like liquid glass. While Ryan and I would have to wear head nets and repellent, thick socks and long sleeves to avoid breaking out in welts from all the biting bugs in the wilderness, Inyo could blink away the gnats with her long lashes. Her well-furred ears and the guard hairs crowning her back and shoulders would prevent the swarms of backcountry mosquitoes from needling her too badly.

Weighing only forty-five pounds and not much taller than my knee, Inyo's body was maturing into more adult proportions. She had wolfy paws, and her tail, bushy as a bottlebrush, hung straight down and close to her hocks like a wolf's. She was long-limbed, with a wolf's narrow chest, not compact with the deeply muscled legs the husky relies on for pulling heavy loads. Other traits were mixed. Siberian huskies have foreheads like a black diamond ski slope, with a pronounced stop between forehead and muzzle, whereas the descent from a wolf's forehead to its longer, narrower muzzle is more gradual. Inyo's skull shape was somewhere between a wolf's and a husky's, just as her triangular ears were too pointy for a wolf but set too far apart on her head for a husky.

On the morning we left for Portland, Inyo lounged on Hanna's backseat, surrounded by backpacks and a jumble of walking poles we'd piled around her. She watched the half-built developments of Reno zoom by, as I imagined wild wolves running there until the 1940s when the last of them were shot and poisoned out of existence. Though they'd killed off all the real wolves, people were still attracted to their romanticized image, dubbing the university's athletic teams the Wolf Pack, and their streets and subdivisions Wolf Run, Lone Wolf Circle, and Wolf Creek Drive.

Our backpacks bulged with sleeping bags and pads, tent, first aid kit, headlamps, and cook pots. We would carry two compasses and a topo map of our backcountry route, which followed a section of the Pacific Crest Trail in the Cascade Range. Into a stuff sack full of string cheese and Clif Bars, turkey jerky and gorp—a custom mix of nuts and dried fruit—I'd loaded Inyo's kibble, pork hocks, and other snacks. Another bag had dinners for Ryan and me, each one carefully planned, plus one emergency ration if we got stranded somewhere. We would sustain ourselves with dried black bean flakes reconstituted with boiling water and heaped onto Minute Rice seasoned with packets of hot sauce snagged from Taco Bell. Along with two sticks of salami and a block of cheddar, we packed in coffee and cocoa—our biggest luxuries—reserved for mornings when we made our poor man's mocha.

During the long drive north, Ryan squirmed in the passenger's seat until the sheepskin cover lay rumpled on the floor mat he'd kicked slantwise. He kept twisting around to stare out Hanna's back window as if keeping track of where we'd come from so he could find his way back. A normal person might have found his inability to sit still amusing. I wanted to hog-tie him. "Quit fidgeting!" I snapped. I couldn't drive another mile with the mat cockeyed. "Lift your feet!" I leaned across him to square the mat, my eyes barely level with the dashboard to keep us on the road.

"You're gonna kill us!" Ryan hollered.

He called me a control freak. I called him a slob. Both were true. By the time we hit Portland city limits we'd broken up and gotten back together three times. When we pulled into my mother's driveway, she looked horrified as we spilled out of Hanna. She glanced at Inyo and her mouth twitched. "I hope she doesn't chew up my house."

But Inyo's chewing wasn't my mother's only concern. "I need a little sit-down with you and your fiancé," she said. That first night at dinner, my mother asked Ryan how he thought we'd manage the stresses of marriage since we each had "personal issues."

"We'll be a tag team," he said cheerfully. "We won't fall apart at the same time. One will prop the other up."

My mother raised an eyebrow but said nothing more.

I changed the subject by asking if Inyo and Lupe could be part of the wedding, but my mother wasn't having it. It was bad enough that I'd shown up with my nose pierced and that my sleeveless wedding dress would display my Celtic-healing-hand tattoo to the dismay of Great-Aunt Clara. No wolfdog was going to chew on her daughter's $900 dress, and no parrot was going to screech while the hired quartet played Pachelbel's *Canon*. At least we were all able to sleep together in my mother's basement guest room.

On our wedding day Ryan struggled to finish writing his vows and I nagged and bitched, but by afternoon, when the ceremony began in a grove of ancient sequoia trees, we forgot our bickering. We paid tribute to both our dead fathers and joined hands while the minister bound us together with a section of climbing rope. The best part was the dancing afterward. Ryan spun and dipped me, whispering, "Forever you and me, Vitamin C." Pictures would later show us grinning and hugging like we couldn't believe we'd made it.

When we returned to my mother's house, Inyo bounded toward me and piddled on my white wedding slippers, whimpering and rolling on her back. We discovered that my mother's worry about her chewing habits hadn't been unfounded. While we'd been eating wedding cake and dancing, Inyo had turned her growing jaw strength and new molars on my mother's antiques, gnawing apart her Victorian Eastlake table. She'd lost several of her milk teeth in the carpet already, and I'd found others in the van's upholstery, embedded in the foam cushions she'd torn up. I remembered what it felt like as a kid losing my baby teeth—I couldn't keep my hands out of my mouth for the throbbing.

At least I had fingers to rub my gums and wiggle loose teeth. Inyo had only objects to chew. I'd tried to keep her supplied with smoked pork hocks and squeak toys to help her deal with the aching and itching. But she'd been so desperately lonesome during the ceremony that the bones and chew toys I'd left her weren't enough.

That night for the first time she slept on the bed between Ryan and me, her body a comforting pressure against my hip and leg. I breathed slowly, in through my nose and out my mouth, not wanting to disturb her and possibly wreck that moment. The next morning, my mother hurried us out her door toward the mountains, happy to see the furniture-chewing wolfdog go.

A year after our wedding trip, federal agents in Oregon would search for the killer of a female gray wolf that had migrated into Oregon. Somewhere between Ukiah and Pendleton the female had been shot with a single bullet from a high-velocity rifle. DNA analysis showed that she was the offspring of wolves reintroduced into central Idaho and Yellowstone National Park in the mid-1990s. Having left her birth pack, the Ukiah wolf swam across the Snake River and entered Oregon via Hells Canyon, a gash in the earth deeper than the Grand Canyon. She'd probably been looking for a mate, although it was unlikely she'd have found one. At the time of her death, wolves had been long gone from Oregon, an incentive for their elimination provided by a bounty in effect from 1843 to 1946, when the last recorded bounty was paid out. In 1913, a person could collect a State of Oregon bounty of five bucks and an Oregon State Game Commission bounty of twenty. Good money for the times.

Since the death of the Ukiah wolf, other wolves have entered Oregon. Some have been killed, but others have survived to produce pups.[1] At this writing wolf numbers in Oregon have reached the midtwenties, and as more animals make their way from Idaho into Oregon and Washington, some people celebrate their return while others brace to fight it. Supporters of wolf recovery champion the predator's role in maintaining a healthy ecosystem. By thinning herds, wolves help prevent deer and elk overpopulation. They also keep coyote numbers in check.

But many livestock growers, who live close to the bone, fear that wolves will destroy their livelihood. Hunters complain that wolves eat all the elk and deer. Those that view the wolf as a wasteful, bloodthirsty predator have vowed to do what they've always done: "Shoot, shovel, and shut up," and hand out free ammunition to anyone willing to do it too.

In other regions of the country, gray wolf populations are much healthier. In Alaska, the Department of Fish and Game (ADF&G) estimates that wolf numbers hover somewhere between 7,000 and 11,000 animals, and wolves are not protected under the Endangered Species Act. In fact, the Alaska Board of Game has authorized reductions in the state's wolf population using controversial methods that include shooting wolves from low-flying aircraft or chasing them from the air until the animals are exhausted and may be more easily shot from the ground. ADF&G and the board justify this method of predator control by citing provisions in Alaska's Constitution and state law for the management of predators and prey for "all users" in the state. In fact, these agencies are required to boost prey populations for the benefit of hunters.

To provide the public with a broad overview of the science supporting these control measures, ADF&G published "Predator Management in Alaska," a thirty-page summary of its efforts to increase the state's moose and caribou populations by reducing the numbers of wolves and bears. According to the document, a collaboration of ADF&G scientists, "a single wolf consumes 12–13 moose in a typical year, and/or 30–40 caribou, mostly calves." These numbers invite the general reader to do a simple multiplication and conclude that the state's wolves are eating a minimum of 84,000 moose and 210,000 caribou a year, twelve times more moose and about eight times more caribou than hunters kill, according to the report. But while wolves might be *capable* of eating that much moose and caribou meat, the fact is that some wolves eat few moose and no caribou at all because not all prey species are available in every part of Alaska. In the interior of the state wolves do feed on moose and caribou—including calves. But in areas without these large ungulates, wolves eat primarily deer. Depending on their location, wolves also prey on mountain goats, Dall sheep, beaver, hare, salmon, and other small animals. The report also fails to mention that hunting is hard work. Healthy adult moose and caribou are quite skilled at defending themselves, so wolves sometimes go hungry.

ADF&G employees I spoke with protested that the report's authors didn't intend for readers to "extrapolate." But despite their best efforts, my contacts at the agency could not find out who had determined the size of the wolf's appetite, how the numbers were calculated, or why they were expressed in such a misleading way. Equally intriguing, by ADF&G's own estimates, grizzly bears outnumber wolves 3 to 1 and black bears outnumber wolves 10 to 1, and yet, predator-control measures discussed in the report focused primarily on wolves.

While wolves in the western Great Lakes region, which includes Minnesota, Michigan, and Wisconsin, number over 4,000 and still have some protections, the Rocky Mountain wolves of Idaho, Wyoming, and Montana, some 1,500 animals, are under constant threat of proposed wolf-kill programs, their endangered status always subject to ongoing court battles.[2] In states where predator-control programs have been too successful, there aren't even enough wolves to qualify as a "population." Although listed as endangered, the Mexican gray wolf, a unique subspecies that lives in Arizona and New Mexico, numbers only about fifty animals in the wild and continues to suffer poaching.[3]

Whereas U.S. Fish and Wildlife biologists could draw on healthy populations of gray wolves from Canada to use in their Rocky Mountain recovery efforts, in the American Southeast they had to trap fourteen of the remaining seventeen red wolves, *Canis rufus,* and put them in a captive breeding program to avoid the extinction of the only other distinct wolf species in North America. The red wolf once populated most of the southeastern United States but was declared extinct in the wild by 1980. As a result of the captive-breeding program, though, more than a hundred wild red wolves now inhabit northeastern North Carolina, part of their original habitat.

These are only small steps in restoring a large predator. Wolves once ranged from the Arctic to central Mexico but now live only in isolated pockets. And wherever there are wolves, there are people who propose kill programs, and where kill programs are at least temporarily stayed by the Endangered Species Act, there are always poachers who make up their own laws.

* * *

After six hours of highway driving, plus one episode of an overheated engine and a leak in the fuel line that sent gas spitting over the highway, we reached the trailhead, filled out a wilderness permit, and strapped on our packs. I clipped the handle of Inyo's Flexi lead to the eye-loop on my pack. Although tethered to me, she could explore sixteen feet in any direction.

We started by following a short spur trail east to a junction with the Pacific Crest Trail. For an hour we climbed through forest, passing shallow ponds and climbing steadily upward to the southern ridge of Three-Fingered Jack, a craggy shield volcano, one of the oldest in the Cascade Range and formed by thousands of flows of molten basalt.

Inyo kept a steady pace on the trail, her tail raised slightly as she focused directly ahead. Occasionally she glanced back at me as if checking to make sure everyone stayed together, her mouth open and relaxed as she floated forward on those long legs, the saddlebags on her back making a gentle swishing sound as they rose and fell with the easy rhythm of her young shoulder muscles. When we'd climbed steadily on the switchbacks, zigzagging up a stretch of steep trail, the forest opened, spilling us out of the huckleberry and rhododendron bushes onto a snowfield, where Jack loomed in all his talus glory.

"Chossy," Ryan said, referring to the loose rock too poor to climb. We dropped the packs to slug water from our Nalgene bottles and gnaw on meatless pemmican bars, compressed cakes of protein made from dried fruit and nuts. Inyo let out a "Whooo!" and yipped, staring into my face, her bushy tail brushing side to side, sweeping pine needles into miniature mountain ranges. Treat time. She inhaled a few chicken strips, immediately poised to move on across the talus slopes and snowfields, her mind always in the moment. No past. No future. No worries. As for me, the panic I felt in the city fell away in the backcountry. My mind emptied of anxiety as my body eased into a rhythm along the trail, no need to tap and circle.

As we traversed the west and north faces of the peak, Inyo tracked true, her hind paws landing in the tracks of her forepaws, making an almost straight line. She trotted along while Ryan and I leaned uphill, kick-stepping into the hard and steep-angled snow. Step. Breathe. Step. Breathe. As we crossed the slope below Jack, I realized that the whole time we'd been hiking, Inyo hadn't pulled. She'd kept a steady rhythm with me, never lunging forward, and it made for pleasant cross-country travel. By dusk, having kept a comfortable pace with each other, we accomplished our goal for the first day and set up camp at Wasco Lake, ten miles from the trailhead.

When we found a tent site where the ground was fairly level and softened by a bed of silver fir needles, I fed Inyo and looped her chain around the base of a fir. She ate and then scratched her bed in the dust, circling and lying down, her chin resting on forepaws, eyelids heavy. She lifted them only slightly now and then when metal pots clanked, and wiggled her black nose at the smell of rice and beans. In the city, she'd been in constant motion, never settling, although we went for our training walks and I'd started taking her on three-mile daily runs along Steamboat and Last Chance Ditch trails, windy creekside paths only ten minutes from home. Sometimes it felt like she was taking me for sprints up those steep cheatgrass- and juniper-covered hillsides where coyotes gathered at dusk and gibbered. Whenever we heard them Inyo gnashed her teeth and tore at the leash, wanting to run to them. Now I wondered if this forest stirred an ancestral memory inside her, if she would dream of deer or elk, although she'd never seen them. After our ten-mile hike, she seemed the most content I'd ever seen her, relaxed and still.

When it was time to climb into our mummy bags, I glanced at her, stretched out on her side, front and back legs extended. She rubbed her cheek in the dust and took a deep breath, smacking her lips together in that contented way dogs do. "Do you think we should bring her into the tent for the night?" I asked Ryan.

"Hell no. There won't be a tent left by morning. She's fine where she is—kickin' it for the night."

I woke several times, strapped on my Petzl headlamp and poked my head out of the tent. Each time the beam of light showed Inyo asleep in the dirt.

The next morning when I unzipped the tent fly, she greeted me with a bow. As I pulled on my boots and fleece jacket to walk her, Ryan filtered water from the lake to brew two mugs of cowboy coffee, made with boiling water and ground espresso roast. He threw in heaping spoonfuls of cocoa powder. When it was done, we slurped. "Stellar," Ryan said. "The coffee of champions."

Over a second cup, this one black, we studied the topo and ate heaping bowls of granola while Inyo gobbled kibble topped with a can of tuna. We'd all need as much energy as we could get to trek twelve miles of mountain terrain. We filtered more water, filling our Nalgene bottles, and guzzled another quart between us. After breaking down the tent and packing our gear, Ryan and I laced our gaiters to wade through the snow. There'd been a high accumulation that winter, so that even in August many trails were still covered. As soon as we climbed the first ridge and crossed an open slope, the Pacific Crest Trail appeared, then disappeared. We used the compass to navigate and slogged for three hours, occasionally falling through to our hips where drifts heaped around the trunks of pine and fir trees had hidden the gaping holes underneath. My hip bones and shoulders were raw from the weight of my pack, leg muscles jellied from exertion, but Inyo didn't seem worn out. Her paws were like a pair of built-in snowshoes with webbed toes splayed for even weight distribution over the ground. She expended less energy than we did because while we post-holed through the deeper sections, she ran along the surface.

"She's in the zone," Ryan said, hauling himself out of another hole.

By noon when we reached Rockpile Lake and filtered more water, we'd lost and found the trail a dozen times, but Ryan's orienteering helped us maintain a steady course toward Shale Lake, our destination for the day. There was little water along a good stretch of the trek between the two lakes. Although we'd filtered plenty at Rockpile Lake for normal summer hiking conditions, these conditions weren't normal. Extended hours of route-finding ate up calories and sucked the moisture from our bodies. We kept just enough liquid water in our bottles to help melt the snow we added now and then. By the time we reached Shale Lake at dark, all three of us had eaten our share of snow, but only one of us seemed unfazed by the grueling day. Inyo frisked around, biting at tent poles and playing tug-of-war with our mummy bags before settling down.

We set up camp and whipped up a one-pot wonder: noodles with olive oil and powdered pesto. With our low blood sugar and seized muscles, we moaned with pleasure at every forkful. Inyo ate a bowl of kibble, a handful of peanut butter dog cookies, a pork hock, and two chicken strips, and as she'd done the night before, dug herself a bed in the dirt. I draped my wet socks on a rock and flipped the tongues back on my boots to air them out. Ryan discovered a hot spot on his foot. "Damn blister boxes," he said, thunking the bottoms of his boots together. I handed him a sheet of moleskin and an army knife, and he wrapped his big toe.

Before bed we hoisted the food sacks into a fir tree with a long cord, careful they didn't dangle too close to the trunk where a bear could easily climb up and bite into them, and high enough from the ground that a bear couldn't stand on its hind legs and claw open the nylon sacks like piñatas. We couldn't risk losing six days' worth of meals twenty-two miles from the nearest Forest Service road. Exhausted, we crawled inside our bags, not bothering to brush our teeth.

The next morning, Inyo woke me by pawing the tent walls. I thought it was a bear until I heard her distinctive whine as she threw herself against the screen door. I bolted upright, realizing that in my exhaustion I'd forgotten to swap out leads and put Inyo on the chain. She must have chewed through the Flexi's nylon cord. I peered through the screen to see the frayed end of the lead dragging behind her in the dust. Just as I was about to unzip the fly and grab her collar, fearing she might run off and I'd never see her again, she raked her nails against the screen, tearing a hole that let in the mosquitoes. When I crawled out she licked my face and tugged on my braids. I kissed her forehead and nuzzled her ears. Pulling a mosquito net over my head, I tied a makeshift knot with the two frayed ends of the leash.

"Ryan, better get up. Incoming," I said, leading Inyo into the brush to pee. He sat up, slapping mosquitoes that had charged the hole in the screen. By the time our coffee was ready, we sipped amid such a swarm we could kill five mosquitoes with one slap.

While Ryan slugged his coffee and read the topo, I broke down camp. We had to get moving. We hoped to reach Russell Creek during the cooler morning hours before sun melted the snow and ice, swelling the crossing with brown glacial water, rapids whisked to such a fury that they obscured the safer footholds. We stuffed gear into our packs, folded the ripped tent, and strapped on Inyo's saddlebags.

We reached the creek later than we should have, having repeatedly lost and then found the trail again with map and compass. By the time we faced the creek it was engorged with glacial melt that had funneled into the streambed up-canyon. The flow gouged the earth and picked up speed as it carried sand and ice down the mountain. Ryan and I dropped our packs, both of us gnawing a bottom lip as we studied the situation, scouting the crossing from a couple of boulders.

There was no particular strategy that would make crossing that torrent any easier, but keeping Inyo on the lead seemed too dangerous. What if the cord caught on a rock during the crossing and she drowned? What if one of us slipped and wolfdog and human tumbled ass over teakettle downstream? I had to unclip Inyo from the leash and allow her total freedom to navigate the stream without feeling tension on her neck, back, or shoulders. I removed her pack and strapped it to mine. Ryan held her collar while I crossed first, balancing on my walking poles and testing the terrain in front of me by jabbing the sticks into the river to check for slippery rocks and sketchy footholds before I made a move. The white water came up to my thighs as I turned to face the oncoming froth, leaning up-canyon to keep from being knocked off my feet by the force of the flow, which seemed to swell by the minute. I teetered under the weight of my pack and almost fell backward. A few steps later, I lost my balance, this time lurching forward, my pack riding up my spine, water pouring in the front of my shirt. When I regained my footing and stood upright, Ryan called out, "You're dialed in, Vitamin C." I tightened the hip belt on my pack, tossed my poles to the opposite bank, and launched myself after them, crawling out of the streambed on all fours.

"Sketchy," Ryan shouted across the creek. "I can make it," he said, then nodded at Inyo. "But I don't know about her."

"She can do it," I called.

"I don't know, man."

"Let her go, Ryan."

He let go of Inyo's collar.

"Inyo, come. Come on, girl!" my voice sounded tinny over the roar of the water.

Inyo hesitated, glancing at the bloated stream and then at me like I was a moron for having crossed and a total lunatic for asking her to do it too. The water churned in front of her, eddied around her paws and flowed on. One more step and she'd have to swim. But in that moment it was as if her mind shifted gears. She took that next step and disappeared ears and all under the foam, then popped up and began to paddle.

"Good girl, Inyo! Go girl, go!"

Inyo's bones and muscles were still finding their shape, developing their strength. But she was strong, stronger than any dog I'd seen at her age. The river boiled and shoved, slamming her body downstream, but she kept swimming toward me.

"Stick it, Inyo. You're golden!" Ryan yelled.

She kept coming toward me, holding her chin above the water, ears twitching when glacial melt splashed them. My teeth chattered from cold as I readied myself to jump back into the water and grab Inyo around the middle. She was so little, but those huge paws paddled fiercely. I held my breath. The current pushed her but she pushed back, keeping that little black nose above the surface. Over the din of the creek, I could hear her breathing, the air forced through her nose in time with her strokes. When she neared the bank, I stepped in, grabbed her around the shoulders, and hauled her out. She shook herself and ran pell-mell around a silver fir.

"Stellar!" Ryan clapped his hands. "You spanked it, Inyo!"

She tore around the fir again. She'd done it. She'd crossed the creek off lead, on her own, and hadn't darted off into the trees and disappeared into the wilderness. Inyo circled me, rubbing against my legs. She scratched in the dirt, turned around several times, and flopped down. Ryan made it across safely and we ate handfuls of gorp and tins of sardines in mustard sauce, while Inyo polished off the chicken strips. We stared at her, lying in the dirt of the wilderness, free and content.

When the chemicals in our sweat attracted the mosquitoes, we prepared to head out. "Let's see how Inyo does without the leash," I said, smashing a mosquito against my forehead.

"You sure? If she runs, that's it. We won't get her back."

"I know, I know. But I don't think she will. Look at her. She doesn't seem interested in going anywhere unless we do."

At the sound of her name, Inyo stood and shook herself.

I hefted on my pack, still wet from the crossing, and shivered from the sweat gone cold on my back. Ryan and I started down the trail and I called to Inyo. She trotted behind Ryan for a moment before cutting in front of him to travel behind me. Then she cut in front of me and jogged ahead on the trail at about the same distance she'd kept when her Flexi was clipped to my pack.

The only time she wandered out of sight was when she spotted a good rock to crouch behind or a fine clump of vine maple or rhododendron bush to hunker under. *Go! Pounce!* She would spring on us when we got close enough, nipping our butts and bounding off. She wanted us to chase her, but there was no way either of us could run under the weight of our packs. I tried once and the heavy Kelty bounced on my shoulders, pounding me downward until I fell on my knees.

We climbed through alpine meadows of Indian paintbrush and blue flax, bushwhacked through snowberry and grayleaf manzanita, and then all three of us stopped to graze on huckleberries, Inyo nibbling them from the bushes. We scrambled up scree slopes to gain a better view of Mount Jefferson and the Cascade Range, Inyo always making it to the top first. But she waited for us, pacing back and forth, *Come! Hurry!* watching as we clambered to reach her. On flatter terrain, she always checked that we were close behind, throwing glances over her shoulder to see which way we intended to go and adjusting her course.

Inyo remained off lead for the rest of the trek. I tethered her only at night. Like the wild wolf pup that accompanies its parents on a hunt, Inyo knew to stay with the pack. The pack was company and survival. The Siberian husky part of her had been bred to work and get along in a group, to travel long distances and remain with the team. Maybe both parts of Inyo were satisfied by this tight formation in constant motion across the landscape.

In the wilderness I'd wagered that Inyo would make it across Russell Creek, and she had. I'd also risked letting her run off lead. I'd won both wagers. Although we had to return to the Biggest Little City in the World, I reminded myself that Reno was a gambling town. With determination and a little beginner's luck Inyo and I could come up aces.

CHAPTER NINE

Limboland

Confusion now hath made his masterpiece.
—William Shakespeare, *Macbeth,*
act II, scene 3, line 72

At home in Reno, when Inyo's eyes were bright and playful, I felt like I was doing something right. But I had to watch out for her wolfy love. When she licked my mouth, sometimes a canine snagged my lip or tongue. If she stood on her hind legs to greet me, placing those giant paw pads with the long splayed toes on my chest, she ripped holes in my sweaters. I cycled through clothing, hitting the Goodwill bins to buy clothes in bulk for $1.29 a pound and turning the ruined sweaters into dust rags. When we wrestled, her spine supple as a Slinky, she could wriggle out of my grasp to mouth my forearms—always with the good grace not to bite down. Pure wolves seven months old have permanent molars able to crack open moose femurs; Inyo could have snapped my arm bones in two.

With her body size catching up to her paws, Inyo grew bolder. Fearing she might get out of the yard while I was in classes three hours a day, I'd wandered the aisles of PetSmart looking at tie-out options, but decided on a trolley system with a swivel pulley and wire cable, which would let her roam around most of the yard. One morning I put her on the trolley and stepped inside to rinse the dishes while Ryan raced around shaving, fixing his tie, and bolting down a bowl of Cap'n Crunch. He'd just laced up his new replacement shoes for teaching and grabbed his briefcase when I poked my head outside to check on Inyo.

63

The highline lay slack on the ground, and the cable, frizzy and kinked where the plastic sheathing had rubbed off, disappeared over the top of the fence separating our yard from Susan and Bill's. The plate I'd been holding shattered on the floor, and I ran to the gate. Her break-away collar should have broken open to free her, but what if it hadn't? I imagined Inyo's body dangling from the cable, muscles jerking in the last moments before death, tongue hanging out the side of her mouth, eyes bugging. But when I reached the other side of the fence I saw her collar hanging there, mercifully empty. How could she have jumped over the fence when I'd measured the cable so carefully?

I sprinted up Riviera toward Idlewild Park and heard the whoops of delighted boys. Inyo was chasing skate punks, willowy boys in flannel shirts, beanies, and Vans, scooping the concrete basin on their boards. A boom box on the lip of the concrete bowl spit out The Dead Kennedys' staccato rage. One of the skaters saw me waving the leash and jumped off his board to call Inyo to him, but she paid no attention. On the heels of another kid as he pulled an ollie, jumping on his board and popping it into the air, Inyo was deep into his boy-smell and colt-ish movements. I ran up behind her and grabbed her collar.

Turned out that the wood post attached to one end of the high-line was rotten. I restrung the highline to another post, doing a load-bearing test by hanging from it. The system was fine for another few weeks, and then one evening I came home from class and found the wire cable chewed through and Inyo gone.

But *why* did Inyo want to leave?

Now when I think about it, I wonder if she'd had the urge to dis-perse and start her own pack. Typically wolves don't start leaving their birth packs until they're eleven to twenty-four months old, but wolves as young as five months have been known to go off on their own, and most commonly in fall and early winter, the time when Inyo began her escape attempts. She acted like the wolfdog version of a "floater," what biologists call lone wolves who float between pack territories the way Inyo skulked the alleyways between apartment buildings. Each time she got out, I went into a panic, circling the blocks, breathless until I found her, blood thrumming in my ears as I imagined the worst—run over, shot, stolen.

The day Inyo chewed through the wire cable, I found her on Foster Road, one block over, her head and shoulders wedged inside a garbage can. When I called her name, she backed out and trotted up to lick me. *Tasty! Have some. Smell it?* I screwed up my face at the stench of rotten meat and moldy vegetables on her breath.

To Inyo, I must have seemed ungrateful, undoing all her good works by pinching steak bones and blackened banana peels between my thumb and forefinger, plunking one treasure after another back in the can. She may have viewed me as a dim-witted dog, pulling my lips back and showing my teeth, strange sounds coming from my mouth. Truth is, the dog in her was doing what all good village dogs have done for thousands of years—cleaning up people's rubbish. But we were in the Biggest Little City in the World, where people tended to frown on the spreading of garbage across their lawns. A Milky Way wrapper stuck to the bottom of my shoe as we weaved home in the dark, my body leaning to one side as I clutched Inyo's collar. The next morning I bought the Beast, an extra heavy-duty dog tie-out picturing a grumpy bulldog on the package, which I'd use until I could think of something better.

When I photographed Inyo and studied the pictures, I glimpsed the dog in her: the husky's distinctive valentine of dark hair that made a V in the middle of her forehead. But like a hologram, Inyo changed depending upon my angle of view. Sometimes when my eyes swept across her image I saw the wolf: thick cheek-tufts and a mantle of tall, bristly guard hairs over her back and shoulders that undulated like stalks of oat grass.

No way around it, at six months old Inyo looked very wolfy—and she was due for her rabies vaccination. I'd been putting off making the appointment. What if the vet identified her as a wolfdog and refused to vaccinate her—or worse? I kept hearing Leda's voice in my head: "Don't tell anyone she's part wolf—not even your vet." I didn't know Nevada law regarding wolfdogs, and I was afraid to find out. But now there could be no more dawdling—if I wanted to take training classes with Inyo, I had to present the instructor with a rabies certificate.

In the waiting room of the vet's office I filled out the usual forms while the receptionists fawned over her, giving her dog cookies from the little tray on the counter and asking if she was part wolf.

"Husky mix," I said.

When the vet entered the exam room, she stopped short when she saw us, glancing at the chart in her hand, and then back at Inyo. "Beautiful animal. Husky mix, huh?"

"Yeah."

The vet looked at me.

"I mean, I think so."

"Where did you get her?"

I wanted to tell her everything—that I'd had Inyo since she was born, that she had a pure wolf father and a wolf-husky mother, that she needed her rabies vaccination so we could attend an obedience class. Instead I said, "I found her. She was a stray in Arizona."

The lie just fell right out of my mouth. I didn't know what the vet would do if I confessed that Inyo was a wolfdog. Maybe she would order me the hell out of her clinic. Or maybe she'd call the police. And if the police came, they'd take Inyo. And then what?

"I've got news for you," the vet said. "Your animal is very likely part wolf. There's no way she's just a husky. You're in for a ride." She explained that there was no law against wolfdogs in the state of Nevada, in the city of Reno, or in Washoe County, where a wolfdog was considered a domestic animal unless it bit a person, a pet, or livestock, and then it would be reclassified from domestic to wild in a blink. Animal control would skip the quarantine period designed to allow for signs of rabies to show up. They would euthanize the animal immediately and send its head straight to the state health department laboratory for a rabies test.

The vet told me that the week before she'd put down a suspected hybrid when the animal bit a six-year-old girl. She'd sent the animal's head to a lab. "I'm pretty sure that animal was a hybrid," she said. "But there have been some sad cases of regular dogs misidentified as wolfdogs. Everybody wants to believe they've got a part wolf." She explained that most people, including animal-control officers, didn't know what a real wolf looked like, and there was no DNA test to prove whether or not an animal had any wolf in it.[1] "Wolfdogs are living in limboland," she said.

I saw visions of Inyo's head on a tray while scientists in white lab coats picked through her brain tissue for evidence of rabies. I could hardly breathe.

The vet gave Inyo the vaccine, saying that it was better she have it than not, but warned me that there had been a few documented cases of vaccinated wolfdogs contracting rabies. Inyo rested a paw on the vet's wrist and licked her cheek.

I told her I understood and explained that we spent a lot of time in the backcountry, and if a rabid animal bit Inyo she'd have a better chance of survival if she'd been vaccinated. I also told her that Inyo would never bite anyone.

I pictured Loop jumping over the backyard fence and nearly killing the neighbor's dog. Remembering that the dog's owner had also been bitten, I wondered then if Loop had done the biting, and if so, had it been an accident? She was gentle, I reasoned. If she had bitten him, it must have been unintentional. But then again, maybe she'd viewed her suburban backyard as too small a territory and sought to get rid of the invading dog. That man had been in the way.

"Um, can we just keep 'husky mix' on that paperwork?" I asked, nodding at the chart.

"Sure," the vet said. "I couldn't prove her identity anyway."

Before leaving the clinic I made an appointment to have Inyo spayed in a couple of weeks. Driving north on Virginia Street past the Jelly Donut and Reno Mega Laundry, I clutched her rabies certificate. Although she usually preferred to sit in the back of Hanna, Inyo rode shotgun that day, gazing out the windshield at a rottweiler pacing the open bed of a Dodge truck with Montana plates. A set of TruckNutz made to look like a scrotum dangled off the tow hitch, and the truck's bumper stickers read The Only Good Wolf Is a Dead Wolf, and Keep Honking. I'm Reloading.

Suddenly danger seemed to be everywhere, and everyone was against us. I slowed way down and switched lanes, letting the truck get two or three cars ahead of me.

Ryan and I didn't plan on living in Nevada forever, so I needed to know the laws about wolfdog ownership in other states. I had plenty of time for uninterrupted research because Ryan had parent-teacher conferences at the high school that night. I stopped at Albertsons and bought a pint of Ben & Jerry's for me and a steak for Inyo. When we got home, I cooked Inyo's steak and dug into the ice cream. The phone rang. A man asked for Ryan, but wouldn't tell me who he was or what he wanted. I wrote down the 1-888 number and hung up.

While Inyo gnawed her steak in the denlike cubbyhole under my desk, I kept my bare feet away from her teeth and spooned Super Fudge Chunk from the carton, surfing the Internet for laws on wolfdog ownership and the rabies vaccination controversy. I didn't think Inyo would ever bite anyone, and I'd said as much to the vet, but what if?

I found a story about a guy in Crown Point, Indiana, who'd gone over to his neighbor's house to borrow a power tool and been bitten by the neighbor's dog. He reported to the authorities that the dog was a German shepherd–wolf mix. The dog's owner maintained that she didn't know whether or not her animal was part wolf or just a German shepherd mixed with some other breed of domestic dog. She might have been stalling, but who could blame her?

Meanwhile, the man who'd been bitten received a series of postexposure vaccinations. He insisted that the animal was a wolfdog, and he wanted it euthanized immediately to know for sure whether it could have given him rabies. "My peace of mind is more important than any animal," he'd said.

According to the article, the dog's owner hired a lawyer to represent her dog and waited while a judge decided if the animal was a domestic dog or a wolf hybrid. Without a conclusive DNA test, the animal could not be proven to be part wolf, so the decision would be based on other evidence—the animal's appearance, behavior, and any breeding records. If he was ruled a wolfdog, the article reported, there would be no quarantine period and he'd be a goner. I searched for follow-up articles but found nothing. I never did learn the fate of that animal.

Inyo had long finished her steak when I heard her chewing on something in the living room and got up to investigate. She'd started gnawing lamp cords, computer cables—even the line to the telephone. I'd been talking with a friend the day before when the line went dead. Puzzled, I looked at the receiver and then over my shoulder, where

Inyo sat with the phone cord dangling from her mouth. Before getting on the computer, I'd unplugged the appliances, lamps, and the television—just in case—and a good thing too. I found her nibbling a lamp cord, and swapped it out for the Ben & Jerry's carton, which had a little melted ice cream pooling at the bottom. While she wedged her muzzle deep into the carton, sticky cream matting the fur between her eyes, I got back online.

The laws governing ownership of wolfdogs varied from one state to the next, one county line and city ordinance to another. The state of Colorado, for instance, had no special restrictions regarding hybrids. They were considered domestic animals. But at the city level, my little family couldn't live in Broomfield or Louisville, although we could live in Boulder or Denver. We could also live in Salt Lake County, Utah, where the only animals prohibited were constrictor snakes longer than ten feet, alligators, grizzly bears, and apes. In Delaware, a state divided neatly into three counties, we could legally live in Sussex, but not in New Castle or Kent. There were grandfather clauses in some laws, none in others. If we'd lived in Billings, Montana, before 1993, we could go on living there. On the other hand, if we'd lived anywhere in Georgia after their state law was passed, we'd have had to pack up and leave. I was starting to appreciate what the vet had meant by "limbo-land."

I found a story in an Arizona newspaper about an ordinance to regulate wolfdog ownership in Tucson. Wolfdogs weren't regulated at the state level, but the Tucson City Council was considering new restrictions in response to more than twenty-six bites by wolves and wolf hybrids in the city within a three-year period. If the ordinance passed, hybrids would have to wear tags around their necks that read Dangerous Animal, be walked on a leash less than six feet long, and wear a muzzle in public. I read further in the article and there was Leda. A reporter had interviewed her as one of the wolfdog owners opposed to the ordinance. She was quoted: "It's not fair to put such onerous requirements on an owner." In the article the reporter noted that Leda had asked not to be named, worried that Loop and Voodoo would be targeted by fearful neighbors. Obviously, the reporter had ignored her request.

The ordinance didn't pass the first time, but several years later a revised version did, this one covering all of Pima County. To find out what Inyo and I would have faced in order to get a rabies certificate in Tucson, I called an animal-control officer who told me that I'd have had to buy a canine-wild-animal-hybrid permit and get written permission from the Arizona State Veterinary Medical Examining Board for Inyo to get the rabies vaccine. Then a licensed veterinarian could vaccinate her against rabies, but would require me to sign a release form declaring that I understood there was no guarantee the rabies vaccine worked in hybrids. If Inyo ever bit someone, she'd be treated like an unvaccinated wild animal and euthanized. Several Tucson veterinarians warned me that if I told the truth about what kind of animal I had, the city and county would be breathing down my neck, inspecting my yard any time they wanted. "If the least thing happens, the county will take your animal."

Reasonable or not, laws were laws, and no matter where we lived, I'd make sure I knew what they were. Inyo was a wolf, but she wasn't. She was a dog too, but she wasn't. So where did that leave her? I decided she'd be safe as long as I kept quiet about her real identity.

Later that night Inyo bounded across the bedroom and jumped onto the bed where I lay snuggled in my great-grandmother's double wedding-ring quilt, reading an old tale about Edmund, King of East Anglia, who was put to death by the invading Danes in the ninth century. When Edmund wouldn't renounce his faith and pledge allegiance to a foreign king, the Danish leader Hinguar beheaded Edmund and tossed his head into a thicket. As the story goes, a wolf witnessed the killing and guarded the head between his great paws until Edmund's companions came looking, following the sound of the wolf's howl. Accompanied by the wolf, they bore Edmund's head and body away and laid them together in a grave. The wolf then returned to the forest. I shivered under the blanket thinking of all those wolfdogs who'd been beheaded for being something they couldn't renounce—creatures of two worlds.

Inyo rubbed her muzzle against me and curled in the crook of my arm. I felt her hot breath through my T-shirt as I stroked her fur and studied the banded guard hairs that formed a cloak across her shoulders. Each black-tipped hair had a lighter band below that, and then a darker band that gave way to gray near the root. By the time snow hooded the Sierra Nevada peaks, Inyo would have her long winter hairs and a double coat to keep her warm when we headed into Desolation Wilderness for a week or two of backcountry skiing and camping.

Still in my clothes, my teeth unbrushed, I let the book slip from my hand and reached up to pull the string on the light. Ryan hadn't come home yet, so Inyo and I lay there alone in the dark. I wondered how long she would let me cuddle her before she jumped down and started eating the electrical cords again. Training would teach Inyo some house manners, I thought, and keep her out of trouble.

CHAPTER TEN

Wolf Whisperer

A wolf's pup will grow into a wolf even though it be raised among men.

—Afghan proverb

To help burn off some of her energy and get us both focused, Inyo and I walked the three miles from home to our PetSmart obedience class. By mile two she pulled less and I could stroll instead of running on my tiptoes behind her on the dark sidewalk. At five feet ten inches I was not a petite woman, but Inyo, weighing in at fifty-eight pounds now, was still the stronger one. If I relaxed for even a moment, she could pull me facedown on the pavement, my arm tangled in the leash. I still had bits of parking-lot gravel buried in my left kneecap from our last walking adventure in the WinCo parking lot, where she'd rushed a flock of Brewer's Blackbirds.

We'd already been running that day, huffing up cheatgrass-covered hills, dodging old bathtubs and televisions on Peavine Mountain northwest of downtown. Among shotgun-shell casings and bullet-ridden bottles of Castrol 20W-50, a dingy gun sock lay in the dirt with the logo "Able Ammo: We shoot all we can and sell the rest." There was a coyote perched on a boulder, eyeing us. It stood and trotted through the cheatgrass in our direction, pausing next to a Magic Chef oven. I'd relented a little on my leash rule, allowing Inyo to run free when we were out of the city. But now I clipped her to her lead, afraid she might chase the coyote and get lost. The coyote watched Inyo's movements more than mine. Inyo craned her neck around to stare, trotting

73

sideways to keep her eye on the coyote as I urged her forward. That had been her big excitement for the day, and by the time we passed El Boracho, a Mexican restaurant lit up for the dinner hour, Inyo was relaxed and ready for our first training class.

Once inside PetSmart we browsed bins crammed with furry candy canes, stuffed reindeer and turkeys, Santa Clauses, and fancy Christmas collars decorated with sparkling red and green gems. When a woman's voice on the loudspeaker announced that the class was about to begin, scrabbling and nail-scritching erupted from the aisles as every dog tuned in to its owner's sudden seriousness. Barks and whines echoed around the store as dogs slid along the glossy concrete, following their people toward the back wall stacked with fifty-pound bags of Science Diet, Purina, and The Good Life. Inside a small ring marked off with orange traffic cones, an Afghan hound looking remarkably like Steve Perry from Journey galloped circles around his owner. I imagined the hound breaking into song, "When the lights go down in the city . . . " and noticed several other owners trying vainly to maintain order with their dogs. I was in good company.

Bonnie, our instructor, was a short, round woman with thick glasses, a quick smile, and an endless supply of dog biscuits in her apron. She seemed perfectly comfortable amid the ruckus of dogs and people, clapping her hands and instructing us to line up so she could greet each dog and owner. She sized up each dog-human duo and gave us all a brief rundown of what we might expect from our various breeds. She told Art that his basset hound Billy was sweet tempered, peaceful, and naturally well behaved, but added that Art might have some difficulty getting Billy's attention if he picked up an interesting scent. Billy looked unmoved by this news, his droopy eyelids giving him a bored expression that would remain unchanged until the hint of some delicious, unknown smell excited his nose.

The owner of Roxy, a long-haired dachshund, told Bonnie that her dog was a chicken chaser and the neighbors were fed up. "They've threatened to call animal control," she said. At the sound of her owner's voice, Roxy wagged her tail side to side like a bell clapper.

"Strong hunting instinct," Bonnie said. "Can't help herself." She explained that dachshunds, bred to hunt rabbits and badgers, were utterly fearless—though not that great on the leash. "Just be thankful she's not going after raccoons," Bonnie said, adding that she'd known a miniature whose jaw had been cracked by a raccoon. "He came home from the vet with a wired chin and went right back to the raccoon's den for another go."

Puffer, a Jack Russell terrier, barked incessantly from his position at third in the lineup. Bonnie instructed his owner to give him the command "Quiet." He was quiet for a minute and then started up again, lurching forward to the end of his leash like a little Napoleon, wanting to rumble with Wolfgang, a young Weimaraner. When he couldn't get to Wolfgang, Puffer lifted his leg on the nearest cone.

Bonnie approached me and smiled. "Well, what do we have here?" Inyo's tail swept side to side at the sound of her voice. Tangled in her lead, I untwisted myself while Inyo chewed on Bonnie's shoelaces.

"Achh! Leave it," Bonnie said. Inyo turned to gnawing on her leash. She'd already chomped through half of it, and I figured I'd have to buy a new one by the time class was over. "Tell her 'Leave it,' when she does that," Bonnie said.

"Leave it," I said and took the leash out of Inyo's mouth.

"Heap on the praise when she stops."

I nodded and smiled, having tried the "Leave it" and "No" commands many times without much luck. Inyo never accepted "no" when she thought "yes" was the right answer. My attempts to anticipate what she might get her mouth on had also failed. Two nights earlier I hadn't been able to find my mouth guard—the three-hundred-dollar dental device that kept me from grinding my teeth to the roots in my sleep. I'd rifled through the bathroom drawer where I kept it stored in a plastic case, but both the case and the guard were missing. The mystery resolved itself the next morning when Inyo and I went for our morning walk. While I rubbed my sore jaw, Inyo squatted, and I saw scraps of opaque white plastic embedded in her stool. A few of the bits were recognizable as tooth impressions. I knew then that she must have watched me put the mouth guard in the drawer and then opened the drawer herself.

"Looks wolfy," Bonnie said. "What is she?"

I hesitated. I was supposed to keep my mouth shut, but I needed help, and if Bonnie knew what Inyo really was, maybe we could get some serious training. "She's a husky-wolf mix."

"Thought so," she said cheerfully, adding that she'd guessed Inyo was either husky-wolf or malamute-wolf.

I'd heard of trainers wary of having wolfdogs in their classes, but Bonnie welcomed us and my breathing relaxed.

Bonnie told me that she'd worked with wolfdogs before and read a lot about wolves. "It pays to read about wolves if you're a dog trainer," she said to the whole group. "All dogs come from wolves."

The owner of a Lhasa apso cringed and stared at Inyo. "She's not dangerous, is she?" Another owner scooped her dog off the floor, a dolled-up shih tzu that looked like Tammy Faye Bakker.

Bonnie ran interference. "This girl seems really gentle," she said, scratching Inyo behind the ears. "You got yourself a good one. I've met some hybrids I wouldn't turn my back on."

I was thinking of a less cordial response to the owner of the Lhasa—something like, "Cool it, lady. Your dog looks like Cousin Itt." But I kept quiet, feeling sorry for her dog who couldn't see through the curtain of hair over its face.

Billy the basset could see all right. He had a decent tail and a finely tuned sense of smell, but his ears were so long and heavy they nearly touched the ground. He couldn't pull his ears back to indicate fear or push them forward to show alertness. Neither could he stiffen those great flapping jowls to bare his teeth. When he let out a deep, throaty bark, that drooping, expressionless face reminded me of someone who'd been to the dentist and had a shot of Novocain.

Plenty of animal behaviorists have noticed that selective breeding has impaired the dog's ability to communicate with its own kind. German ethologist Dorit Feddersen-Petersen has studied how dogs socialize with one another compared to the way their closest wild relatives do. Wolves, coyotes, and golden jackals are canines with a highly developed social repertoire of sounds, as well as facial and body expressions. Compared to their wild relatives, dogs have few of these tools, but pet dogs live with people, not in a wild pack, and don't need such an elegant vocabulary to survive.

Bonnie finished greeting the other dogs and their owners and instructed us to walk clockwise in a circle, following the set of cones. I didn't mind the circle, as long as Bonnie would have us reverse direction at some point so I could unwind myself. "Give the person in front of you plenty of room," she said. "You're the leader. You set the pace." The owner of a standard poodle struggled to stay on her feet as her dog leaned heavily against her. "That's a sign of dominance!" Bonnie called out. She took hold of the poodle's leash to demonstrate. Shaved in the traditional lion clip, the poodle looked like Carmen Miranda in *Down Argentine Way*, right down to a match for Carmen's tutti-frutti hat—a cheerful topknot. Bonnie nodded at Inyo. "Wolves don't get nasty about their personal space very often. The alpha wolf uses its body to move a lower-ranking animal out of the way. *You* do it by lifting your knee."

While Bonnie lifted her knee, making it uncomfortable for the poodle to lean, I started getting antsy. We'd made four clockwise circles, and all I could think about was when she would send us the other direction. "I'll let you in on a little secret," Bonnie said, handing the leash back to the poodle's owner. "This class is not really about training your dog, it's about training you. Obedience class is ninety percent training the owner and only ten percent training the dog. If there's one thing I want you to take from tonight's class, it's this: If your dog isn't performing a command correctly, ask yourself if you gave the right cue."

Finally Bonnie had us turn and walk in a counterclockwise circle. With Inyo on my left-hand side, her shoulder parallel to my thigh, I gave the heel command and stepped forward with my left foot. When she surged ahead as she'd done in the park, I gave a gentle tug on the leash and released the pressure immediately. "Good girl, Inyo!" She walked next to me for a few seconds and then rushed forward again.

"That's okay," Bonnie said. "You'll get it. Bring her back to your side. Just keep doing that, and don't stop walking." I was supposed to bring Inyo back to position while keeping my pace, praising her when she walked quietly. Bonnie assured me that Inyo would learn to walk on my left side if I was consistent.

Many years later when I met Pat Goodman, curator at Indiana's Wolf Park, she told me that she doesn't expect the same level of obedience from a wolf that she would from a dog. She and the other wolf handlers use heavy seven- to nine-foot-long chain leashes with snaps at each end to make a one-size-fits-all collar for the wolf and a loop at the other end for the handler. (Nylon and leather are out for good reason: They're chewable and edible.) Goodman explained that leashed wolves are allowed to explore their environment, moving to the left or right side of the handler, rather than staying on the left at the heel and paying strict attention to the person walking them. The wolves go where they want, within reason, but they go at the pace the handler sets—at a walk or very slow jog. But apparently even this latitude doesn't always make for a pleasant walk.

"When your dog stays at the heel, praise it," Bonnie said, explaining that to get cooperation from our dogs we had to be good leaders. By teaching them to heel, to remain at our sides or slightly behind us, we were establishing our leadership position. "Don't miss any opportunity to develop the good feelings between you," she said. At the time, I appreciated Bonnie's positive training techniques, but when she called out, "Dogs love this kind of work. It stimulates their minds," I couldn't agree that Inyo found this training very stimulating. Going around a set of orange traffic cones just wasn't her thing, and come to think of it, mine either. Both of us would have preferred running up Peavine Mountain in a snowstorm. But the reality was that Inyo and I lived in the city, at least for now, and I couldn't deny the practical applications of a basic obedience class. One screwup and we might find ourselves in a parking lot, living in Hanna again. However, my dreams of graduating into the advanced class were fading. Newfoundland and basset hound, Weimaraner and dachshund, each one had its share of doggy attention deficit disorder or stubbornness, but each also saw its person as the quarterback of every play and watched for cues. Once the people got their cues right and the dogs understood what was being asked of them, most of them responded eagerly, as if to say, "Well sure! Why didn't you say so in the first place? That's a great idea!"

Although Inyo did understand my requests (I swear I was asking correctly), she thought heeling was nonsense and going around a circle the most frivolous waste of energy imaginable. *Not fun. Stupid wolf, YOU go around in circles.* When I looked over at Roxy or Billy, I could see that although they'd walked the circle a dozen times by now, the terrain remained fascinating and full of new promising scents with each go-around. Inyo didn't see the point of looping around bags of Science Diet over and over. *Rip-tear the bags!* She pulled me toward the treat aisle. *Cow hooves! Bins and bins!* I pulled her back and she lurched toward the horse tack, toward all those delicious bridles and saddles, the unbearably wonderful scent of tanned cowhide. She clacked her jaws in frustration as I steered her toward the circle and Billy the basset with his dragging ears.

When Bonnie told us to stop we were supposed to turn abruptly to the left and halt, putting our dogs into a sit. When people turned, their dogs bumped into their thighs and sat, except the Lhasa apso and the shih tzu, whose owners tripped over them. If our dogs kept going, we were supposed to give a gentle correction, but before I had a chance, Inyo pulled me straight into Wolfgang's owner. "I'm so sorry," I said. Lucky for me the floor was slick. Inyo scrabbled and scraped, but I had the advantage of wearing sneakers with traction. I planted my feet and leaned backward. Inyo finally spun around, stopped, and began chewing her leash, staring into space as if dreaming.

"Who's walking whom?" Bonnie said, smiling at me.

I smiled and shook my head, blowing out a puff of air. The other dog-owner teams seemed to be having a ball, the dogs nearly knocking their owners over with the sheer joy of being close to them. I was not the center of Inyo's world. She seemed to look through me to someplace else, and walking her felt like driving a hot rod with the gas pedal floored and no steering wheel.

At the end of the hour Bonnie dismissed the class for the night, and when everyone had dispersed except for Inyo and me—and Puffer's owner, left wiping up his piddle with a paper towel—Bonnie said, "Wolf hybrids are just harder. They're more intense than dogs." She told me that dog owners have to stay one step ahead to be good leaders, but their dogs want to please them. "You need to stay three steps ahead," she said. "Wolves and wolfdogs are always wondering 'What's in it for me?'" I wasn't entering Inyo in a dog show so I didn't need a competition-grade heel. "We'll work with her wolfy ways," Bonnie added. "She'll walk quietly at your side at least some of the time." Then she laughed. "And we want you to look comfortable, not like you're water-skiing on pavement."

I had to admit that Inyo would never upstage the shih tzu and the poodle in the training ring, but she could follow any command that a regular dog could—if she was in the mood. And none of those dogs had anything on Inyo in the backcountry.

As I led Inyo to the exit, she suddenly dashed into the aquarium aisle. *Finned things!*

I tightened my grip on the leash. "Inyo, leave it."

Fish-fish, dummy! She strained toward the rows of gurgling tanks.

I waved a snack bag of chopped hot dogs in the air, coaxing her through the automatic doors into the parking lot. A man leaned out the driver's side window of his van and said, "That a wolf you got there?"

I told him that Inyo was a husky mix.

"She might have a little husky in her, but I bet she's mostly wolf," he said. "Better be careful. She might turn on you."

When I started to walk away he called out, "She got five toes or six?"

I counted the toes on her front paws. "Five."

"She's a wolf then. Dogs got six toes."

People had some peculiar notions—a dog with six toes? (Turns out one breed, the Norwegian Lundehund, does have six toes.)

"The roof of her mouth black?" he asked.

I'd never looked.

"If it's black she's a wolf," he said. "A dog's is pink." He added that the proportion of black to pink would tell me how much wolf Inyo had in her. He also told me to look at her gums—the blacker they were the more wolf blood she had. I nodded politely, thanking him for the information.[1]

"You take care now," the man said, starting his engine.

Inyo peed in a concrete-rimmed flower bed occupied by one of those scraggly deciduous trees trying to grow in the harsh conditions of the high desert. Outside the Jelly Donut I overheard a homeless man tell his buddy, "Hey, dude, that girl's walking a wolf on a leash."

Back in my well-lit kitchen, I pried open Inyo's clackers to have a look at the roof of her mouth. It was dark, just like the man had said, but there was some pink too. I pulled a package of pork neck bones from the freezer, and as I wrested one of the bones from the frozen clump, Inyo let out a deep, throaty howl. My shoulders hiked up to my ears, and I winced at the thought of Bill and Susan on the other side of our thin shared wall. Any minute now Bill would march over and bang on the door. "Get out!" he'd holler. "You and your dog are a nuisance to the neighborhood!" Then I remembered they'd gone to their vacation home for a week, and swallowed with relief.

When I finished drying the last of the dinner dishes and there was no more clatter of crockery or the tinny sound of silverware clanking in the drawer, an unnerving silence filled the house. I knew Ryan was in the bedroom, engrossed in Thomas Pynchon's novel *Mason & Dixon*. I heard the swish of a page turning. He'd disappeared into the bedroom when I told him that the same man from the 1-888 number had telephoned that afternoon and insisted, "Your husband needs to call me." This time the man left his first name, Kevin, but would not tell me what the call was about, and neither would Ryan. When I pressed him, Ryan blinked his long, dark lashes and set his mouth. "They're probably just trying to sell me something."

I didn't want to believe Ryan was hiding something from me, but I'd gone to Raley's for groceries a few days earlier, and the cashier had frowned at my check and said she was sorry, she couldn't accept it. My account had been flagged because Ryan had bounced two checks there recently. The next customer sighed and raised his eyebrows. I was sure everyone in line behind me could hear. I had to leave the bagged groceries and walk out, feeling all those eyes on my back. When I'd confronted Ryan he shrugged and said he didn't know what I was talking about, and did I want to climb at River Rock that weekend?

From under the blanket covering his cage, Lupe emitted a contented sleepy gurgle, but where was Inyo? Surely she'd finished her bones by now. Maybe she was curled on her cedar bed, sacked out after a day of exercise and all that contact with new people and dogs. At least the silence meant she wasn't chewing electrical cords, or her newfound interest—windowsills. That had made a terrible sound, and I'd been sure Bill and Susan had heard the wood splintering through the walls.

I threw the dish towel over my shoulder and peered into the living room. Surrounded by several mutilated pairs of my underwear, Inyo sat proudly chewing the crotch out of a pair of lemon-yellow bikinis.

I guessed then that under Ryan's nose she'd knocked over the hamper to root through the hill of work shirts, jeans, and socks. Silently she'd lifted one pair of undies and then another and another, making trips from the bedroom to the living room with her contraband. While Ryan read about frontier encounters with Native Americans, Inyo had settled in to make alterations to my undergarments. I clapped my hands to my knees, feeling a bead of gravel rotate just under the skin, and collapsed on the floor in a fit of giggles. Thongs were popular, but crotchless panties?

I managed to save two pairs and scrapped the others, stowing the hamper in the bedroom closet. Ryan's newest teaching shoes were still intact, and the fact that we couldn't afford a new pair weekly had helped him remember to tuck them safely on a high shelf. Meanwhile, I would try to follow Bonnie's advice: "Stay three steps ahead."

CHAPTER ELEVEN

In Yo Face

Calmer than you are.
—Walter Sobchak (John Goodman),
The Big Lebowski

One afternoon when I came out of Raley's and slid open Hanna's side door with a fresh package of marrowbones, Inyo leaped from the rear seat and tore the package from my hand, her teeth barely missing my fingers. When I reached over to snatch it back and redo the whole here's-your-bone-that's-a-good-girl routine, she growled and her hackles pricked. The skin of her muzzle wrinkled and her canines, sharp as scythes, made me hesitate, exactly as they were meant to. Leda had told me that I had to be alpha in the relationship, but in this case I didn't know whether to assert authority or back down.

In the 1940s animal behaviorist Rudolph Schenkel coined the term "alpha" to account for the dominance contests he saw in captive groups of unrelated wolves. He thought that wild wolves must also live in a system of dominance and submission, with all the attendant violence he had observed in captive wolves. When geneticist Robert K. Wayne wrote "Dogs are gray wolves, despite their diversity in size and proportion," dog trainers naturally assumed that their methods should be based on wolf behavior, and since *captive* wolf behavior was all people knew about at the time, for a while the alpha roll was one of many popular techniques to remind the dog that the human is boss.

More recently, wolf biologist L. David Mech has called the whole alpha concept into question by pointing out that wild wolf packs are made up of mom, dad, and kids, so applying the term "alpha pair" to the breeding male and female makes about as much sense as referring to human parents as alphas. Yes, they're in charge, but they don't abuse their children physically or psychologically to make them behave. According to Mech, when a wild wolf displays a submissive posture, such as rolling on its back, the gesture is voluntary and serves to maintain friendly relations within the pack.

In her lecture "Wolf or 'Woof,'" dog trainer and wolf-behavior specialist and educator Beth Duman comes right out and says, "That alpha stuff is garbage." Dogs naturally look to their people as leaders. They are not trying to dominate us. They don't understand why they're being flipped over on their backs and growled at. This treatment, she says, terrorizes dogs and in some cases makes them aggressive. Its prominent advocates, the Monks of New Skete, now regret recommending it. "People who work with captive wolves found out a long time ago that if you pick on wolves, they'll pick on you back," Duman says, "so you'd better let go of that dominance model unless you want to die young."[1]

Many wolfdog owners I later encountered hadn't figured this out. One owner wore lambskin slippers around her wolfdogs as a litmus test of their respect for her alpha position. "They know better than to steal from me," she wrote, explaining that wearing the slippers around the animals taught them how to handle their temptations and develop self-control. Just in case any of her animals harbored notions of moving up in rank, another owner made a habit of dragging a deer carcass into the wolfdogs' pen and petting her animals while they ate. If they exhibited any threatening behavior toward her, she would haul the deer out. "Wolves and wolfdogs will test your alpha status to see what they can get away with," she wrote. "They push until you push back." One man claimed to wrestle what he called his "monster child" into a submissive position to remind the animal of his lower rank in the human–wolfdog pack. "You have to believe you're a badass to really be one," he said.

For the most part I trusted in positive-reinforcement training rather than punishment to get the behavior I wanted, but standing in the

Raley's parking lot that afternoon with the cold wind blowing through my thin cotton slacks, I couldn't see a safe way to apply either method. Inyo was going on nine months old now, and something inside her had definitely changed. Many wolfdog owners claim that their animals test human authority, and if the owner doesn't pass the smaller tests when the wolfdog is still young, she can look forward to more severe challenges later. If Inyo was testing me, then I failed—because I backed off. I chose to keep all of my fingers and refused to wrangle with her over a bunch of goopy marrowbones.

I wasn't doing very well with Ryan either. When a Raley's cashier refused my check a second time and I'd had to leave behind another cart of groceries, I called the bank and discovered our checking account was overdrawn and Ryan had drained the savings. Turned out he'd been going to Cashco and Moneytree for payday loans, hoping I wouldn't notice a couple hundred dollars missing every month when they collected what he owed, plus a hefty amount of interest. When I demanded to know what the hell he was trying to do to us, Ryan just looked at the floor and shrugged. "I needed stuff." I decided to take control of the budget, assigning Ryan the electric, phone, and other utility bills, and giving him an allowance to spend on whatever he wanted. I would write the rent check and buy the groceries. I could tell he didn't like my new plan, but later that night he offered to brush my hair, patiently working the tangles out with his fingers. The next morning he left me a few lines from a Pablo Neruda poem:

> *Take bread away from me, if you wish,*
> *take air away, but*
> *do not take from me your laughter.*[2]

I softened, but the fact was, Ryan just couldn't handle money very well. To get through the rest of the month, I called my mother and stepdad for a loan.

One night, not long after the episode in the Raley's parking lot, I heard glass shatter and sprinted toward the kitchen, my ankles rolling on cracked cow femurs. Inyo stared at me from the countertop and let out a mournful howl. She crouched with her tail tucked between her legs, lips pulled back, ears flat, and just the tip of her tongue poking out between her front teeth. Her head lowered and slightly cocked, she seemed to be trying to appease me. I almost yelled, "Get down, goddamn it!" but caught myself. She looked like a kid whose ice cream had just tumbled off the cone and landed with a *splat!* Glass shards, stray egg noodles, and flecks of tuna covered the linoleum. At least somebody liked my casserole. For dinner Ryan had eaten three bowls of Cap'n Crunch and washed them down with a 40-ounce bottle of Miller High Life. "Honey, it's the Captain and the champagne of beers," he'd said.

I held my palm near Inyo's face, not wanting her to leap down and cut her paw pads on the glass. "Wait," I said. But she wasn't planning to abandon her post no matter what I said. I rushed for the broom, and although I felt like chasing her with it, I swept up the shards of Pyrex. She watched as I sponged shiny splinters mixed with noodles off the linoleum. Once satisfied that I'd picked up all the glass, I pointed my finger at the floor. "Inyo, off!" She stood her ground and uttered a high-pitched whine.

Even through his headphones, Ryan heard the sound and swiveled in the computer chair. "What's the rumpus?"

"Never mind."

"Roger that," he said, and swiveled back to his game.

Inyo and I were in a face-off—eye to eye, an arm's length apart. Something was wrong. What did she need? Although Leda had said that high-quality kibble supplemented with bones would be a good diet for Inyo, I found myself doubting it. I'd tried the expensive kibble. I'd tried the cruddy cheap stuff. But Inyo often flipped her dish upside down, pawing through the brown nuggets as if looking for the prize in the Cracker Jack box.

Although I didn't want to reward her little countertop caper, I also didn't want the situation to deteriorate into another contest of wills. The whine was not aggressive, but plaintive, a plea for food. To entice her off the counter, I rummaged through the crisper for one of the pig feet I'd bought her. Holding the foot by its longest digit, all pink and powdery, I crouched on the floor and pretended to eat the pasty hoof, smacking my lips. Inyo paced the countertop and howled. I decided to time my command with her movements, so that she connected my asking her to get off the counter and the tasty reward. Just when she tensed her muscles to jump off and go for the hoof, I said "Inyo off," as cheerily as I could with a pig foot in my face.

She trotted over and sat back on her haunches, both front paws on my shoulder. She licked my lips and nibbled my chin. I made a grill out of my front teeth, a gesture someone had told me would satisfy my obligation to wolfy social graces while sparing me a mouthful of wolf-dog spit. "Good off," I said, and put the hoof in front of her.

When she finished, leaving only a nubbin of bone on the carpet, she mussed my hair with her nose and rubbed against my fleece pajamas before flopping down on her side to show me her belly. I patted her barrel and cradled one of her big paws in my hand. I gave her another pig foot, but instead of eating it as I thought she would, she tried to bury it in a corner of the living room, digging at the floor where a small section of carpet had come unglued.

When wolves are full, they often cache leftovers underground, but looking back on it now, I wonder if Inyo's hunger had made her stash food to supplement the inadequate kibble diet she'd been on. A few days before the tuna casserole incident, I'd stepped briefly out of the kitchen to get the mail, and when I came back the whole chicken thawing in the sink had disappeared, giblets and all. I hadn't bothered looking for the bird, thinking Inyo must have eaten it. But she hadn't. I found the chicken the next day when I followed the stench to a spot behind the sofa pillows where she'd cached it, pimply skin intact. Had she been saving the meat for a time when hunger became too much?

Digging furiously into the floor, she'd eventually use her teeth to rip the carpet, so I shooed her away. She tried to bury the pig foot behind the sofa cushions as she had the chicken. Better she slime my thrift store sofa than shred Bill and Susan's carpet, I thought, but Inyo decided the couch wasn't a safe hiding place and buried the pig foot in our bed sheets. I was too tired to care.

Ryan, still engrossed in his game, gave a quick wave good night. Computer-generated characters ran back and forth across the screen, casting spells and dying. Earlier in the evening he'd tried to entice me to play by creating a character he thought I'd like, a druid that could shape-shift into different animals and had a magical talent for influencing an animal's behavior. But I had no appetite for pretend. I switched off the light. Soon we'd be in the backcountry again, where our lives made more sense. Lupe would go to the parrot sitter, and Ryan, Inyo, and I would be trekking—this time in Desolation Wilderness. I could feel Inyo's ribs through her thick fur. I needed to get more weight on her. She was too ribby for a multiday trek through deep snow in freezing temperatures.

The next day, walking the aisles of a boutique pet supply store, I browsed the shelves of kibble, peering at the bags that pictured wolves and promised to replicate the dog's "ancestral diet." But I couldn't believe that by themselves a bunch of brown pellets, no matter how pricy, could satisfy Inyo. There had to be something I could add. Mounds of hamburger filled a freezer in one corner, but I worried about the bacteria in raw meat. Cans of tripe, their labels featuring a howling wolf, were stacked near the checkout. No way I'd buy canned guts filled with grass. I left disappointed.

In the ensuing years, I learned that the Smithsonian Institution's reclassification of the domestic dog as a subspecies of the wolf had prompted companies selling raw-meat products for dogs to peddle their wares more vigorously with the claim that dogs are domesticated wolves and should eat like their wild relatives. Even companies selling kibble eventually cashed in on the reclassification, declaring that their products also emulated the "ancestral diet" of dogs, one dictated by their genes. Some dog owners have added unwashed green tripe— the stomach and its contents, the partially digested grasses and grains of cows and other ruminants—to their animal's diet with the assumption that the dog's instinct is to mimic wild wolves and eat the fresh steaming gut contents of a prey animal. But when wolves bring down a large ungulate like a moose, bison, or caribou, they eat the organs, muscle meat, fat, connective tissue, hair, and bone—just about everything *except* the contents of the stomach and intestines. In fact, wolves shake out as much of the actual contents of the intestine and stomach as they can before eating only the lining. According to

L. David Mech, plant material makes up a very small part of a wolf's overall diet, "perhaps as little as 1–3%."

It may also be hazardous to assume that since wolves eat raw bones, dogs can do the same. The wild wolf's intestinal tract and organs are better protected from punctures than a dog's because the prey animal's hair (or fur) wraps around bone fragments like a cocoon and acts as a buffer down the short but delicate chute of the intestinal tract. Besides, the action of the digestive tract is only one part of the process. Dogs' skull shape and jaw structure (of even the most wolfy-looking northern breeds) differ from those of wolves and vary radically from one breed to the next. And while both dogs and wolves have forty-two teeth, those teeth aren't of the same size or spaced alike in the mouth and will grind bones differently. In other words, safety has as much to do with what happens to bones *before* they reach the stomach as it does when they get there.

Not only are dogs designed for a different diet from wolves, they don't share the wolves' eating schedule. In fact wolves don't have a schedule because their hunting efforts aren't always successful. When they do make a kill, they eat all they can, for tomorrow they may go hungry. According to educators at the International Wolf Center in Ely, Minnesota, a wolf is capable of eating 20% of its body weight in a single sitting, which for the average human would be the same as eating 133 McDonald's Happy Meals. The design of a wolf's stomach allows it to expand to hold that enormous quantity of food. Dogs don't have that capacity, and vomit if they eat too much at once. Anyhow, dog owners don't limit their dogs to one giant meal every few days.

All I knew at the time was that Inyo was hungry, and I would have to improvise. For treats I'd stick with thick-walled beef bones, but for regular meals I decided to concoct a stew to top her kibble. I drove to Raley's and bought two chickens, a heap of vegetables, and a bag of potatoes. As I was chopping carrots, Inyo gnawing a marrowbone at my feet, the phone rang. Caller ID told me it was Kevin from the 1-888 number. Ryan was at work, so I decided to get to the bottom of the mystery. I felt a twinge of guilt posing as Ryan to get information, but I did it anyway, making my voice deep and manly to answer all of Kevin's questions: date of birth, mother's maiden name, Social Security number. "You're in some serious trouble, son," Kevin said. "You've let your student loans go into default, and now you owe a lot of money." I asked him how much "I" owed. In a steady, practiced voice he replied that the principal, plus interest accrued since the loans had slipped into default, came to well over a hundred thousand dollars.

"Hello?" Kevin said when I fell silent. I couldn't breathe. "Hello? Are you there?" I hung up the phone and gasped for air. No amount of circling or tapping would calm me down. I dialed the high school where Ryan taught and asked the secretary to page him out of class. When he came to the phone, I said, "I just found out about the hundred grand you owe."

"I already told you about that. You just don't remember."

What was he trying to do—make me crazy? "Bullshit!" I yelled.

"It's not a big deal," Ryan said.

"Not a big deal? You've wrecked our lives! I'm going to fucking kill myself." I slammed down the phone.

Fifteen minutes later, there was a knock on the sliding door, and when I pulled back the drapes I found the glass filled with two large police officers. Officer Dan and Officer Tim told me I had to go with them.

"Go where?"

Ryan had called the cops, thinking that I'd gone bananas and would hurt myself. What he didn't know was that when you call the Reno police with a claim like that, even if the person isn't serious about doing herself in, the responding officers may haul her away at their discretion.

"I was pissed off," I said. "I wasn't planning to do anything." But arguing was useless. I had five minutes to gather my belongings. Putting Lupe in his cage with a handful of parrot kibble, I clipped Inyo to her Beast tie-out and dumped a whole package of marrowbones in the backyard, hoping they'd last her until Ryan got home. The officers escorted me in the back of their patrol car to a local emergency room and from there to the state mental hospital.

Ryan met me at the hospital. "I'm sorry," he said, his chin quivering, eyes full of tears. "I was worried about you."

I gave him a stiff hug. I couldn't speak.

Nurse Tina told him he could visit me the next day during family hour, and the heavy double doors clicked shut behind him. She made an inventory of my personal effects—one pair of Levis, one Tom Waits T-shirt, one pair of blue underpants, one smoking pipe and small bag of tobacco, one lighter—and informed me that I'd have to surrender my nose ring. That first night in 8-North Ward, I wore a green hospital gown and slept in a locked room with four beds, only one other bed occupied. My roommate, Jane, who'd been admitted the day before, told me that her husband had kept her locked in the house and beat her for imagined transgressions. She'd taken to quiet cutting sessions with a butter knife, until this last time when she'd decided to use his hand drill. The fluorescent panel-lighting stayed on all night, and cameras mounted in the corners of the room kept an eye on us. Pulling the sheet up to my chin, I thought about Inyo tethered to the Beast. Ryan would have brought her inside the house by now, wouldn't he? I couldn't sleep. I wanted to do my circles, but if the nurses saw me on camera they'd keep me locked up longer. Squeezing my eyes shut, I got some mild relief by imagining myself circling clockwise and then unwinding myself, but by the next morning when I saw the bars on the windows, the compulsion overpowered me and I had to do it for real. I circled and unwound myself twice. The cameras caught me.

When I met with my appointed psychiatrist, Dr. Hill, a bald man in a wrinkled lounge suit, I told him that my being in the hospital was the result of a misunderstanding. I explained about the student loans and told him that I'd just been angry when I screamed what I did, but that I hadn't been serious. He jotted a few notes on my chart and then informed me that he was prescribing Luvox for obsessive-compulsive disorder and lithium to stabilize my mood. When I started to cry, he said, "I'm not letting you out of here anytime soon, if that's what you're thinking." When I told him I was working toward a Ph.D. and had a school schedule to keep to, he scoffed. "You won't be going home tomorrow or the next day." In fact, he wouldn't discharge me for at least a week, he said, which made me cry harder. All I could think about was Inyo at home alone while Ryan was at work. What if he played War-craft all night and forgot to feed her? What if she got out and got hit by a car? My sobs turned into hiccups. Dr. Hill gave me a tissue and sent me down the hall to another member of my treatment team.

Dr. Taylor, a psychologist, tested my clarity of thought by asking me to explain the maxim, "People who live in glass houses shouldn't throw stones." Then he asked me to subtract seven from one hundred, and then seven again, and so on until I reached seventy-nine. Then he asked me what a table and chair have in common. "Symbols of organization, of culture, a place to sit and eat." I didn't know what he wanted me to say.

"Very good," he said. "Look at it this way—you're not psychotic or schizophrenic. You're just neurotic. Women with OCD usually do well in this society. They tend to be high achievers." He had me transferred to 8-South Ward, where patients could wear their street clothes, visit the hospital library, and watch movies. I took my first shower in days, washing my hair with generic shampoo from a dispenser on the wall. The morning of my third day I asked Nurse Della for cotton balls to stuff in my ears at bedtime because my roommates were noisy. Candice snored and Debra farted. Dinisha, the third roommate, overheard my complaints. "Hey, Miss Thang, it's the meds," she said. "And you're *not* the queen of quiet." She told me that I snorted and was given to bouts of shouting that woke everyone up.

During smoke breaks, the floor manager Earl, who stood six feet five inches and had tattoos of jaguars on the insides of both forearms, put me outside with the other patients. Some played basketball. Some leaned against the steam pipes, stared at their shoes, and drooled. A tall, lean woman who never spoke and always wore a white hospital gown, drifted back and forth across the basketball court like a specter. Other patients called her "The Swan." Don, a man who looked like Humphrey Bogart, only with a face even more wrecked, would claw at the door, pleading with Earl to be let in. "Don't leave me out here," he said. "I'm scared." Debra would call Greg a gimp—he was missing his left arm to the shoulder and his left leg to the hip—and he'd chase her across the court in his wheelchair. "I'll catch you, you goddamn bitch!" he'd yell. I'd stand in the quadrangle and puff on my pipe—the rummy smell of Cavendish comforted me—staring through the chain-link fence at the Reno Hilton and The Nugget. Beyond, I could see the

Sierra Nevada range. In those moments, I wished that I could shape-shift into a wolf, leap over the fence, and run and run.

One of our late-afternoon smoke breaks was cut short when Sarah set her hair on fire. She walked toward me with her hair ablaze and looked into my eyes. "My hair is on fire," she said, in a near whisper. "I'm trying to burn my eyes out." Lori, whose meth use had rotted her teeth, asked Sarah if she was trying to roast marshmallows or something. Johnny, high on Depakote, stared at the singed hairs, strings of spittle soaking the front of his "I Believe God's Promises" T-shirt. Earl tossed a bucket of water on Sarah's head and ushered all the patients inside. He lined us up for medications, but Kimberly wouldn't accept the Dixie cup of water to help swallow her pills. She called it Satan's water and gnashed the chalky tablets between her teeth while glaring at Earl, who'd dragged her away earlier that morning during arts and crafts therapy.

We'd been given a photograph of the Jarbidge Wilderness with its blue peaks and fields of harlequin lupine, and told to paint a likeness of it. I'd started to paint a picture of Inyo and me running through the lupine, when Kimberly dipped her feet in the Folgers can of blue paint and marched around 8-South like Darwin's blue-footed booby, snapping her fingers and singing the *Batman* theme song. She growled and spit when Earl picked her up and carried her to a small windowless room at the end of the hall, where he put her on lockdown for five hours. "Let me go, you goddamn bastard!" she'd shouted. Lori and I mopped up some of the paint with paper towels while Jane ignored the commotion, engrossed in a *Cosmopolitan* article, "Six Best Sex Positions."

Jane had been transferred to 8-South, and I'd begged the staff to let us room together. At 6:30 every morning, Nurse Della would wake Jane and me chiming, "Okay, ladies, time for breakfast." Breakfast meant Cheerios soaked in fat-free milk. I was hungry again in less than an hour. Jane and I joked that if all the computers went down, the doors on 8-South would slide open and we'd skip down the sidewalk to IHOP for a Rooty Tooty Fresh 'N Fruity and the tallest stack of double blueberry pancakes we could get. We talked endlessly about buttermilk pancakes smothered in cinnamon-apple compote and whipped cream.

Jane dabbed foundation on her wrists every morning to hide her scars. I could see them in the mirror when she braided my hair and powdered my cheeks before breakfast, loaning me lip liner and a miniature tube of Clinique's fierce rouge. "Samples rule," she said. We both knew that wearing our normal street clothes and putting on makeup made us feel different from the guild of mentally ill.

All the meals on 8-South were an anorexic's dream. For lunch, the cafeteria staff served cottage cheese on a bed of iceberg lettuce with a tube of fat-free French dressing, a carton of milk, and choice of an orange or an oatmeal cookie. When I went back for seconds, the cook glared at me, saying I'd had a decent lunch and what did I want more for? Anna, another patient, wasn't shy about asking for food. She went from one table to the next: "Are you going to drink your milk? Can I have your cookie? Can I eat your orange?" I watched her fill her pockets with cookies and oranges, and later stash them under her mattress. I leaned over my tray, guarding my cookie and hard-won second helping of cottage cheese.

If Anna tried to take my food, I would bite her.

I had to get out of there.

During his daily visits Ryan smuggled chocolate chip cookies to me in our Yahtzee game. He'd never baked anything before, but he was trying hard to show he was sorry for getting me locked up. I never talked about it. I just wanted to go home and couldn't think about anything but Inyo and huge debts. Each time he came to visit my first question was "How's Inyo?" He assured me that she was fine. He'd been taking her for regular walks, and she'd been riding in Hanna to the hospital for visiting hours. I missed her horribly and worried that she was lonely and not getting enough to eat.

My second question was always, "Why didn't you tell me about those loans?"

"I did tell you," Ryan said, shaking the dice in the red plastic cup. "You just don't remember."

"You think I wouldn't remember a number like a hundred grand?"

"Well, I did tell you."

I sighed. "We have to pay them back. We both need decent credit or we'll never be able to own a house."

"Yeah yeah, I know."

Around and around, getting nowhere.

I called a meeting with Dr. Hill the morning of my fourth day in the ward and told him that the hospital was starving me and did he know I had a history of anorexia? Nurse Della backed me up in a meeting with my treatment team by pointing out that as someone with OCD I would take my medications religiously. Dr. Hill wrote up my discharge papers.

Packed and ready to leave, anxious to start cooking for Inyo, I felt bubbly and suddenly social. I turned to Maxine, who sat with her chin on her knees in one of the orange vinyl chairs, and asked her how she was doing.

"Go to hell," she said.

That afternoon I said good-bye to Jane. She'd asked Dr. Hill to keep her in 8-South a few more days. Maybe she preferred hunger to her husband's beatings. She reminded me of the wolf that chews off its own leg to escape a trap. I gave her my phone number and walked out. Ryan met me at the entrance, but I ran from him toward Hanna, where Inyo was pacing from front to back and circling. "Inyo girl!" I called, sliding open the side door. She put her paws on my chest to lick my mouth. I couldn't help but hug her hard. She let me.

CHAPTER TWELVE

Pink Slip

Live with wolves and you learn to howl.
—Spanish proverb

Near the end of my first year in grad school, not long after Inyo's first birthday, I came home from class to find a pink slip wedged in the door, a citation from Washoe County Regional Animal Services for Keeping of Noisy Animals.

> It is unlawful for any person to keep, harbor or own any animal or poultry which by loud or frequent habitual barking, yelping, braying or other noise causes annoyance to the neighborhood or to any persons in the vicinity.

The animal-control officer had penned a note at the bottom of the ticket: "Neighbors complained of howling."

Well muscled, with a healthy gloss to her coat, Inyo didn't howl from hunger, happy with the stew I made for her. I was sure she howled out of boredom, so I added two pork hocks and a marrowbone to her stash of distractions. They didn't work. A little more than a week later I came home to find another pink slip for howling. These citations were warnings to me, but residents of the Riviera Apartments, whose living-room windows overlooked our backyard, had given Inyo more than a warning. When I heard gnawing and ripping, I dropped my schoolbag and let the pink slip flutter to the pavement as I hurried to unlock the door. Trying to take cover, Inyo had chewed a hole in the back door. I found her crouched and shaking, wood chips and splinters all around her. From an upper-story window, a resident in the apartment complex had chucked a full can of Folgers at her with such force that the can had made a divot in the lawn. Someone else had lobbed milk jugs and 7UP bottles that now lay strewn in Susan's flower bed. Tomato guts splattered the siding.

To calm Inyo, I dumped the hamper full of dirty clothes on the living-room floor and let her roll in them. She seemed to forget the coffee can and milk jugs launched over the fence as she snuffled the laundry with a pair of Ryan's boxers on her head. When I carted out the week's recycling, piled high with flattened Cap'n Crunch boxes, a guy marched out of his apartment in flip-flops and a bathrobe, black chest-hair curling above the terry cloth. "People are trying to sleep," he shouted, his face so close to mine he could have licked my eyebrows. He was a blackjack dealer at the Eldorado casino, and a few other residents worked the Peppermill, and who the hell did I think I was? "We work all night," he hissed. "Then we have to listen to your dog or wolf or whatever the hell it is howl all day while we're trying to sleep. Fix it, or I'll fix you!" He turned and stomped off. I tried to apologize but nothing would come out of my mouth, and then he was gone.

Although wolves and many wolfdogs do bark—contrary to popular belief—they do it differently and less often than dogs. Their bark, more of a deep throaty *woof!*, communicates alarm. But what they do more often is howl, and that's what we were in trouble for. I hadn't known how to curb Inyo's howling. Biologists say howling probably serves at least three functions in wolf packs: to convey a wolf's location to other pack members, to rally before a hunt, and to prevent conflicts by warning rival packs that other wolves are in the area. As a wolfdog Inyo hadn't needed to communicate her location or assemble a hunting party, but she had definitely broadcast our location to the rival "pack" in the Riviera Apartments.

In addition to boredom and loneliness, Inyo's howling was provoked, I suspected, by anxiety. Wolves can hear up to ten miles in a clearing, six miles in a forest, so as a wolfdog living in a forest of buildings buzzing with human activity, Inyo could hear too much going on—human chatter, a game show on television, a man's shout, highway traffic, a dog's bark—the collective rasping of souls living in that gambling town. Unable to explore the source of any of those noises, she may have been driven more than a little mad.

Many years later, I met Ed Bangs of the U.S. Fish and Wildlife Service who told me about a Tennessee man spotted by rangers running through Montana's Glacier National Park with two wolves on his heels.[1] The rangers discovered that the "wolves" were really wolfdogs that the owner had set loose, sneaking out of camp when the animals weren't looking. Having bonded with the man, the wolfdogs hadn't wanted to be left behind and had tracked down their owner. The man claimed to have taught the animals how to hunt raccoons and squirrels, and thought the park would be the safest place for them to "go back to the wild." Maybe he figured his wolfdogs would start out hunting small prey as he'd taught them, and would eventually learn how to hunt larger prey on their own.

"He was threatening the gene pool of the wild wolf population," Bangs said. "Not to mention giving those wolfdogs a death sentence." The animals would not likely have survived on their own. Wild wolves might have killed them as intruders, and while the wolfdogs might have been adept at hunting raccoons and squirrels, they wouldn't necessarily have learned the skills needed to hunt larger prey. Also, having been raised by a man, the animals lacked the natural wariness possessed by wild wolves and might have drifted dangerously close to humans to attack easier prey, like livestock. Bangs added that if the man's wolfdogs had killed any livestock, wild wolves would have been blamed.[2]

The rangers fined him and gave him a choice: Take the wolfdogs back to Tennessee or have them euthanized. As far as the rangers knew, he took them back to Tennessee. But what had made that man drive his animals all the way from Tennessee to Montana? Had his neighbors complained about howling? Had he believed that his animals longed for the wilderness and decided that the kindest act would be to let them go?

Two Kongs stuffed with peanut butter and four hedgehog squeaky toys later, I came home from school to find animal-control officer Tanya scribbling our third noisy-animal citation. This one would cost us $195. I invited her inside to meet Inyo, who gave her a thorough tongue bathing. "Beautiful hybrid," she said, wiping her lips. "But your neighbors have been calling our office every day. Can't you get her a buddy or something?"[3]

I told her Bill the landlord wouldn't allow it. Besides, I wasn't sure how much good it would do to get a dog chum for her. I'd taken Inyo to the dog park near Virginia Lake a few times, and while she would romp with dachshunds and Labs, chasing goldens in hot pursuit of tennis balls, she tired of them within minutes. She would fix her gaze on the palomino and Appaloosa browsing tall spring grasses in the field adjoining the park. The horses felt Inyo's heavy, pressing attention as they swished their tails to brush blackflies from their hocks. Sometimes they spun around to face her and snorted, or they trotted from one end of the pasture to the other, their heads held high, nostrils flaring. When I patrolled the fence line between her and the horses, Inyo would dash to the other side of the park and vault over a section of fence there, then head toward Virginia Lake to paddle after American coots. Occasionally I could catch her when she waded back to shore and shook the water from her coat, but mostly she was too quick, dodging my grasp and sprinting up the street. By the time I caught up she might already be on Plumb Lane in front of Shenanigans, the Irish pub, or be heading toward Battle Born Tattoo, a quiver of breast feathers sticking out of her mouth.

Almost apologetic, Officer Tanya handed me the citation. She liked Inyo and gently encouraged me to figure out how to keep her quiet. I decided that although we ran daily in the hills surrounding Reno, Inyo needed a novel experience. I began driving her to Pyramid Lake on the Paiute Reservation northeast of Reno. Through a narrow chute in the Virginia Mountains, we coasted over Mullen Pass to Wino Beach and Indian Head Rock, or drove farther north to Warrior and Spider Points, where she could sprint along the beach and paddle in the lake. We scrambled up white tufa mounds and raced each other through the soft plumes of cheatgrass, careful to skirt the barbs of Russian thistle. Inyo would pin her ears and swallow ground with galloping strides. I ate her dust. When it was time to go home a few hours later, evading departure became the new game. Sliding open Hanna's side door, I called to her, knowing she wouldn't come right away. I would start the engine and roll along the dirt road in first gear while Inyo peered from behind a clump of sagebrush. Through a cloud of dust, I could see her eyes blink with recognition. "Bye-bye, Inyo!" I'd call, and she would bolt for the van. Shifting into second, I let her race alongside Hanna for another hundred yards, then downshifted to give her a chance to leap in. Sometimes she did. Other times she veered off, not ready to end our game, and I sped up—second gear, third. Her interest piqued, and the race went on, around and around the dusty loops of road until I'd downshift again and tap the brakes, slower, slower—and finally she would spring through the side door, ready for a ride in her moveable den.

Our trips to Pyramid Lake, in combination with daily runs and walks, seemed to help Inyo relax, and several days went by without a complaint. Just when I thought she'd stopped the incessant moan-howls, I found a letter tucked in the door. This one wasn't pink, but white and fearsome. In scrawled print the note read, "Shut your fuck-ing dog up or I will."

Staring at the tower of apartments next door, wondering if the writer of that note was watching me, I decided it wasn't safe to leave Inyo home. She would have to go to school with me. The students loved her—until she rifled through their backpacks and chewed off the shoulder straps, or played tug-of-war with their tube socks. I tried keeping her in the teaching assistants' office while I was in class, but she rummaged through garbage, chomped electrical cords, and eventually figured out how to open the door to roam the halls of Frandsen Humanities.

I resorted to wrapping a simple tie-out cable around the trunk of a cherry tree outside the building (at home the Beast was still holding its own against her teeth) and left her with water, plenty of shade, and friendly students who locked up their bikes and cooed at her. But I could hardly sit still in class. During a short break I ran down the hall and out the door to find the frayed end of the wire cable lying on the grass. Stupidly, I'd thought she wouldn't have time to chew through the cable in one class session. While I raced around campus calling her name, another student flagged me down. "Hey, you missing a wolfy-looking dog?"

He told me that he'd seen Inyo running through the quad toward the rose garden, and one of the maintenance guys had taken her to the Buildings and Grounds office. I found her there eating a cheese and pickle sandwich. Larry, from the grounds crew, had tried the number on Inyo's tag but unable to reach anyone and not knowing what else to do, called animal control to pick her up. "She's friendly," he said, as I leashed her. "She came right up to me."

No doubt Inyo was easy to catch. If a person was new to her, she'd approach to smell his feet and shins and knees, then rub against him or stand on her hind legs to nose his cheek. The total stranger was novel and wonderful, and Inyo came readily. But with Ryan and me, she would remain just out of reach of us—the wreckers of her fun.

I hated being a wrecker of fun. At Home Depot, a man in an orange "I put customers first" apron helped me cut a ten-foot section of chain to secure Inyo to the cherry tree during class. With the chain coiled in her water dish and stowed at the bottom of my backpack, I stacked my lunch and schoolbooks on top, and Inyo and I walked to school by way of Center Street, passing Mexican women hired as room cleaners at the Flamingo Motel and The Shamrock Inn Motel with their curtains slumped off the rods and 1960s signs that didn't light up anymore. People lived for months at a time there, cooking on hibachis outside their rooms.

One morning on Liberty Street, I spotted Don, confused at the crosswalk. I hadn't seen him in five months, not since my last day in the hospital. He strode to the middle of the street and stopped, turned around and shouted, "Oh no, I'm stuck!" He lifted one foot and put it down again as if trying to avoid a land mine, hands pressed to his chest, fingers clenched like claws. People honked their horns and yelled at him. "Get the hell out of the street, you faggot!"

Another morning, a woman with two black eyes hobbled up to us and asked for money. A block behind her a man shouted, "Get back here. Hey, ugly, where you goin'?" I smelled stale Southern Comfort on her tattered clothing. It was Maxine from 8-South. She didn't recognize me. I gave her five bucks and asked if she wanted help. She stroked Inyo's head and waved the five-dollar bill. "This'll do it."

Outside the humanities building I looped the chain around the base of the cherry tree and clipped the end to Inyo's collar with a carabiner. She had a full water dish, three Greenies, and a stuffed Shrek. The chain held. I breathed a sigh of relief.

But one afternoon when I walked Inyo home from school and

checked the mail, I found a white envelope with a pink notice showing through its window. It was addressed to Ryan, but pink was a bad
color. While guilt niggled at me, I ripped open the envelope. The paper
notified him of an administrative wage garnishment due to defaulted
student loans. In thirty days the U.S. Department of Education would
deduct 15% of his disposable income every month to repay the debt.
My knees wobbled and I felt dizzy. I didn't even have the energy to tap
and circle. I sat on the pavement and let Inyo chew the envelope.

Ryan had told me he'd called and set up a payment plan. Maybe
the letter was a mistake, but if it wasn't, then I might say something I
couldn't take back. I left a brief note on the kitchen table, loaded Inyo
into Hanna, and drove a hundred miles north—past dry Winnemucca
Lake and the towns of Gerlach and Empire—to the Black Rock Desert, part of a dry lake bed from late-Pleistocene Lake Lahontan that
once encompassed more than 8,000 square miles. Some people have
used the Black Rock to race cars and launch rockets; thousands have
congregated there for the annual Burning Man festival. I fled to that
remnant of an inland sea to get my thoughts together.

Near a crude sign for Rainbow Opal Mining I turned onto a dirt
road and parked Hanna among the saltbush and greasewood, rolling
out the awning and setting up the cooler and stove. Then Inyo and
I headed out to explore the top of a boulder-strewn hill, clambering
over rocks split by hard heat and water. I listened for rattlesnakes as
we waded through four-winged saltbush and iodine bush, their new
spring succulents sprouting in place of last year's dead leaves. From
that height I spotted a train speeding along the Union Pacific railroad
tracks on the eastern edge of the playa, the Jackson Mountains with
their chinks and gouges rising behind it.

We didn't see people for two days, and although it was the perfect
place for Inyo to howl and yip, I heard only the contented raking of
her teeth on marrowbones. Once I tried a moan-howl of my own,
breathing deeply through my nose, making an O of my lips, and jut-
ting out my chin. Inyo's moan-howl always started low, like breath
blown over the mouth of a pop bottle, before rising in pitch. I raised
my eyebrows as if that might lift the sound and send it farther, my
voice like the bawl of a dying cow. I winced and bit my lip, sneaking a

sidelong glance at Inyo. Unimpressed, maybe even irritated, she trotted through the brush to lie down some distance away.

For the long hours of each day, we explored, napped on Hanna's foldout bed, then crawled into abandoned miners' shelters with their split, weatherworn beams and dirt floors strewn with beer cans and rusted mattress-springs. We wandered the playa where Inyo poked her nose into the cracked alkaline hardpan under our feet.

Although we had to go back to Reno, after two days of silence, I convinced myself that if Ryan would just do what I told him instead of ruining everything, we'd be fine.

"We're moving," I told him, when Inyo and I burst through the door. "We're paying back those student loans. There'll be no wage garnishment, and those debt collectors won't be calling anymore." I beamed a smile. "We're going to be normal people and rent a whole house, a *real* house, not part of a house, not a carpeted garage." My plan would work. I was sure of it. I told him that we'd get another dog, a companion for Inyo, and that way she wouldn't howl when we were gone and wouldn't try to escape. The dogs at the park hadn't been helpful because she didn't live with them. A doggy roommate would show her how things were supposed to go in a human household. "We'll rescue an older dog at the pound and buy a kennel with a roof." There wouldn't be any more notices shoved in the door, no more citations or fines, no death threats, no cruddy looks from the neighbors and scary men in bathrobes with hairy chests and halitosis.

"Well?" I said. "What do you think? Isn't this great? Are you listening?"

But Ryan had departed into his gnome-warrior avatar in the World of Warcraft. "Sure, honey," he said, deep into his slaughter. "Sounds like a plan."

Bill was one step ahead of me. He left a message on our phone saying we needed to have "a little talk." By his tone, I could tell that this was one of those serious conversations—the kind you feel you should get dressed up for. That night he said, "I can't have trouble with my neighbors. You have thirty days."

Time for a fresh start.

CHAPTER THIRTEEN

The Wolf and
the Housedog

*Feed the wolf as much as you like. He will always look
toward the forest.*

—Russian proverb

Ryan set up loan payments before his thirty-day grace period ran out, and he promised not to go to Cashco again. Late one afternoon I came home from school to find that he'd made dinner. Pasta carbonara steamed on the plates as Ryan whisked hot bread from the oven and poured the Chianti. While we ate, he rested his slender fingers on my arm. "Thank you for being patient with me," he said, and presented me with a "Super-Duper Spouse" certificate for "great patience, skills, and loving behavior." He told me he'd been strained at his teaching job, where there were so many papers to grade that he'd fallen behind. He just couldn't seem to get organized. I knew that some mornings he searched frantically for his glasses only to find he'd been holding the pair in his hand. He often misplaced his wallet and lost the house keys.

Organization was frighteningly easy for me, and ever the Mrs. Fix-It, I told him we'd make a filing system for his classroom. Leaping from my seat, I grabbed a basket off my desk and designated it the official wallet and keys holder. We'd solve this problem!

Crystal, a fellow teaching assistant at the university, pretended to be our previous landlord, giving us and our well-behaved pets a glowing recommendation for a new rental house. We moved into a craftsman bungalow with a wrought-iron fence and a front door of wood rather than sliding glass. Instead of shag carpeting stapled over an old garage floor, we had hardwood that gleamed when sunlight spilled through the picture window in the living room. Overlooking the backyard with its six-foot wooden fence, the window above the kitchen sink allowed me to keep watch on Inyo. We also moved the top tier of our wedding cake, fourteen months old now, its little bride and groom listing heavily to the left in their new freezer. Ryan and I had planned to mark our first anniversary with a candlelit dinner when we'd cut the cake together. But when the day came, it was obvious Ryan had forgotten. I was stubborn and thought it wouldn't be a real celebration if I had to remind him, so I gritted my teeth and kept quiet. When we emptied the old freezer during the move, he saw the cake and felt bad for forgetting. "We'll have that dinner as soon as we get settled," he said.

The bungalow was the kind of home that might inspire some to start their first vegetable garden and fill the window boxes with pansies and snapdragons. I moved ahead with my plan to adopt a dog from the local animal shelter. When I told Leda she didn't sound convinced that a plain old dog would satisfy Inyo's "intellectual needs." She advised that if I insisted on getting a dog instead of another wolfdog, then I should at least adopt a puppy so Inyo would bond with it.

The animal shelter on Longley Lane brimmed with pit bulls, Lab mixes, spaniel types and Dobermans, a chow chow–Akita mix with matted hair, and a basset hound that bayed at me as I passed. A boxer mix wagged its nub of a tail. All eyes followed Ryan and me as we wandered up one row of kennels and down another. Even after everything these dogs had been through, they never eyed us with suspicion, only hope, wondering if we might give them a second glance. Some of the dogs shoved their paws under the gates of their kennels so we might touch each other. Others pressed their wet noses through the chain link to sniff the air. They smelled our eagerness to take one of them home.

Although the 400 or so dog breeds currently recognized today are relatively recent, according to some scientists the human-dog relationship started at least 15,000 years ago, with some estimates reaching as far back as 100,000 years and more. Scientists continue to wrestle with the where, when, and how domestication took place, and frankly, when it comes to dogs, scientists almost never agree. New genetic research continues to emerge, and theories are in a constant state of revision.

Studies conducted by molecular biologist Peter Savolainen caught a lot of media attention in 2002 when he and his team analyzed mitochondrial DNA in hair samples from 654 dogs around the world and announced that the dog originated somewhere in East Asia. Then in 2009, he and a group of thirteen other scientists made a startling declaration, the most specific of any research team, about where and how domestication took place. Based on additional assays of mitochondrial DNA extracted from hair and blood, the dog, they said, originated 5,400–16,300 years ago in China, south of the Yangtze River, when rice farmers began domesticating the wolf as a food source. They claimed that domestication of the Chinese wolf would have been "a widespread and important custom" practiced "at a large scale." Although they acknowledged that such an undertaking would have been neither easy nor safe, the researchers offered no insight into how rice farmers thousands of years ago could have pulled off such an enterprise (other than the fact that ancient and modern wolves in East Asia were smaller than European wolves and presumably easier to handle) or why they would have bothered. The fact is, competing theories of dog origin abound, and with ongoing genetic advancements, new theories emerge frequently. In 2010, geneticist Bridgett vonHoldt and her research team announced that their studies showed that dogs originated in the Middle East.[1]

Some scientists argue that domestication happened only once. Others suggest that domestication of dogs occurred multiple times in different geographic regions. But no matter how domestication happened, no matter who the dog's ancestor really was, Buddy, listed at the shelter as a five-year-old Lab, couldn't have been less wolflike. He stood at the fence quietly wagging his thick cream-colored tail and panting a smile. His body was solid and powerful, with a thick barrel covered in short, dense yellow hair. He gazed at me with bright brown eyes set on a blocky head, and his wet black nose shone. Rubbing his ears through the wire, I spoke softly to him, and he pressed closer, floppy ears rising and falling with each panting breath.

One of the staff explained that Buddy's original owner had brought him to the shelter because she was moving and couldn't take him with her. He'd already been adopted and returned three times, each person fed up with his whining and scratching when left alone too long in the backyard. "This is his last chance," the woman said as she hosed out the adjacent kennel. "We're short on space." As Buddy licked my hands through the chain link, I remembered Leda's words: "Get a puppy." But how could I leave Buddy at the shelter knowing he'd be put down? I gave Ryan a pleading look and saw that he'd already decided Buddy was coming home with us.

Worried that Inyo might see Buddy as an intruder, I kept her on a tight lead when Ryan walked Buddy through the door. But Inyo's tail wagged. She nosed Buddy's ears and licked his mouth, then rolled on her back. Buddy didn't care one way or the other about Inyo. He made a beeline for the food bowl.

The week we brought him home I changed Buddy's name to "Panzer," German for "armor." Somehow a new name, one with some steel in it, would have the power, I thought, to erase his unhappy past and shape his future. I wanted that for Ryan too. One day, not long after we'd adopted Panzer, Ryan came home devastated, almost in tears. He'd lost control of his classroom when the students refused to work and mocked him for the way he dressed, offering to take him clothes shopping so he didn't look like such a geek.

"Honey, you're the teacher," I said. "Send those punks to the principal's office."

I'd never seen Ryan break down like that before and asked if he'd taken his medication that morning.

"I was late for work. I forgot."

I would help him remember.

Not wanting Ryan or me out of his sight, Panzer followed on our heels from one room to another, a behavior that puzzled Inyo. She wanted to play with him, but he preferred to put his head in my lap or rest his chin on my foot. Frustrated, she would pounce on him and nip his butt. He would give her a look—*Do I know you?*—and then glance at me for help. Inyo was lightning—powerful, unpredictable, mysterious—while Panzer was like the 110-volt electric socket in the house, steady and reliable. Although popular media encourages people to believe that their dogs are just well-adjusted versions of those supermodel wolves in the wildlife calendars and might just have a twinkle of that wildness left in them, Panzer was anything but wild.[2] He reminded me of the dog in Aesop's fable, "The Wolf and the Housedog," content to wear the collar and receive free meals, caresses, and kind words. Inyo could have been the wolf in the tale who, on seeing the collar around the dog's neck, exclaimed, "A collar and a chain! You mean you are not free to come and go as you please? Dog, I would rather starve and remain free than to be a fat slave." But Inyo was partly like the dog too. She enjoyed (and expected) her meals, and she could be deeply affectionate, occasionally somersaulting into my lap to have her belly rubbed. Still, appalled at Panzer's acceptance of the collar and leash, she invented a new game—chew off the dog's collar and set him free!

Now I realize that Inyo was not a fully domestic animal. How could she have been when none of her wolf ancestors had been selectively bred to live in a household or to thrive on the jobs given them by their human owners? So how did dogs become dogs, those firm friends that aren't constantly trying to pack up and leave us?

Although many popular dog books I've read and even a recent pithy collection of scientific papers on dog behavior start with phrases like: "When humans began domesticating wolves . . ." Beth Duman, dog trainer and wolf-behavior expert, calls this idea "the Fred Flintstone Fallacy." For her, it's ludicrous to imagine that early humans—struggling to survive and having an average life span of thirty years—would make an organized effort to create the domestic dog by stealing wolf cubs from dens, weeding out the aggressive and otherwise unsuitable animals to breed a population of calm and reliable domestic companions. "Are you crazy? Have you ever tried living with a wolf?" she asks. "They're unmanageable the moment they open their eyes. There's no way those early people would have tolerated wolfy behavior—eating their clothing constructed of animal hide, stealing precious and limited food resources, some showing aggression toward people."

Biologists and dog trainers Ray and Lorna Coppinger espouse the theory that wolves *turned themselves* into dogs. Calmer animals, those with less fear of people, hung around the village dump providing a sanitation service, and over successive generations acquired more dog-like physical and behavioral characteristics. However, Duman sees a problem with that theory too. She argues, "Wolves that are used to hanging around people and associating them with food are more apt to be dangerous." For example, in Points North Landing, Saskatchewan, Canada, several generations of gray wolves no longer hunt for their food, but live on the garbage of a local mining camp. Accustomed to the presence of people, these wolves are less fearful of them and willing to defend their food source. Documented incidents of aggression by these animals cast serious doubt on the theory that such trash-eating wolves would eventually turn themselves into dogs. If the dog's ancestor *turned itself* into a human companion by living off the village dump, then it was a creature behaviorally very different from the modern gray wolf.

Biologist and dog behaviorist Jan Koler-Matznick disputes another popular theory, that people domesticated wolves to act as guard animals and assist them in hunting large prey. Wolves don't make good guard animals, she says. And even if tamed wolves had helped to bring down a prey animal, "humans would have had to fight them for it."

Whether or not humans actively domesticated the dog, domestication did occur, and Russian geneticist Dmitry K. Belyaev theorized that selecting for one basic trait—tameness—the tolerance or even desire for human contact, had been the key. In 1957 he began a breeding experiment with the farmed fox *Vulpes vulpes,* a member of the family Canidae and a distant cousin of the dog. Belyaev set out to replicate the domestication process as he imagined it took place over many thousands of years, eliminating all the sloppiness, dead ends, and inefficiencies of chance and human blunder. His goal: to create a domesticated fox in *one human lifetime.* He believed that by pulling off such a complicated experiment he could reveal the genetic mechanisms that led to the creation of domestic animals. To begin his experiment, Belyaev traveled to several fur farms where foxes had been bred in captivity for more than a hundred years, choosing 130 of the calmest animals he could find and bypassing the process of lure, capture, and confinement that would have traumatized wild foxes, and in some cases literally scared them to death. By 1978 he and his colleagues had produced more than 10,000 foxes, ranking each animal according to its response to a human experimenter who tried to touch and feed it. Only those foxes that showed tolerance for the nearness of people were selected, while aggressive or fearful animals were culled. As the experiment continued, each successive generation of foxes grew calmer and more approachable, some showing not only a tolerance for human contact but an inherent eagerness for it, whining to attract attention and "licking experimenters like dogs." Many of the foxes responded to their nicknames, even jostling one another for human affection, and Belyaev argued that their more doglike interest in people was genetic, not learned.

What Belyaev produced before his death in 1985—when his research partner, Lyudmila Trut, took over—was a population of genetically tame foxes, animals who had inherited tame behavior from their ancestors who'd been consistently selected for this quality over multiple generations. The terms "population" and "genetically tame" are critical here. A person can tame an individual animal that, despite its genetic programming to the contrary, *learns* through early socialization and training to tolerate human presence without cowering or becoming frantic. But this animal won't necessarily exhibit tame behavior reliably and will certainly not pass on tame behavior to its offspring. It may also revert to "genetic wildness," a term behavioral geneticists have used to explain the anxiety that even captive-raised animals often display around humans or unfamiliar objects.[3]

Belyaev believed that only a *genetically tame* population could develop into a domestic one that wouldn't need coaxing to accept human contact.[4] To be absolutely certain that two genetically tame foxes would reliably produce genetically tame offspring every time, researchers bred some 50,000 foxes tested for their friendliness to humans. (Even so, these foxes exhibit tameness within a certain range; not all of the foxes want to be cuddled.)

The differences between Panzer's and Inyo's behavior puzzled me for years. When I learned about the fox experiment, I thought the foxes, heavily selected for tameness, might represent the missing link between my thoroughly domestic yellow Lab and my part-wild wolfdog. I had to meet those foxes for myself, so in fall 2009 I packed nineteen rolls of film, pocketed my visa and plane ticket, and caught a flight to Novosibirsk, a region in Western Siberia bordering Kazakhstan to the southwest and Mongolia to the southeast. There, researchers at Belyaev's experimental fox farm have been selectively breeding foxes for more than fifty years. At the airport in Portland, Oregon, a security guard, whose accent sounded either Russian or Ukrainian, hand-checked my film and asked my reasons for flying to the Russian Federation. I told him about the fox experiment and mentioned that it might shed some light on the origin of the domestic dog. "So they screw up one animal to understand how another got screwed up," he said. "It's cold there. I hope you have a coat."

I took Aeroflot Flight 809 to the city of Novosibirsk, at one time the "special pet" of the Soviet government, but largely neglected after perestroika. A Russian man across the aisle leaned over to tell me that in Russia you needed initiative and plenty of luck. Other passengers seemed to think so too—when the plane landed, everyone on board clapped as if landing safely were an unexpected surprise.

Anastāsiya Kharlamova, a researcher who worked with the foxes, clutched a heavy coat around her slim frame as she held up a sign with my name printed on it. She met me with an easygoing and sleepy smile, curling a strand of shoulder-length brown hair behind one ear. It was five in the morning and still dark. A cold, dry September wind met us as we loaded into a van owned by the Institute of Cytology and Genetics, part of the Siberian Division of the Russian Academy of Sciences. The institute's official driver whisked us through the dark streets toward Academgorodok, Academic Town, the scientific center of Siberia, where I checked into the Golden Valley Hotel. After I rested and had a meal, Kharlamova would introduce me to Lyudmila Trut, Belyaev's longtime colleague, and the three of us would visit the fox farm together. I slept a few hours and woke with a rumbling belly, wondering if I'd need any luck to order a meal in Russian. I imagined that I could almost read the Cyrillic alphabet if I stood on my head and used a mirror. Fortunately, the menu arrived in English, and I ordered "toothsome pork chops served with green stuff, deep-fried onions, branded gravy, and pickled garbage."

The weather was perfect as I walked to the institute along a well-worn path that meandered through a forest of birch, chamomile, and wild nettles. I smiled at everyone. I'd made it to Siberia, and I was going to meet the foxes! The Russian faces did not smile back, but seemed heavy and solemn as I stood in front of a cluster of raspberry bushes, nibbling on the warm, sweet fruits. (A Russian colleague of mine would later tell me that random smiling was considered ill-mannered on the one hand, and on the other a sign of possible mental deficiency, in which case I'd be taken very good care of.)

The institute's building was worn, with paint peeling from the walls. Inside the research office, dishes filled with different varieties of apples the size of ping-pong balls decorated the desks and provided the only color in the room, save a child's crayon drawing of a green fox with one eye in the middle of its forehead. Most people in Academgorodok walked to work from their apartments, so the apples came in pocket-fuls, probably plucked from trees planted along the roadways and forest trails. Anastãsiya Kharlamova offered me an apple and led me down a long gray hallway to Lyudmila Trut's office. Trut, a petite woman in her late sixties wearing a blue pinstripe jacket and light gray pants with white leather flats, looked up from the scientific paper she'd been reviewing for one of her colleagues. She held the document close to her face, because as I found out later, she had a detached retina, which made it difficult to see. She peered at me through thick glasses. "I don't know what we're doing here," she said, meaning she didn't know what *I* was doing there. My reply, translated by Kharlamova, was that I'd read every scientific paper that had come out of Belyaev's fox experiments and that I'd traveled thirty hours to meet the foxes myself and gain a better understanding of *genetic* tameness. This response passed muster. Trut clapped her hands and smiled, instructing Kharlamova to call the institute's driver and have him shuttle us to the fox farm on the outskirts of town.

The Volga, a battered white van, bounced along cracked and buck-led roads that had frozen and thawed over the long Siberian winter. The driver delivered us to the farm's entrance where a dented metal gate opened onto dilapidated rows of narrow, barracks-style sheds. Upkeep had fallen off due to funding shortages, leaving morning glories to sprout from cracks in the plank walls. The farm currently housed 3,000 foxes, each open-air wooden shed holding 100 or so animals in adjacent wire cages, each measuring one cubic yard. All wire above, below, and on both sides, the cages held no toys, no stimulation of any kind, except for a cast-aluminum food tray that rotated like a lazy Susan on an axis so that food could be placed on the tray from outside the cage. Muscular women with gold-capped teeth wheeled carts down the rows and slopped a thick gray mush onto each tray, spinning it around to the inside of the fox's cage. As the three of us put on white lab coats, Kharlamova pointed out the sheds containing foxes selected strictly for aggressiveness and those that remained unselected—both populations used for comparison and breeding in other genetic experiments.[5]

The main goal of the original experiment, selecting animals for one trait—tolerance and even longing for close human contact—had produced not only friendly foxes but changes to the foxes' appearance. For the most part, however, I found that scientific papers and the popular media had overemphasized the resemblance of the foxes to dogs, making too much of floppy ears and curly tails. Few of the tame foxes I saw had either. Kharlamova explained that those characteristics had mostly appeared in the earlier generations and then largely disappeared. On the other hand, pigmentation changes in those earlier generations had persisted. I met a few foxes with one or two blue eyes, and while many of the genetically tame foxes retained the silver pelt of farmed foxes, some had piebald coats (those with large patches of white fur) that looked a bit like the coats of border collies.[6] Otherwise, the foxes still pretty much looked like foxes, but many of them now yearned for contact with people.

As we walked down the rows, the genetically tame foxes mewed for attention and rattled their metal trays, pawing them wildly until they spun on their axes. Some of the foxes mirror-danced with their neighbors in adjacent cages. A few whirled in perpetual circles, while others shoved their paws under the wire doors to make contact with us, just like the dogs on Longley Lane the day I'd adopted Panzer. *Pick me! Pick me!*

We paused in front of one of the cages, and Kharlamova flipped open the latch, scooped one of the tame foxes into her arms, then passed the trembling creature to me. It shivered and moaned, teeth chattering as I held it. She explained that I was giving the animal what it wanted, and that the fox had become "very emotional." (She was referring to "emotional excitability," a term scientists use for the dog's capacity for emotional arousal—not just the joyful wiggling of happy dogs, but a heightened emotional response of any kind.) During the week of my visit, I held many of the genetically tame foxes, stroking their fur and cooing to them. Many were eager for touch, approaching me readily. Others were timid at first, hanging back when I opened their cage doors, but when I reached my hand inside, they would cackle and pant, rolling on their backs and whining in delight as I rubbed their bellies.

Murmuring to a fox that felt so light in my arms and stroking its downy fur, I gazed around at the magnitude of this experiment, sensing the heartbeats of 3,000 animals that would never leave their cages, never touch the grass, and wondered how rice farmers thousands of years ago could possibly have managed such a complicated project with wolves. Thousands of the more than 50,000 foxes produced during the experiment have flunked out, unsuccessful at getting along with humans on human terms. Failure = culling = death. In that year alone, 300 or so would be euthanized, a few of those the very animals I held during my visit. Smelling musky from all that nuzzling, I trudged back to my hotel each evening with fox fur stuck to my lips and tiny hairs wedged between my front teeth. As I ate traditional Russian *okroshka,* served with sour cream and "garbage," I fantasized about smuggling home a couple of those crazy foxes spinning in their lonely circles.

Although the researchers in Novosibirsk sometimes interchanged the terms "genetically tame" and "domestic" when referring to the foxes, these terms are not synonymous. Genetic tameness has produced foxes with consistently lower levels of cortisol and epinephrine, stress hormones involved in the fight-or-flight response, and higher levels of serotonin, the natural opiate known as the "happy hormone." The genetically tame foxes are calm enough to pay attention to people. The foxes I met were even able to follow my visual cues like pointing, a skill normally attributed to dogs. In fact, anthropologist Brian Hare and his colleagues at the Max Planck Institute for Evolutionary Anthropology in Leipzig, Germany, believe the foxes are almost as skilled as dogs at "reading" human glances and gestures to figure out what we want. Nevertheless, the genetically tame foxes are not yet *domestic* by the standard of dog behavior, the standard Belyaev set when he devised the experiment. To date, only a few foxes have been placed in homes as pets, and as Trut said, they are "not so submissive to man as the dog." To validate any claims of their domesticity, thousands of these foxes would have to show that they can be successfully trained to respond to commands a dog could typically master.[7] Training requires attention to humans and willingness to obey their commands as dogs do, a quality wild animals don't have. Inyo certainly didn't have it. When my desires and hers coincided—great. When they didn't, forget about it. At present, the Novosibirsk experimenters lack funding for trainers and facilities, so we don't yet know the foxes' potential. But cradling those gentle, eager creatures in my arms, what I could say for sure was that in their present state the foxes represented an intermediate step between part-wild Inyo and domestic Panzer.

Before my trip to Siberia, I'd met Terry Jenkins, a former wolfdog breeder and superintendent of Folsom City Zoo Sanctuary, who had created a wolfdog exhibit called "Leading Double Lives," the only one of its kind in the country, to educate visitors about the consequences of breeding wolfdogs. As a breeder, Jenkins had tried to produce an animal that looked like a wolf, to satisfy the urge some people had to own an exotic pet, but that behaved like a dog—friendly and trainable—so the animal could get along in human society and not be subject to wild urges. But she didn't succeed. "I never attained that goal, not even once," she told me. "Most of the pups I sold were dead before they were two years old. Most of those that lived beyond that were consistently misunderstood, misjudged, and/or mistreated. And many of them were in breeding programs as well. I could no more control what happened to the next generation than I could with the ones I sold directly. As much as I loved and respected the animals I had known, I had created a Pandora's box situation that I couldn't retract. But at least I could stop and try to convince others to stop as well."[8] Of course she hadn't achieved her goal. She hadn't selectively bred her animals for genetic tameness on the vast scale of Belyaev's experiment.

Belyaev had been right. Panzer's ancestor, whatever it was, had evolved from a wild animal to part of a genetically tame population, and finally to a member of a vast and diverse group of companionable *domestic* canines that didn't need any coaxing to dive into the blankets. Panzer certainly hadn't needed any coaxing. He always came when I called him, and slept on the bed or climbed into my lap every chance he got—all eighty pounds of him—and he didn't let me out of his sight, worried he'd be abandoned again. Slowly, though, he became more confident. When we took him climbing he began to figure out that when Ryan and I mantled onto a ledge out of sight or vanished into a crack in the rock face, we always reappeared. We went up. We came down. That's how it was.

One weekend in midsummer, when we'd had Panzer for about a month, we took him and Inyo rock climbing at Lover's Leap near Lake Tahoe. While we climbed routes like Pop Bottle and Bear's Reach, the Farce and Harvey's Wallbangers, Inyo and Panzer would explore the scrub or nap under a juniper tree. At night in the campground we organized the climbing rack, separating cams from nuts, adding a few slings and a cordelette in preparation for the next day's routes. We cooked our pasta and beans on a fire while Panzer patrolled the perimeter of our camp, marking bushes. He recognized the bounds of the temporary home we'd established, lying at our feet while we ate. Inyo recognized no such boundaries. The whole world was community property to Inyo, and finally I had to chain her to a juniper so she wouldn't steal other campers' food. When we passed out in our sleeping bags from the exertion, Panzer slept in the tent with us, pressing close to my body, while Inyo, as usual, preferred to stay outside.

Sunday morning, I heard shouts from another climber's tent. "Wolf!" I kicked off the sleeping bag, groped for the zipper on the tent door, and clawed my way out. Inyo had wiggled out of her collar and dug a guy out of his bivvy sack in a nearby campsite. She'd knocked over an open bottle of beer left on the picnic table and lapped up what was left. She'd also plundered the guy's food bags, devouring a bag of KETTLE Chips, two Clif Bars, and a bag of beef jerky. I apologized to the man and clipped on Inyo's collar to lead her away. The camper growled and flipped the lid of his bivvy over his face. I came back later with some of our extra food to replace what Inyo had eaten.

From the campground we hiked half a mile to the weekend's finale, an easy climb called Knapsack Crack on the northeast face of a granite outcropping called the Hogsback. Inyo loped ahead on the approach to the climb, leaping from ditches and bushes to pounce on Panzer, who remained behind me for some protection. I don't think Inyo understood Panzer's reluctance to leave us. Frustrated, she occasionally uttered a high-pitched whine and nipped his butt. *Hurry! Let's go!* But he wouldn't budge—another hopelessly stupid wolf for her to deal with. When I reached back to pat Panzer on the head, I noticed that his neck was bare. Inyo had chewed off his third collar in a month.

We reached the base of the climb near a stout juniper and flaked out the rope, passing it through our hands into a gentle coil on the ground to make sure there were no kinks or tangles. I gave Panzer and Inyo a Greenie apiece and filled their water bowls, then tied in to the rope and locked my carabiner, threading the rope through my belay device and slipping on my climbing shoes. Ryan tied in to the sharp end, the end of the rope knotted to the lead climber's harness. I would follow and remove cams and nuts as I went.

"On belay?" Ryan asked.

"Belay on."

"Climbing."

"Climb on," I said, letting Ryan know I was firmly anchored at the belay station and he could start the first of three pitches, which followed a crack and a right-facing dihedral. He chalked up his hands for better traction on the granite and began the climb, gardening along the route, pulling weeds out of the crack in order to place a cam. A climber should never take her eyes off her partner when he's on belay, but I couldn't help scanning around for Inyo. She roamed and explored. As she'd grown older, she'd started to travel farther afield while we climbed, always orbiting us and aware of our location, but coming back when she was ready. Panzer rested in the shade, watching us keenly, glancing up to check on Ryan as he heel-hooked and hand-jammed into a crack.

118

I braked with my right hand while Ryan set us an anchor on a ledge and I prepared to follow, glancing around to make sure Panzer was still in sight and hadn't wandered off after Inyo and become lost. I chalked up my hands and began the climb. "Climbing!"

"Climb on, Huevos Rancheros!" Ryan called down. For the three-pitch climb, we continued up the dihedral to a steeper section of rock. While I climbed, hand-jamming in the crack and foot-smearing on the smooth granite face, maximizing contact between the sole of my climbing shoe and the rock, relying on friction to hold me, I peered down into the scrub and saw a gray-blond streak stalking squirrels and rabbits in the brush, a yellow torpedo in tow. With Ryan and me out of sight, Panzer had decided to follow Inyo. I felt guilty letting her hunt—on a recent trip into Desolation she'd eaten a Nuttall's cottontail and a mountain pocket gopher, both vulnerable species whose populations were declining. But what could I do, keep her on a chain all the time? I cleaned the route, removing the protection Ryan had lodged in the cracks. I knocked a hex loose and then a cam, clipping the pieces to the loop on my harness. But when I reached for the next hold my foot slipped and I slid down the rock until Ryan put on the brake. Thinking about Inyo, I hadn't been paying attention to the climb. Then the Elvis Leg started, and I wanted off that rock. "Can I do this?" I called.

"Go for a knee jam. Stick it!" Ryan yelled back.

I wedged one knee, jammed the opposite foot into the crack, and hauled myself up.

The rock felt greasy under my sweaty palms. I was nervous about Panzer because I didn't know what trouble Inyo might get him into. As I dipped my hands into the chalk bag, white powder clouds rose in the air and made me sneeze. "Up rope!" I shouted through the wind, and Ryan took up the slack. If I slipped, the rope would hold me.

We face- and crack-climbed the next pitch. This time I led, smearing up the granite slab. I used a narrow crack above me for fingerlocks and placed two nuts. My fingers, swollen from the heat, made crimping on a tiny ledge of rock difficult, but we made it, topping out on the shoulder of the Hogsback after the third pitch. I was surprised not to see Panzer. I'd been so sure he'd be there waiting for us, as usual.

119

"Panzer! Hey, boy!" I whistled and clapped, peeling off my climbing shoes to let my toes uncurl. Ryan butterfly-coiled the rope to strap on his pack and we guzzled water. As I took a swig, I heard a whimper in the brush. With Ryan behind me, I ran barefoot toward the sound. Panzer appeared, weaving, and then fell on his side. He got up yelping, then wobbled and fell again. "Stay down, boy," I said, placing my palm on his chest. Frantic, I scanned his body for injury and saw two puncture marks on his nose, which had gone completely dry. "Ryan, look at Panzer's nose!"

Ryan leaned over Panzer to get a better look at him and stroked his head. Panzer yipped. "Whatever it was, it really tagged him," Ryan said.

The two puncture marks were perfectly aligned. Snakes! Rattlesnakes! Panzer's whole head had started to swell. Rattlers were shy and struck only when they felt imminent danger. Their first line of defense was actually silence. Panzer had probably stuck his nose into a mammal burrow, and when the snake rattled a warning he'd kept on poking.

Stuffing the rest of our climbing gear in the packs, we prepared to descend the rocky trail. Ryan squatted and I made a forklift of my arms to scoop Panzer and drape him as gently as I could across Ryan's shoulders. I hefted a pack onto each of my shoulders and walked behind Ryan, spotting him as he carried Panzer along the ridge. Any missteps down the rock-strewn trail and they'd both tumble. Inyo showed up with a squirrel in her teeth, and followed us in the pressing heat as we hiked down the shoulder of the Hogsback. It was a half mile back to the campground and the van, but the adrenaline gave Ryan the strength to carry Panzer all the way.

Panzer exhibited all the typical signs of a rattlesnake bite: panting, restlessness, drooling, and muscular weakness. By the time we laid him in the back of Hanna, his whole head had swelled and his body was limp. "Jesus Christ, his head is the size of a fucking television!" Ryan said, and tried to stroke Panzer, but Panzer nipped at him out of pain. I traded Inyo a marrowbone for the squirrel and coaxed her into the van. We drove the forty-five miles back to Reno as fast as Hanna would go without overheating or jostling Panzer too much. Every jerky downshift or tight corner made him cry out.

Pulling into the parking lot of the vet clinic, we strapped Panzer on a gurney and wheeled him in. The waiting room smelled like bleach, dog hair, and fear. A receptionist wearing a flower-print smock and a name badge—"Hi, my name is Mindy"—took down our information. I paced the brown floor tiles, turned in a clockwise circle when Mindy wasn't looking, then unwound myself. Circle, unwind. Circle, unwind. Under a drawing of a boy pulling a wagon, his spotted dog barking and running alongside, a placard read: "A good dog brings so much to a family." The sliding wooden door to the exam room opened and Dr. Burke came out. "We'll need to keep Panzer for at least twenty-four hours to monitor him."

While Panzer was set up on an IV pump and injected with cefazolin, an antibiotic, and butorphanol, an opioid analgesic for the intense pain, I drove to PetSmart and bought him a new collar and engraved tag. "Hi, I'm Panzer. Please call my mom." Buying the collar and tag meant he'd pull through, his beingness in the world undeniable, and this time I bought a studded collar because the studs might deter Inyo from chewing him out of it.

In a day or two, when Panzer stabilized, the vet removed the IV and sent him home with instructions to watch him carefully because venom could cause severe tissue damage and bleeding disorders, as well as long-term heart and nerve damage. Spooning sweet-potato turkey mash onto his kibble and holding the water dish under his nose, Ryan and I cooed to him as he rested on his bed. As the days passed, he stood for longer periods of time, and was finally able to pee without wobbling and falling over. After a couple of weeks of coddling and quiet, he fully recovered.

One afternoon, just when I thought the worst was over and life had returned to normal, I saw a terrible stain in the middle of Plumb Street on my walk home from school. When I rushed through the door, I found Ryan crying. "I'm sorry, I'm sorry," he said.

"What? What is it?"

"I didn't want you to see him."

"Who? What are you talking about?"

"Panzer got out, he got hit."

Ryan had been playing Warcraft and ignored Panzer's clawing at the

121

back door, figuring he needed to stay out to keep Inyo company. Inyo had chewed through the Beast tie-out cable and dug a hole under the gate to the front yard. Panzer had followed her. While she'd dodged the afternoon traffic, Panzer got creamed by a 4x4.

I slumped on the couch and sobbed. Panzer had loved us and relied on us to keep him safe, and we'd failed him. I'd failed him. I thought his name would give him power, my stupid fantasy, a hope for him, but it hadn't worked. We'd been in the new house more than a month, and I should have bought a kennel. I'd intended to, but hadn't gotten around to it. I had no excuse. My face still hot from crying, I took the shot of Bushmills Ryan offered, and we toasted our dog and stared at the wall.

Although Inyo had escaped a rattlesnake bite and skirted the cars, she hadn't evaded animal control. She'd be in lockup until the next day.

CHAPTER FOURTEEN

Happy Hormones

Who's the midget?
—J. J. Gittes (Jack Nicholson),
Chinatown

Panzer had held up his end of the domestication bargain. He instinctively, genetically, knew how to be a dog, and what a good dog he'd been—he'd come when called, he'd known not to eat the furniture. When I told him the vacuum cleaner was okay, not a dog-eating monster, he believed me. He'd been a trusting follower who'd trotted right into rush-hour traffic. On the other hand, Inyo was an independent adventurer with a wolf's wariness that she carried with her into each new environment, always alert for any change that might signal danger.

The next morning I posted bail for her: a first-offense $34 impoundment fee for "animal running at large," plus $9 for overnight kenneling. The officer behind the desk asked if Inyo was part wolf. Wolfdogs were notorious escape artists, she said, and during her night in the Big House Inyo had climbed out of her cell. The staff had found her roaming the aisle looking for a way out of the building. Shaking my head, I scribbled out the check and thought of Cochise—the hours he'd passed alone, waiting for his owner, damned by the label "wolfdog." I hadn't wanted Inyo to spend one second in a place like this, and before now, I'd always been able to catch her before she got pinched. But there must have been a paddy wagon somewhere in our neighborhood, and Inyo had probably been easy to net because she'd readily approach strangers.

With Inyo riding shotgun, I drove straight from the pound to Home Depot to buy a kennel. Taking her to school was a thing of the past. She'd started howling and I'd had to leave class too many times. I found a twenty-by-ten-foot dog run with a UV-coated gauzy fabric roof for shade. Stretched tight and wired to the side panels, the cover was also supposed to prevent escape. At home Ryan and I spread out the panel walls, sorted through the mess of washers and cotter pins, brackets and clamps. Squaring up the panels on a concrete pad to prevent Inyo from digging out, we slid on the stiffener brackets, ratcheted the corners tight, and wired the roof taut all on sides. I spread loose straw on the concrete for a softer surface and constructed a straw-bale den in one corner of the kennel so Inyo could hide whenever she wanted. I hoped that Halloween pumpkins and stuffed Kongs hidden in the straw would keep her occupied for the two to three hours I was gone each day.

Though we were still grieving for Panzer, whose ashes rested in a box on the mantelpiece, Ryan and I waited just two weeks before returning to the pound. Inyo needed a canine companion, but this time we'd adopt a puppy as Leda had recommended.

The pound bustled with people dropping off stray animals and families wandering the aisles looking for a new pet. Combing the rows, I read each tag. Most dogs were unnamed strays, but a few had names and stories. Fritz, a six-year-old cocker spaniel mix who suffered from occasional seizures, had been dumped off when his owner died. A dachshund mix named Patsy Mae had been abandoned in a basement when her owners moved out of state. She trembled as I murmured to her, her ratlike tail vibrating like a tuning fork. A tricolor beagle mix named Johnny Cash had been confiscated in a neglect case. None of these animals were puppies or even adolescents. One little boy pointed to a twelve-year-old red and cream-colored Pomeranian named Stevie, and said, "I want that one!" His father peered over his glasses to read Stevie's description and clacked his tongue. "Too old," he said in a thick Russian accent, and jerked the boy by the hand. "You want he should die tomorrow?" I felt a moral obligation to adopt a creature who would otherwise be euthanized, but Leda had insisted that a puppy would arouse a sense of wolfy duty in Inyo, who would see the pup as part of her pack and stick around to care for it.

Hearing a cough at the end of the aisle and then a sneeze, I turned to see a black and tan paw poke out under a kennel door. The tag read "Male shepherd mix. Stray. Four months old." When I sat on the concrete floor in front of him, the pup pressed his forehead to the chain link and I waggled my fingers through the wire to give him a good scratch. His breath sputtered, and he retched, hacking up white foam. He pushed his big black nose through the diamond-shaped hole and sneezed again. Touching his nose, I felt the fever on my fingertips and pulled the bandana off my head to wipe away the snot. One of the shelter staff told me he'd been found wandering the streets with his mother and brother, both kenneled across the aisle from him. All three had been starving, lurking around a 7-Eleven, eating out of trash cans. With his handsome tuxedo markings and white spats, floppy ears and pips—fawn-colored spots above each of his orange eyes that gave him a severe look—he appeared to be a cross between a German shepherd and a Doberman, but with the coat of a husky. Still young, he was a good candidate for some family to adopt, but because he was sick he'd have only the briefest chance in the pound before they put him down. "I'll get you out, little guy," I said, hoping he was still puppy enough for Inyo to bond with him. He licked my fingers, and I stood to find Ryan.

At the opposite end of the hallway he was looking at a five-week-old Catahoula leopard dog–pit bull cross—or something like that. He could barely say it all in one breath. "A lady already placed a hold on her," he told me, but added that the woman had seemed creepy and the shelter staff didn't want her to adopt the dog.

The officer standing next to Ryan explained that she thought the woman bred fighting dogs and was looking for cheap fresh blood. "This little girl is one of the sweetest pups we've had in here," she said, nodding to the puppy curled on a pillow and looking tiny inside that giant cell. "I don't want to see her ruined or dead."

Sitting cross-legged on the floor, I called the pup to me. She walked quietly into the lighted hallway and climbed into my lap. She didn't wrestle and leap around and explore, but neither was she listless or sick—just incredibly self-possessed, dainty and careful in her movements, in striking contrast to her slapdash markings, black splotches on a basecoat of sienna. With that coat and her ears rounded like a bear's, she looked like a little hyena. I held her up as she looked at me quietly, panting fresh puppy breath into my face. "She's like a little adult, all serious."

"She couldn't have been more than four weeks old when somebody dumped her here in the middle of the night in a cardboard box," the officer said.

When I held the puppy to my face, she licked my nose, and the officer added that she didn't think the other woman would be back. "I asked her too many questions and made her nervous," she said, chuckling.

I told Ryan about the other pup at the end of the hall. "He has kennel cough," I said, and added in a low whisper, "He's really sick. I'm sure they'll put him down."

We ended up putting a hold on the male dog and a second hold on the female pup in case the other woman didn't come back. We could adopt only one dog, and we needed to sleep on the decision.

Late that night, while Inyo gnawed a knucklebone, we lay in bed, determined to make a choice by morning.

"You awake?" I said, smelling my fingers, the scent of warm fur and dog dander still lingering.

"Yeah."

"We can't adopt both dogs, can we?"

"Hell no."

"Right. Totally crazy. Never mind."

By the next morning, still undecided, Ryan and I figured that the Catahoula-mix pup would probably be gone, making choosing between the two dogs unnecessary. But when we drove to the shelter that afternoon, the officer told us that the other lady had never come back for the puppy, so we could adopt her if we wanted. Ryan and I gave each other a long, knowing look. We filled out adoption paperwork for both dogs, and three days later, picked them up from a local vet after they'd been spayed and neutered.

When Inyo met the Catahoula puppy she nosed her roughly around the living room and tried to chew her ears. "Easy," I said, and scooped the little pup we'd named Thelma into my arms. Inyo was supposed to take these puppies into her care, not bully them. She stood on her hind legs to smell Thelma, who'd hidden her head in the crook of my arm. When Inyo settled down, I put Thelma on the floor, but she wasn't taking any chances and scrabbled under my desk to hide. Inyo wedged her snout between the thick walnut legs, wiggling her butt, and I could just imagine poor Thelma staring at Inyo's head, which was bigger than she was. *She'll eat me!* Frustrated by the desk, which was keeping her from her new toy, Inyo bit the wooden leg, raking her canines against the walnut, and Thelma cringed next to the wall vent. Inyo wanted to chew on Thelma's ears with her wolfy teeth, to nibble and gnaw them. *Where's Midget? Come here, Midget.* I pushed her away and cradled Thelma in my lap.

As the days passed, Thelma grew a bit braver, even when Inyo got that I-want-to-eat-your-ears look in her eyes. She followed Inyo around the house and tried to mimic her low, throaty rumbles, even managing a yipping howl. These would become the sounds Thelma would make her whole life.

Inyo showed little interest in the wheezing male we named Argos, from the Greek myth of Odysseus's loyal dog who waited twenty years for him to return from the Trojan War. Weak and thin, lying on a heap of manure and riddled with fleas, the mythological Argos was the only one to recognize Odysseus disguised as a beggar. The old dog lifted his head, making a great effort to wag his tail, and relieved that his master had finally returned, exhaled his last breath.

But this Argos would not die. Several times a day I dosed him with a bitter tincture of thyme, and as a preventative, I medicated Inyo and Thelma too. Ryan held them while I slipped the dropper between their flues, green juice running over their tongues. Within a few days, Argos breathed normally. The sound of fluttering air in his lungs and the terrible hacking stopped.

A shrill bark replaced Argos's wheezing. When I walked to the mailbox, gone at most three minutes, he let me have it. Bark! Bark! *Where have you been?* Home from work, Ryan would barely set foot inside the door. Bark! *How dare you leave me!* Bark! I'd retrieve a wrench from the garage, and when I slipped through the kitchen door, Bark! *You left me. I knew you would.* Bark! *You don't want me after all.* Bark!

Inyo body-slammed Argos or shook him by the scruff when he launched into one of his barking tirades, and he squealed more in terror than in pain. But Inyo wouldn't let go. She would utter a deep scolding growl until Argos quieted himself after one last barely audible whimper. When Inyo released him, he forgot all about having been "abandoned" and then scolded, leaping to his feet. *Hi! How ya doin? Glad to see ya. What are we doing next?* All was forgotten. I mean really. His brain rewound itself.

One afternoon, when I'd spent half an hour lining our shoes in perfect rows, crouching low in the bedroom closet to check that each heel exactly aligned with its mate, not a fraction off, I went outside to find Thelma and Argos inside the kennel with the door wide open and Inyo gone. She'd unlatched the "dog-proof" gate and taken off.

Perched on a straw bale, Thelma watched me for a cue, her tail circling like a propeller. She lifted her right paw and waved. Argos crawled out of the den and shook the straw from his coat. Had the pups simply been too dim to unlatch the gate as Inyo had? Were they even duller for remaining inside with the door wide open instead of exploring the whole backyard? It turns out that until recently, many scientists have interpreted the dog's apparent lack of initiative as a sign of mental dullness resulting from domestication. That's what Leda had meant when she said dogs were "developmentally retarded." Others attribute it to perpetual puppy syndrome, meaning that while domestication may not have made our dogs stupid, it has made them the Peter Pans of the canine world. They never grow up and always look at their humans as mom or dad.

It just isn't fair to compare the intelligence of wolves and dogs and conclude that dogs suffer from mental deficiency or perpetual adolescence. Wolves and dogs occupy different ecological niches—dogs in human society, wolves in the wild—and each niche requires a different set of skills to survive and succeed. Hungarian ethologist Ádám Miklósi put it this way: "I wouldn't say one species is smarter. If you assume an animal has to survive without human presence, then wolves are smarter. But if you are thinking that dogs have to survive in a human environment where it's very important to follow the communications of humans, then in this aspect, dogs are smarter."

Domestication has not dimmed dogs' intelligence, only shaped it in complex ways. Ethologist Vilmos Csányi and his colleagues in Hungary have done experiments with dogs and with captive-bred, socialized wolves, in which the wolves unlatched a gate after watching a person do it one time, whereas the dogs in the experiment didn't, even after several repetitions. Csányi wasn't satisfied with the explanation that dogs simply weren't smart enough to figure out the latch mechanism. His team discovered that domestication has its trade-offs. Much of doggy intelligence is devoted to figuring out what people want rather than solving problems independently, and the dogs were content to let the gate stay latched since that was the way their humans seemed to prefer it.

Thelma and Argos hadn't left the kennel because I, the human they innately viewed as the leader, had put them there, so I would be the one to let them out. They would not let themselves out. (Of course, without an owner's presence, some dogs will dash out immediately, and others will wait only briefly for a cue, depending on the attractions outside. On the other hand, no wolf would care whether a person was present or not. Its focus would be on the opportunity offered by the open gate.)

Years later, when I learned about Csányi's experiments as well as those conducted by Miklósi, I understood more clearly why the pups waited for me instead of following Inyo out of the kennel. When Miklósi put wolf puppies in the exclusive twenty-four-hour care of women handlers and later compared the wolves' behavior to the behavior of identically reared dogs, he discovered that when given the choice to approach a human or another dog, the hand-raised wolves always chose the dog, whereas the dogs always chose the human. He concluded that wolves, even those intensively socialized to humans, were hardwired to prefer other canines, and early bonding between a wolf and a human could not guarantee that the wolf would maintain that emotional connection as it matured.[1] In contrast, dogs have undergone heavy selection pressures that have hardwired them so that they often prefer the company of people to other dogs. (It should be noted that a wolfdog's response to humans can be similar to a dog's or to a wolf's—or somewhere in between.)

In another experiment wolves and dogs learned to remove a piece of meat from under a cage by pulling on a rope. Both performed equally well. In the next phase of the test researchers anchored the rope so that removing the meat was impossible. While the wolves ignored their human caregivers and focused exclusively on the meat, yanking the rope until they tuckered themselves out, the dogs tried a few times and then looked to their human handlers for help.

Just as those dogs had looked to their people for direction, Argos and Thelma were eager to learn anything I wanted to teach them. Thelma had mastered the sit command quickly, and after only three attempts, she nailed the down and stay cues. Argos learned the heel, sit, down, and stay cues within a few days, and even when his separation anxiety flared and he launched into a tirade of shrill barking, he would try to follow my directions. Even outdoors with kids and their bouncing balls—any distraction but squirrels, which he simply couldn't resist—he was near perfect on the recall, one of the most difficult commands to teach a dog. "Come!" I would say, and slap my thigh. He would wheel on his haunches and bound toward me without fault. When I kneeled to praise him, he would burrow his head into my chest or place his paws on my shoulders, giving me the closest thing to a dog hug. Both dogs obeyed willingly—often for praise alone—and did not mind repetition. During walks, they would glance back at me. *Like this? Is this right?*

Inyo was incredibly smart and could and did learn, but on her own terms. She would sit and lie down when she felt like it, would come when it suited her and the wind was blowing west. Her compliance had been much like that of the wolves I would later visit at Indiana's Wolf Park, whose tameness was learned, not genetic. They accommodated their handlers when in the mood and rewarded with food. From Renki's balancing act on a wooden teeter-totter to Wolfgang's performance of "Leaping Lizards," a duet performed by the handler and wolf, complete with a bow and a backward leap through the air, the wolves complied for strips of jerky hand-delivered to them after every fair performance. The wolves were never forced to do anything. These behaviors developed naturally in each individual wolf; the handlers merely cultivated and reinforced them. As handler Pat Goodman told me, "We demonstrated to the wolves that these are behaviors we're willing to pay for."[2] Kent Weber, cofounder and director of Colorado's Mission: Wolf, put it to me simply: "Wolves do what *they* want. Dogs ask 'What do *you* want me to do?'"

Thelma and Argos had often demonstrated their doggy eagerness to please. When I told them "Leave it," they would drop Ryan's tube sock or my underpants and accept a toy in trade, and after only a few times, they left those items alone permanently. Inyo didn't pay any attention to the "Leave it" command. No matter what I said, everything was fair game. *Eat the peanut butter! Stalk the bird! Gnash the pencils! Chew the computer cords! Peel the wallpaper! Eyeglasses, toothpaste, chair, rug, and fluffy pillows—feathers flying!*

While happy hormones raced merrily through Thelma and Argos, and Inyo's wild streak took her rambling as usual, my own brain chemicals were about to explode. A few days before I found the kennel door wide open, I'd come home to a dark and freezing house. When I flipped the light switch and heard only a dull click, I rummaged through a kitchen drawer for a flashlight and found the phone. Sierra Pacific Power hadn't received a check from Ryan, who later admitted that he hadn't paid the bill because he'd needed the money to close the deal on a used pickup, which he'd financed by agreeing to pay 22.9% interest. To top it off, he'd also borrowed money from Cashco again, arguing that his allowance wasn't enough, and since we'd been making payments on his student loans there was never money to buy anything, so what else was he supposed to do? Cashco had collected what he owed, plus interest, leaving no money in the bank. The checks I'd written to cover our other bills were bouncing all over Reno, and I realized that Ryan couldn't be trusted with money at all. And now Inyo's latest little breakout—just the kind of double whammy to send me back to the nuthouse.

I called Thelma and Argos out of the kennel, praising them for waiting, and put them in the house. Argos nosed the kitchen floor for crumbs, always hungry even with a full belly. I gave him a carrot, a favorite treat, and sent him to his bed. Ignoring her fancy cedar bed, Thelma had recently adopted the bathroom rug as her sleeping pad, dragging it from room to room to lie down near Ryan or me. Now she appeared in the kitchen, blue shag in tow, waiting for me to settle down.

Calling Inyo's name, I sprinted next door where my bald and gangly neighbor in a Hawaiian shirt was yelling and waving his arms. Apparently Inyo had trapped his cat Pepsi under a garden tractor, and unable to reach her prey, she'd bitten the tractor tire instead. As the black donut hissed, leaking out its air, Pepsi streaked for a crawl space under the house with Inyo in pursuit. When I came on the scene I found her crouched at the mouth of the hole, ripping vinyl siding off the man's house.

Dragging her home, the neighbor shouting after me to keep my dog in my own damn yard, I told myself to hang in there six more weeks until Christmas break. Then Ryan and I, the dogs and Inyo would head for the Sierras where the snows would be piled high. Thelma would be old enough to follow us on the smooth cross-country ski trails, and Inyo could ghost across the frozen lakes to her rambling heart's content. The presence of two puppy friends hadn't diminished Inyo's howling in the least, and I'd have to think of another solution to that problem. Meanwhile, I'd padlock the kennel door just as I'd seen Leda do.

CHAPTER FIFTEEN

Crapshoot

It's hard to be brave when you're only a Very Small Animal.
—Piglet, from *Winnie-the-Pooh* by A. A. Milne

Our adventure in the Sierras would be the pups' first backpack experience and their first contact with snow. They each had a pack, although Thelma's contained only a handful of peanut butter dog cookies. At four months old, she was still too little to carry much weight, so she'd wear the saddlebags just to get used to the idea. I filled old bread sacks with kibble, dividing the weight between Inyo and Argos, and sewed neon yellow reflective tape onto each pack to make the dogs visible day and night.

We packed Hanna with skis, poles, goggles, fleece balaclavas, our Scrabble game, and the topo map of the Homewood Quadrangle. Along with packages of pork neck bones and whole-grain dog cookies, I stuffed baguettes, hard cheese, whiskey, foot-long Christmas sausages, and a bottle of wine into my pack.

On the west side of Lake Tahoe we parked at the end of Rubicon Avenue, shoveling the oil-stained snow along the roadside for a parking space. Before strapping on my skis, I greased the puppies' paws with Vaseline while they sniffed snow mixed with fir needles and mud. Thelma growled when the cold whiteness bit her paws, and she sat on a hump of snow to nibble her toes. When he landed in snow Argos shrieked in delight and surprise, then buried his black head in a drift with only his pips showing, and snorted. Completely at home out here, Inyo belly-slid down a steep bank, plowing the snow with her muzzle.

Breath fogged my glasses as we trudged along under the weight of our packs, lifting one heel and then another, sliding our skis forward along McKinney-Rubicon Springs Road, heel lift-slide, heel lift-slide. Soothed by the scuffing of our thin red Fischers through the powder, we made our way toward Ludlow Hut, a rental cabin owned by the Sierra Club and hidden deep in the backcountry near Richardson Lake on the north edge of Desolation Wilderness.

Inyo shot ahead through the trees and crouched down in a snowy bowl, her tail sweeping side to side like a cat's on the prowl. Then, rocking back on her haunches, she leaped from her frozen hole to pounce on Argos first. He tucked his head to his chest and winced as she danced around and batted him with a forepaw. *Chase me! Chase me!* Next, she body-slammed Thelma. *Bite me, Midget!*

"Get her!" I said, pointing at Inyo, and the pups ran after her. Thrilled, Inyo allowed Thelma to seize her by the end of the tail. Thelma dug her heels into the snow and pulled, while Argos grabbed a thick tuft of Inyo's neck fur in his teeth. Almost six feet long nose to tail tip, Inyo hunched, curving and twisting her long spine while uttering a high-pitched whine. Although to my ear the whine-moan sounded like displeasure, even pain, I knew this was her version of good play. Pulling out of their grasp, she bounded across the snow in a boxy run, and the pups raced after her.

Thelma and Argos, with their dainty, narrow paws and small toes, weren't as supple or coordinated on the snow, but they pushed ahead cheerfully, naturals at this wilderness business despite their youth and inexperience. For her part, Thelma took on the task of herding us together if she thought we'd drifted too far apart. Bounding ahead, she nudged the leader to slow down while urging the lagger to catch up, traveling double the miles for her efforts. Argos trotted dutifully at the leader's heels, never breaking ahead—a steady traveler. Eager for adventure, both dogs helped me put on their packs, nosing through the chest straps after each rest break.

Inyo tried to jaw-wrestle with Thelma and Argos in the way I'd seen captive wolves do, her growls and shrieks rising to a near screaming pitch. I'd thought those wolves would rip chunks of flesh out of one another's flanks and necks, but they never did; it was all just intense, wolfy play. But when Inyo displayed her teeth, Thelma and Argos crouched low to the ground, the skin of their brows knitted into worried triangles when she growled and whine-moaned. They seemed to experience her behavior as a sign of aggression and hid behind me for safety.

As suddenly as she wanted to jaw-wrestle the pups, Inyo forgot about them and whirled around, chasing her bushy tail and nipping her own butt—*Go, go, run faster!* She chased pinecones down a sunlit snowbank and then collapsed on her side, tongue lolling, and rolled on her back in a wolfy version of a snow angel. When she stood and shook herself, she fixed her gaze on Thelma, sidling up to give the pup a swift hip-bump that knocked her off her feet. *Now chew Midget's ears. Hold still, Midget!*

"Shoo! Leave it!" I said, pushing off on my skis and sliding full speed toward them, waving a pole in the air. Thelma lay still on her side, frozen in fear, and Inyo slunk off. I put Thelma at the heel and praised her. At only four months old and leashless, she heeled faultlessly.

The vet had told me that Thelma didn't have a yeast infection in her ears, and it wasn't likely that Inyo was attracted to earwax, which left both of us perplexed about her motive for ear-chewing, especially since she never bothered Argos. Much later, when I learned that from ear secretions (other than wax) wolves get information about the sex, health, strength, and social status of another animal, I thought that as a maturing female wolfdog, even a spayed one, Inyo might have viewed Thelma as a potential rival and chewed her vulnerable ears to cow her.

As cheeky and forward as she was with Thelma and as unfazed as she'd been when the neighbor screamed and waved a push broom at her, in certain situations Inyo had begun to show timidity that reminded me of earlier episodes when she was a pup. Startled when a car backfired, she would skitter across the floor and hide behind the futon, and once, when a friend visited with her infant son, she took one look at the baby and scrambled for the bedroom where she hid under the bed and wouldn't come out. At three months shy of her second birthday, why would she regress?

It wasn't until many years later that I found clues to the reasons for her new behavior. Although the dog and the wolf are closely related, their mitochondrial DNA almost identical, their gene expression patterns—which genes blink on or off at what times—are very different. Geneticist Peter Saetre and his team have discovered that this difference in gene expression helps explain the behavioral differences between dogs and wolves. Thousands of years ago, the ancestor of the dog (whatever it was) evolved into an animal that from puppyhood through adulthood possessed a higher tolerance than the wolf for certain kinds of environmental stress, particularly stress associated with human activity.[1]

But what about a wolfdog, an animal that is both wolf and dog? How will gene expression changes, particularly at maturity, affect the behavior of these animals, animals like Inyo? The answer isn't simple or predictable. Even if we know an animal's ancestry, we may not know its genetic composition. Genetic makeup is very difficult to determine unless we have puppies with one pure wolf and one pure dog parent. *Ancestrally,* those puppies would be 50% wolf and 50% dog. *Genetically,* they would also be 50% wolf and 50% dog, because each pup in the litter receives exactly half its genetic material from mom and half from dad. This is the *only* instance in which we know with any certainty that ancestry and genetic makeup match.

But how does knowing the pups' ancestry, or even their genetic composition in the case of the genetically 50% wolfdogs, tell us anything about how the animals will turn out as adults? In the case of the 50% wolfdogs, the common misconception is that the pups will represent a happy medium between wolf and dog in temperament and behavior. But the myth of the happy medium is just that—a myth. Just because we know that a litter of wolfdogs is genetically 50% wolf, we cannot know how any of the puppies' genes will express themselves at maturity. Will the mature wolfdogs exhibit the dog's expression, sending happy hormones through their brains, or will they have the wolf's more wild expression, their systems flooded with cortisol in response to a perceived threat? Or could the animals display some combination of the two? As geneticist Jennifer Leonard told me, "A true wolfdog hybrid would likely have a gene expression pattern in the brain which was different from both the wolf and the dog, somewhere in between, but not at all the average. It is impossible to predict what it would be."[2]

In the 1930s Russian zoologist Leonid Krushinsky crossed pure wolves with pure dogs and studied the responses of these genetically 50% wolfdogs to environmental stressors. The animals, he reported, overreacted to their environment, showing extreme stress and agitation in response to humans. Krushinsky concluded that the genes of emotional excitability inherited from the dog parent combined with the genes of natural shyness inherited from the wolf parent created wolfdogs that were more potentially excitable and more potentially shy than either of their parents.[3] Likewise, when the wolf's fight-or-flight hormonal system (more cortisol, less serotonin) and its lower tolerance for certain kinds of stress mix with the dog's emotional excitability, the outcome may be an increase in defensive reactions like agitation and aggression.[4]

But I was certain that if I figured out the right formula, I could make Inyo as loyal and obedient as Thelma and Argos—and as happy. Meantime, I had to keep her away from Thelma's ears, or Thelma wouldn't have any ears left at all. As I shuffled along, I noticed that she had begun to develop "cauliflower ear," the flaps folding in on themselves the way a boxer's ears, punched too many times, shrivel permanently. I would have to be more protective of her.

When we reached McKinney Lake, we dropped our packs for water and a snack break. Ryan sliced cheese with his Swiss Army knife while Inyo pounced on air pockets and pressure bubbles suspended under a thin crust of ice along the shoreline. She pawed loose a flake and took it in her teeth, parading in front of the pups. They watched her, fascinated—she'd killed the icy beast and wrenched it apart. I gave each dog a hunk of Uncle Sam's Duck Jerky for dogs. While Thelma and Argos sat a few feet from us, gnawing their treat, Inyo gulped down her wedge and slipped up behind me—her paw pads silent on the snow—to snatch a whole block of cheddar from my hand and scamper off delighted with herself.

Our skis glided easily over Lily Lake, last year's rumpled yellow lily pads crisped and glowing just beneath the surface. At Miller Lake, the ice groaned under our weight and a loud *crack!* echoed in the hushed and snowy basin. But the surface held, and I slipped my skis forward.

Inyo slid on her belly, and the pups followed, cautious and shaky. When we reached Richardson Lake, we started backtracking through the woods looking for Ludlow Hut, fanning out to cover more ground. Ryan spied the cabin first and called to me. Following the sound through the trees, I found him standing in front of a giant A-frame construction so covered with snow it blended into the landscape. We lifted, slid, and dragged our skis up a short slope to the entrance and dropped our packs to dig a path to the door. It opened on a single room with two heavy wooden tables carved with the initials of previous visitors, and a pair of woodstoves. Black-and-white photographs, taken in 1955, showed the cabin in various stages of construction. A ladder led to a loft where a stack of foam sleeping pads lined one wall and a hinged section of the second-story floor swung open to allow heat from the woodstove to rise and warm the loft.

Ryan and I set up housekeeping. While he started a fire in one of the two woodstoves, I chose a couple sleeping pads, including one for the dogs, unpacked the Scrabble game, and fired up a pot of cowboy coffee with whiskey on our propane stove. Inyo was more content outside than in, but checked on us from time to time, standing on her hind legs to scratch at the cabin door. Once inside, she stayed long enough to smell the Scrabble letters and our coffee mugs, scan for unattended food items, or take a quick nap on a mattress near the pups, but not touching them. (If they got too close, she would let out a high-pitched whine of irritation and snap at them.) Soon she'd scratch to be let out again. When I didn't hear from her for a while, I poked my head out and saw her curled in the snow, the tip of her tail shielding her nose from the cold.

We spent the next few days skiing along the flanks of Sourdough Hill and around Richardson Lake and Miller Meadows, with their wide bowls and snowy ridges. Afterward Ryan and I huddled around the woodstove sipping cowboy coffee with cocoa as the black tin stovepipe radiated heat and dried our boots. We sorted our Scrabble letters and made words like YODEL and DIZZIED and SH.

Christmas morning I unlatched the wood shutter from the loft and gazed down on Inyo. She lay curled on the snowy slope in front of the cabin, blinking her eyes at the sound of the creaking hinge, her lashes flecked with fresh powder. We had two more days in this cabin, two more days of solitude with no kennels for Inyo to escape, no cats for her to chase, no neighbor yelling at me, and no freezer-burned wedding cake to obsess over. We still hadn't eaten that anniversary dinner, but we would, I thought.

I slept for what must have been another hour. The next time I peeked outside Inyo was gone. Had she scratched at the door to be let in, and getting no answer wandered off? I tugged on my boots and tumbled down the snowy hill from the cabin calling to her. I found her stalking snowballs along the edge of Richardson Lake, a few hundred yards away. When she spotted me running toward her, it was as if we'd been apart for months. She rocketed across the snow and caromed into my chest. I flew backward and she stood on my belly, licking my mouth and nibbling my chin. *You! You!* When I got to my feet we trudged uphill together from the lakeshore, Inyo's breath hanging like smoke in the air.

I heard Ryan call to me from the cabin. "We're coming!" I shouted into the early gloom, my voice echoing off the trees. Suddenly I took a misstep and lurched forward, doing a face-plant in the snow. I coughed and sucked in a breath, and in that instant Inyo leaped onto my back, pinning my shoulders to the ground with her forepaws and those long, arched toes. Her canines, curved slightly toward the back of her mouth, were long and knifepoint sharp, but her teeth barely grazed my skin as she cradled the nape of my neck in her jaws and uttered a low growl. I froze. She was playing. I was sure she was playing. Of course she was. Wasn't she?

Inyo mussed the cap off my head with her nose and bounded off with my hat in her teeth as I pushed myself up and sat back on my heels. While she ran in circles around me, I grew cold wondering what had just happened.

CHAPTER SIXTEEN

Terrible Twos

*There's no reason to become alarmed, and we hope you'll
enjoy the rest of your flight. By the way, is there anyone on
board who knows how to fly a plane?*
—Elaine Dickinson (Julie Hagerty), *Airplane*

As I sat in class one afternoon in early spring the secretary of the
English Department slipped me a note. The principal of Jessie Beck
Elementary, a few blocks from our house, had called the university,
desperate to reach the owner of the wolf running loose on his school's
playground. Apparently one of the teachers had read the name tag on
Inyo's collar and noted the university number before Inyo darted for
the jungle gym where screaming second graders hung from the monkey bars. The principal had pulled all the children in from recess and
called animal control.

By the time I arrived, the paddy wagon had already whisked Inyo
off to the jug. The principal told me that he couldn't take any chances
with the kids, but that Inyo had been "a very friendly wolf," and he'd
told the animal-control officers as much so they wouldn't hurt her.
(Animal control doesn't have to impound an animal deemed a threat
to public safety; officers can shoot it on sight.)

At home, I found Argos and Thelma curled in the warm straw and
the kennel gate padlocked, just as I'd left it. They rose yawning when
they saw me. Thelma waved and Argos burrowed into my shoulder as I
checked the wire lacing running along the top and bottom of the kennel. It remained intact, along with the extra tension bands. My two-

year-old Houdini child seemed to have vanished like a musical note on the air. Then I saw it—a gash on the rear wall of the kennel where she'd tugged and twisted the 11-gauge chain link, gnawing until it surrendered and she could wriggle through.

Hanna rumbled down Longley Lane to the county animal shelter, a route that had become too familiar. I knew all the stoplights, the Pioneer Inn Hotel Casino, Amelia's Mexican Steakhouse, M & M Fish & Chicken Shack, the FedEx Ship Center, and the Wave Car Wash. I wanted to spring Inyo from the clink and go home, but somehow her license, along with her rabies tag, had fallen off her collar, and the woman behind the desk informed me that until I could prove her identity and vaccination status, I couldn't retrieve her. Grumbling, I drove back to the house and rummaged through the vet records for Inyo's rabies certificate. Two round-trips and she was free. Her second offense cost $50 plus $8 for a replacement license. That night, by the light of my headlamp, I fixed the hole in the kennel wall, fingers fumbling like a nervous surgeon's as I stitched the gash with 9-gauge wire. The next day I drove to Home Depot and bought a hotwire system as a backup, securing one strand of wire at knee height and another at chin level around the perimeter of the yard. The controller box hummed, its red eye blinking.

The next time, instead of chewing through the kennel wall, Inyo gnawed a hole in one corner of the roof and climbed out. I sprinted across the yard in time to see her flatten her torso to skim between the top of the fence and the hotwire, her shoulders shivering as she made contact. I grabbed her bushy tail and pulled, my forearms pressed against the pulsing current, but Inyo's head and shoulders were already over the fence, and gravity did the rest. I lurched backward, landing on a pile of scrap wood.

Probably still angry about his cat and his siding, my neighbor hollered over the fence, "She just doesn't want to stay home, now does she?" He chewed the end of a cigar, his breath hanging in the air. I was thankful it wasn't his yard Inyo had jumped into, but the weedy lot of a sweet college kid with a goldfish.

"You got yourself a real problem animal there."

I told the neighbor that I appreciated his concern but that I had things under control.

"Sure you do," he said.

I took deliberate, calm strides into the house so he wouldn't have the satisfaction of seeing me panic, but once out of his sight, I grabbed the leash, yanked a block of cheddar off the refrigerator shelf, and dashed out the front door.

Considering Inyo's challenge of the hotwire, not even those shock collars I'd found online—Tri-Tronics, Innotek, Dogtra, collars that sounded like they'd been designed by the Department of Defense—would have worked. Terry Jenkins told me about a wolfdog puppy she'd sold to a man who lived in a neighborhood where the homeowners' association prohibited fencing higher than four feet. As an alternative to fencing, the man had strapped one of those high-tech shock collars on his wolfdog. When she approached the boundary of the yard, the collar would beep a warning, and if she didn't retreat within a few seconds, the collar would shock her. But the man always found her roaming the neighborhood or locked in the pound, and when he checked her collar, he'd find the batteries dead. She kept escaping even though he'd replaced the batteries numerous times and even strapped on a second shock collar. Totally perplexed, he hid in the house one day to watch her. Trembling, the wolfdog approached the boundary and the beeping started. When the two collars screamed into her neck, she only stood there shaking until the batteries in both collars wore down, and she could run free again.

That afternoon I found Inyo two streets over and held out the block of cheddar. She turned her nose and ran on. Finally I caught her by getting down on my knees and pretending to dig in someone's lawn, shrieking with excitement. She couldn't help herself, trotting over to see what all the fuss was about, and I slipped my fingers under her collar. I sutured the new hole in the kennel wall, stretched a third strand of hotwire around the yard—which worked for a while—and carried a leash to class in my backpack. My literature professor forged ahead while I watched the door and waited for a phone call.

Sometimes I got lucky. "I've got your wolf locked in my garage," the voice on the phone would say. "I'll keep her until you get here." Other times the voice would say, "I saw your dog go by here. I tried to catch her but she took off. Say . . . is she a wolf?" Then it would be a race between me and the paddy wagon.

A patched-up kennel and four strands of hotwire seemed to work, and my spirits lifted. That is, until the ice storm, when Reno experienced a citywide power outage. This time the paddy wagon won the race. When I arrived at the shelter, the patrolling officer chuckled. "Wolfdogs know when the power's out. I've scooped up every wolfdog inside the city limits today." Bail was set at $100 for Inyo's third offense. From now on, every time she landed in the pokey, the fee would be $100.

The winter storms that year made the electricity unreliable, so I kept Inyo in the house until she chewed a hole in the bottom of the back door just large enough to squeeze through, and I had to put her back in the kennel with the pups. My cigar-smoking neighbor had his own ideas. I came home to find the padlock on the kennel door cut, the front gate ajar, and Inyo gone. When I knocked on his door to ask if he'd seen her, he said innocently that he'd seen animal control outside the house. Inyo had been loose in the front yard, so they picked her up. By the smirk on his face, I figured he'd probably let her out and then called animal control to get her.

Another $100. I replaced the padlock, and soon the ice melted, the electricity hummed, and Inyo was secure again—until a few days later when I found her weaving, unable to walk straight, and vomiting. Scribbling a quick note to Ryan, I carried Inyo to Hanna. As I sped toward the vet, I took deep breaths, reminding myself that Inyo was tough.

The vet ran tests while I answered questions. No, I didn't have any containers of pesticides lying around my yard, in the garage, or anywhere else. Yes, I kept aspirin, Tylenol, ibuprofen, and other medicines where Inyo couldn't get to them—stuffed into our backpacks stored in the garage! No, I didn't use flea and tick products, no dips or shampoos.

When the test results came back the vet told me that Inyo had ingested some kind of tobacco mixed with raw meat, not enough to give her seizures or put her in a coma, just enough to make her stomach upset and cause an irregular heartbeat. She asked if I had any reason to believe Inyo might have been intentionally poisoned. A picture formed in my mind—the neighbor tinkering with his big Ford truck and smoking a cigar.

While the remedy for Inyo was hydration and quiet, the prescription for my neighbor came to me in a dark moment. I smeared Crisco under the door handles and on the side mirrors of his truck, and squirted Gorilla Glue into the locks. He called the property management company we rented the house from, complaining that Inyo was a menace who howled constantly, and that Ryan and I had wild parties with drinking and drugs. I gave his door handles a second dose of Crisco and watched him from my bedroom window as he had a fit in his driveway.

The company sent us a warning letter, demanding that we get our animal under control and behave like respectable citizens. To needle us, the neighbor stood across the street and videotaped Ryan and me as we came and went, so I videotaped him yelling at his wife in their driveway. His face reddened and he swore at me. His wife cussed me out in Romanian before disappearing inside the house.

I filed a restraining order when the bald man spit, "I'm going to get you."

He complained to the property management company a second time. "Looks like you'll be moving," he said, as I stood on the porch reading the pink eviction notice tacked to the front door. That color pink again.

We fought the eviction in court. In a gush of emotion, I told the judge that the neighbor had poisoned my dog, and I'd had to call the police on three different occasions because he beat his wife. The judge yawned as if he'd heard plenty of cases like this one. Our day in court gained us nothing; Ryan and I now had less than thirty days to evacuate the premises. The judge added that to prevent further escalation between the parties, the animal in question would have to be kept elsewhere, and if found on the premises, she would be confiscated.

While Ryan painted a battalion of miniature orcs and goblins in chaos black and bloodred for his next tabletop Warhammer Fantasy

Battle, I stood in front of the freezer, an icy fog wafting over me as I fiddled with the wedding cake, going on two years old now. I imagined that if I nudged the cake a quarter inch left, then right, making certain the center leaf on the frosting-rose arrangement faced precisely front in the middle of the shelf, Ryan would get his troubles straightened out and we'd find a place to live. But with an eviction on record, plus three canines and a parrot, it was impossible to find anything. And where would Inyo stay for the next thirty days? I called friends and professors who lived farther out of town to see if someone could house her temporarily—a ridiculous notion—and finally resorted to putting an ad in the paper:

> *HELP! Part-wolf needs foster care.*
> *Desperate situation.*
> *Temporary home only.*

A call came from a woman named Shirley in Virginia City, a tiny slice of the Old West in the hills southeast of Reno, where rugged individualism prevailed and there were few rules. "No one worries about dogs," Shirley said. "People pretty much leave you alone." She'd fostered several dogs, she said, and although her kennels were full, if I had nowhere else, I could take Inyo there. The weather was good and there were plenty of trees where I could tie her out.

When the phone didn't ring and the neighbor threatened to call the police if I didn't get Inyo out of there, I loaded her in Hanna and drove to Virginia City. Hanna chugged up Geiger Grade Road, popping and sputtering when I downshifted on the hairpin turns, winding upward toward the old mining boomtown. Shirley, a short, plump woman in her fifties, invited us inside her house where every room was cluttered with cat carriers and cats, empty aquariums, guinea pigs in a cardboard box, and a mouse running on a wheel. She introduced me to her pregnant sixteen-year-old daughter and the daughter's boyfriend. "They're living with me until they can get on their feet," she said. They nodded hello and disappeared into the daughter's bedroom.

"We should probably go back outside," I said, tightening the leash as Inyo strained toward the guinea pigs and cats.

Shirley led us out back where boxer mixes, German shepherd types, and mixed terriers were housed in kennels strewn across the yard. The acrid smell of urine stung my nose. A rusted yellow wheelbarrow piled high with dog shit sat in a corner of the yard. A rake and shovel leaned against one of the dog runs, as if someone had started to clean and been distracted. In order to allow myself to chain Inyo to a tree trunk in the hilly yard behind Shirley's house, I vowed that she would be there only a short time, that I would find another rental by the end of the week.

Girdling the base of a juniper trunk with one end of a twenty-foot chain, I used a carabiner to clip the other end to Inyo's collar. "You'll have to unwind the chain often," I said, explaining that Inyo would wrap it around the tree until it got too short for her to move around. "You're sure you can keep an eye on her?"

Shirley nodded and smiled, but I wasn't so sure. I told myself that I had no other choice but to trust her, and I'd get Inyo out of here as soon as I could.

Handing Shirley written instructions about Inyo's meals, I retrieved two twenty-pound sacks of kibble from Hanna and filled Shirley's refrigerator and freezer with tubs of turkey-vegetable mash. "She gets a pork hock in the afternoon and a beef bone at night," I said, giving Shirley a satchel with four packages of pork hocks and beef bones, a Kong, and a jar of Jif. "Keep her Kong full of peanut butter and kibble," I said. "She's calmer if she has to work at something." When I ran up the driveway to get a package of pig ears I'd forgotten, the van already felt lonesome. Starting Hanna's engine to leave, I heard Inyo howl and I could hardly breathe, putting a hand on my belly where a knot had formed. She would be all right, I told myself. This was an emergency measure.

The next morning, I scanned the rentals in the *Reno Gazette-Journal*, but all the ads vetoed dogs. When I visited Inyo two days later, winding up Geiger Grade with a fresh package of pork hocks, she pawed the air and whined when she saw me. Her chain, wound countless times around the base of the juniper, left her only a couple of feet to move, and her water dish was empty. Rubbing her wolfy cheek tufts, I kissed her wet black nose and loaded her in Hanna. I left a brief note for Shirley and drove off.

Inyo and I ran and ran on Peavine Mountain and didn't go home until after dark, when the flickering blue light of the neighbor's television splashed against his living-room curtains. For the next ten days, I managed to sneak Inyo out to Hanna in the early morning, when the sky was still black, and bring her back at night undetected.

When I still couldn't find a new rental and we had only five days left to get out of that house, my friend Crystal came to the rescue, generously offering us the spare bedroom in her house. We could stay there with all the animals until we found our own place. The neighbor videotaped us as we lugged boxes into our third U-Haul in two years. One of Ryan's coworkers bought the patched kennel, neither strong enough nor big enough for Inyo, and the wedding cake, its frosting roses beginning to sag, rode shotgun to its third freezer.

CHAPTER SEVENTEEN

Noah's Ark

They say marriages are made in Heaven. But so is thunder and lightning.

—Clint Eastwood

Thelma and Argos slept in Crystal's spare bedroom with Ryan and me. Inyo had to stay outside on a chain except for short supervised visits indoors, and though I took her for rides in Hanna and our daily runs, I was gnawed by guilt. I added ten feet to her tether as if that made any difference. Chaining was supposed to be a temporary measure, but "temporary" was getting longer and longer.

For a month I searched the ads in the *Reno Gazette-Journal*, *Reno News & Review*, and the *Big Nickel*, looking for rental houses with fenced yards. Dizzy with advertisements, I saw their headlines in my sleep: "Rent Reduced!" "A Real Charmer." "Doll House." "Summer Special." As I scanned the ads, inevitably reading "no pets" or "small dog ok," empty hangers in the guest-room closet made a *tin-tin* sound when the dry summer wind blew through the window. I kept my clothes in a cardboard box and my doctoral exam books stacked on the floor in tidy columns, as if by staying always ready to go, we'd find a home faster.

A sign for a new housing development off U.S. 395 read, "If you lived here, you'd be home by now." Other developments sprang up all over Reno, expanding farther into the sagebrush. Coyote Ridge Road and Cedar Waxwing Court appeared overnight. Leveled and staked, lands once covered in sagebrush and shadscale now lay smooth where new homes would go. At the finished houses, sprinklers soaked the carpets of newly unrolled sod. I took Inyo running in one of the neighborhoods under construction. Clouds of hot dust carried the arrhythmic clanking of hammers and the groan of heavy machinery down the slopes of Peavine. As we jogged up a recently paved swath of desert, automatic sprinklers pumping *cht-cht-cht* all night had created a steady runnel downhill, filling the gutter along a newly poured sidewalk. California quail chicks with their bobbing teardrop plumes floated like tiny sailboats, spinning down Archimedes Lane, unable to escape the flood. I tied Inyo to a pole and scooped up one quail chick, and then another and another, cradling them in my shirttails. Their chests heaved from exertion as I set the faint chicks under a clump of sagebrush in hopes that their parents would find them. Inyo watched me, quiet and intense. If she'd had her druthers, she'd have gobbled them.

Although I wouldn't have wanted to live in one of those developments—the houses packed close and the "gorgeous view" soon to disappear once the next development crept up the face of Peavine— it occurred to me that if we bought our own place far outside the city, there wouldn't be any neighbors to complain to animal control, no poisonings, no eviction notices, no more sleeping in a kind friend's spare bedroom, no more phone calls—"I have your wolf in my garage." And no more chains! I skipped the rentals and went straight to the For Sale ads.

Over breakfast at the Pneumatic Diner, I tapped the newspaper, showing Ryan ads for homes with acreage and others for raw land. "I'll build a fancy run for Inyo," I told him. "Three or four acres with mazes and hidey-holes and a pond. We'll have our own land to run on—forty acres, eighty acres, maybe more!" I added that his credit should be repaired now that he'd been making payments on the student loans.

Ryan took a bite of sausage and peered at me over his reading glasses.

I called Crystal's real estate agent and told her what we wanted. She showed me one- and two-acre parcels in Cold Springs and Silver Knolls, Stead and Sun Valley. She just didn't get it. As far as neighbors were concerned, I told her, I should be able to see them only with a pair of binoculars. I found a new agent, and Inyo and I spent whole days trekking twenty-, forty-, and eighty-acre parcels in Antelope Valley, Spanish Springs, Palomino Valley, and the Virginia City Highlands, some places so remote the roads had neither names nor numbers.

Driven to find land, a place of our own, I developed nervous habits. Scanning ads online, I would tug strands of hair until they fell out and scratch my scalp until it bled. My front teeth were loose from nights of grinding, and when I talked or chewed, my jaw made a crunching sound like gravel underfoot. I also became forgetful. Before meeting with the agent one morning, I stopped at the ARCO station to fill Hanna's tank. Inyo lounged on the backseat while I went inside to pay, and when I came out Hanna was gone. I'd already lost my keys twice, misplaced my wallet, left my computer in a coffee shop, and wandered into rooms having forgotten what I'd gone in there for. Now I'd misplaced Inyo and Hanna. I'd left the key in the ignition, but who'd steal an old van with a wolfdog in the back? I ran to the pump, as if by standing in that spot, I could make Hanna and Inyo suddenly reappear. I went from one customer to another, my eyes wide with fear, asking if they'd seen a blue Volkswagen van. They all shrugged and shook their heads. Then a woman pointed. "Is that it?"

Hanna sat about two hundred yards away in a large undeveloped field. I sprinted toward her, leaping over balls of Russian thistle, to find Inyo sitting at the helm of her movable den, looking bored. Hanna looked like a Chia Pet with stalks of cheatgrass poking out of her grille and a thick film of dust clinging to her windows. I hadn't set the emergency brake, and she'd just rolled out of the station.

Other days I felt focused and hopeful. When Ryan and I walked the perimeter of a spring-fed twenty-acre parcel overlooking Palomino Valley, I was sure we'd found home. With only seasonal vehicle access—during winter months the road so rutted and slick that not even a four-wheel-drive vehicle could navigate it—I figured we could park below the property and cross-country ski up the mountain to the old trailer we'd buy and power with a generator until we could afford to build a house. Anything that had to do with climbing a mountain was boss to Ryan, as long as he could play World of Warcraft once in a while.

But there was a hitch. The banks wouldn't give us a loan for raw land. We'd have to pay cash or ask the owner to carry a loan. Since we didn't have $42,000 up front, paying cash was out, but I'd seen plenty of ads with "owner will carry," so I kept my hopes up. While our new real estate agent contacted the landowner, I scanned *Deals & Wheels*, the local automotive rag, and found a 1975 Traveleze trailer with fridge and water pump for $2,400. Home felt closer than ever, and my plan seemed perfect—until it crumbled. It turned out the owner wasn't in a rush to sell his land and didn't want to carry a loan. We kept looking. I daydreamed about winning the lottery and thought seriously about becoming a nude dancer to make some fast money.

Meanwhile, the safeguards we'd decided on in our own place couldn't be applied in our cramped temporary quarters. One afternoon as I changed into running clothes, I heard a panicky wing-flutter behind me and turned to see a spray of feathers hit the air. Tired of his shrieks going unanswered, Lupe had kamikazed off his rope swing to get my attention, and Inyo pounced. I dove on her, wrapping my arms around her barrel to haul her off. Lupe lay crumpled and blinking, orange and green feathers strewn on the carpet around him.

Ryan, who'd been reading a book of Jorie Graham's poems, rushed out of the bedroom and kneeled over Lupe, while Inyo sat a few feet away, head down, ears up, waiting to spring forward and try again.

Lupe closed his eyes.

"He's dead," Ryan said.

"Wait!"

"What?"

"He moved."

"I don't see anything."

Lupe opened his eyes and stood up.

"He might live."

"Doubtful," Ryan said.

Lupe shook like a dog and stretched his wings, letting out a piercing screech.

"This world is a predatory holocaust," Ryan said, scooping Lupe into his hands. Easing the parrot into his fleece tent, Ryan draped a thick blanket over Lupe's cage for darkness and quiet to help him recover.

* * *

Ryan and I looked at properties almost daily, winding through miles of sagebrush and juniper to remote acreage within an hour's commute of Reno. One afternoon we drove Inyo and the pups out on Morning Star Road until we reached a steep gravel drive marked on the plot map the agent had given us. Parking on the cleared and leveled homesite overlooking a forty-acre apron of land that adjoined Bureau of Land Management (BLM) property, I could see juniper trees for miles. "This is it," I said, not waiting for Ryan to comment. Pacing the dusty site, I spun my plan. "We'll put our new home right here," I said. The ad had specified that the owner would carry the loan with 15% down. I dug in my pocket for the calculator I always carried and punched in the figures. "We have to come up with $9,750."

Ryan raised his eyebrows. "How do you figure we'll raise that kind of money? Hold a bake sale?"

When I called the real estate agent to ask if there were any other options for us, she uttered the magic words—Land-Home Package Deal. If we found a parcel of land we wanted and bought a manufactured or modular home, we could get a bank to finance the deal as long as the home sat on a permanent foundation.

Although a manufactured home was not my first choice, I'd live in a shoe box to get Inyo some land. Ryan and I walked through two- and three-bedroom modular homes, learning all about tape and textured walls, Hardie trim and simulated stone, goal-post kitchen entrances, toe-kick heat vents, and porches with "hip" roofs. Ann, our manufactured home agent, told us that since we'd already picked out the parcel we wanted on Morning Star Road, we could choose the home model and get started with loan prequalification. As a graduate teaching assistant, my salary was low, but my credit score was excellent. Ryan had a good salary and had been making good-faith payments to get his loans out of default and his credit score up.

Ann suggested that we attend a meeting of the Morning Star Estates Property Owners Association. "Get to know those people," she said, explaining that the association could be strict about the kinds of structures it allowed, and she'd had problems with the committee before. "Just check it out before you settle. Meantime we'll start the loan paperwork."

The following week I tethered Inyo to one of the picnic tables outside the meeting hall on Morning Star. While she lounged in the grass chewing a marrowbone, Ryan and I poured ourselves cups of Folgers and found our seats. I smiled at everyone, but there was a strange tension in the air, couples huddled together whispering. For the first time in a while though, we weren't the ones in trouble. The president of the board, seated at the front of the room, called the meeting to order, and seconds later, accusations flew. Apparently, one homeowner had planted a tree in front of his kitchen window without going through the proper channels to have the species and the planting location approved. The tree had grown taller than expected and blocked the view of the adjacent neighbor. To make things worse, the color of the tree's blooms clashed with the house paint, tarnishing the aesthetics of the neighborhood. "Who does this jackass think he is anyway?" shrieked the offended neighbor, red-faced, his neck veins bulging.

The man accused of breaking the rules kicked a folding chair at his accuser, yelled, "Screw you," and stomped out. Ryan and I looked at each other. The president banged a gavel on the Formica table. "This will have to be settled at another time," he said. The meeting continued with other business—voting to raise the annual assessment by 10% for capital improvements to the common area—and adjourned early. Two couples introduced themselves after the meeting and reassured us that what had happened that night was a rare incident. Usually people were much more polite and tolerant. "We all get along for the most part," one woman said. "These two have had it in for each other."

Inyo howled when she saw Ryan and me exit the building. The man who'd planted the wrong sort of tree approached us. He flicked a cigarette into the dust, grinding it out with the heel of his boot. "That your dog?"

I nodded.

"She's pretty. Better make sure she isn't a nuisance. People got livestock around here, and they'll shoot her. Most of them in there wouldn't even bother to tell you about it. They'd just bury her and that'd be it."

"Let's go," Ryan said.

On the way back to town, I told Ryan Inyo wouldn't be a problem, she would have too much to do to bother people's cows. We'd manage out there.

"You bet we'll manage," he said. "We'll manage by staying the hell away from those people. I'm not trading one landlord for twenty."

I had to admit that at times Ryan had more common sense than I.

We found another parcel at the base of Fred's Mountain, twenty minutes from downtown Reno. On our way to see it, thousands of shield-backed katydids moved down the dirt road in an undulating brown wave, attacking and eating one another, leaping and flying forward to keep from being devoured by the one behind. A few of them got stuck in the windshield wipers, their guts smearing the glass. We pulled over, katydids crunching under our feet as we walked the parcel, a mere ten acres. But the property adjoined BLM land, and best of all, there was no homeowners' association. I got so excited I drove to the nearest neighbor and introduced myself.

I could hardly wait for our next appointment with Ann, who'd been working on our loan application. The floor was spongy in the old modular business office, and the walls shook as Ryan and I strode down the hall toward her cubicle. In the middle of a phone call she motioned for us to take a seat. A calendar on the wall behind her featured June's modular home of the month, a Weston Xtreme. The water cooler gurgled in the hallway.

When Ann put down the receiver, she told us that we were closer to putting something together. "We have a few more background details to look into, but it's looking like we can get you qualified for a total of $130,000." That amount had to cover land purchase and the cost of the manufactured home, as well as land preparation including well and septic. The land cost $40,000, the home $65,000, and land preparation would run about $25,000. The total came to exactly $130,000. There would be additional fees, but she told us we might be able to roll some of the costs into the loan package. There was no wiggle room, but things were looking good. Check back in a week.

Certain this deal would go through, I bought wooden stakes and orange flagging, crushing more katydids to mark the tall sagebrush shrubs I didn't want the construction crew to pull out. I referred to the land as "our home," and told friends we'd soon have our own address.

But when Ann phoned a few days later to say she needed to see us, I felt like I'd been summoned to the principal's office.

"We've got a problem," she said, and looked at Ryan. "You didn't mention that your wages were being garnished."

"What?" I turned to Ryan.

"The government and the loan companies have been garnishing Ryan's wages for the last three months," Ann said.

"But I thought we'd been making payments on those loans to fix your credit!"

Ryan opened his eyes wide and turned down the corners of his mouth. I knew that expression. It was the expression of a man getting caught and trying to look as surprised as the rest of us. Then he stiffened. "Well, it was cheaper than paying back the loans. I'll be dead before they get paid off anyway, so what's the point?"

CHAPTER EIGHTEEN

Location, Location, Location

You have brains in your head. You have feet in your shoes.
You can steer yourself any direction you choose.
              —Dr. Seuss, *Oh, the Places You'll Go!*

While Ryan drove, I stared out the side window, grinding my teeth. *I can't believe this is happening.* Ann had told us that originally we'd looked good for a $130,000 loan at a 9% fixed rate for thirty years, but that deal was off the table now. She'd call a few private lenders who might give us a loan with a variable rate.

In a moment of conciliation Ryan took his eyes off the road and patted my shoulder. "We'll make it through this, honey," he said.

"No, we won't," I yelled, shoving his hand away. "It's not like we're a match made in heaven, and now you've ruined everything." I'd gone over the edge, said something terrible I couldn't take back. I felt cold and tingly and ready to fight. Both of us fell silent the rest of the way to Crystal's house.

When I slid open the glass door to the backyard and called Inyo, Thelma and Argos rushed forward, their bodies wiggling in joy. Thelma greeted me with *"Arruuh!"* and waved her paw. Argos circled my legs and whined. I stroked his head and scratched his ruff, then called Inyo again. No response. I picked up the anchored end of her chain. It glided over my palms as I followed the tether link by link to the edge of the deck, where it disappeared underground. Several deck boards had buckled, the ends gnawed to splinters, and clumps of sod lay strewn around the yard. Though I felt wretched, I got down on my knees and called cheerfully into the hole. Yawning, Inyo crawled from her den and kissed me.

Later that night, over Lupe's screams for attention, I showed Crystal the gnawed deck boards and destroyed sod. She shook her head and told me that her neighbors had complained about Inyo's howling. Although she didn't ask us to leave, and in fact insisted that we were welcome to stay until we could find another rental, I knew it was time to go. A loan had to come through—it just had to.

We sat in Ann's office with a view of the WinCo parking lot through one of the torn shades, as she told us that Ryan would need to make nine months of good-faith payments on the student loans to get them out of default and off his record. She also informed us that apparently he also owed several thousands to the IRS. "Get your credit in good standing," she said, "and the underwriters will have another look." Ann picked up the phone to call another customer, our signal to leave.

Listening to the thrum of the truck's engine, I kept silent on the ride back to Crystal's. I wanted to yell, but instead I clacked my front teeth together and curled my toes. Where would we live while I tried to convince Ryan to reenroll in debt rehab? We couldn't stay on at Crystal's house, and there weren't any rentals—at least none that would take dogs and tenants with evictions on record.

Then I got an idea.

I pulled a city map of Reno from the glove compartment and scanned the surrounding areas for public land where we might be able to set up camp and live in Hanna for the rest of the summer—or at least until I could figure something out. Thirty minutes from town, in the Humboldt-Toiyabe National Forest outside Verdi, California, a place called Dog Valley had several undeveloped campgrounds. Inyo and I had hiked there. It was secluded, quiet—and best of all it was free.

We left Crystal's without offering to pay for replacement deck boards and sod, a negligence she never held against me. Just before we left I rummaged through her freezer for the wedding cake, now crushed and grayed, and pitched it in the trash.

Caravanning west on I-80 past Mogul and Boomtown Reno Casino and Hotel, we crossed two slim bridges spanning the Truckee River and took Dog Valley Road uphill until the pavement turned to gravel.

A sign on the road announced our arrival: Entering the Toiyabe Forest, and read to me like Welcome Home. Hanna's wheels spit gravel and dust, and the temperature cooled by ten degrees as we climbed, escaping Reno's heat.

As long as we moved our campsite every fourteen days, we could live in Dog Valley as long as we needed to. We parked Hanna under a limber pine and wheeled Lupe's dome-top cage across the pine needles to give him a view of the creek.

True to the name Dog Valley—so called for the pack of feral dogs that had run free there at one time—Thelma and Argos chased Inyo around the aspen woodlands, darting in and out of marrow-red ponderosa pines. When they'd exhausted themselves, all three drank from the creek, then flopped down in the dirt for a nap. Near dark, I set up two folding chairs and a card table for Yahtzee. Ryan and I drank Moose Drool Brown Ale from the icy cooler and played two rounds before falling silent and staring into the campfire.

I blew over the mouth of my bottle, whistling, while Ryan peeled the label from his, waving it over the fire. It fluttered down to rest on the embers and then shriveled. The fire spit. Ryan recited "Hurt Hawks" by Robinson Jeffers. "I'd sooner, except the penalties, kill a man than a hawk . . ." Moments like those I felt close to him, admiring.

The aspens rose out of the valley, their slim, white trunks gleaming in the firelight, green leaves rustling on their branches. Those leaves would change to yellow in a month, and eventually the snows would come.

We couldn't stay there forever.

We spent the next two weeks reading and walking and checking the newspapers. Ryan would bird-watch in the early mornings, stalking downy woodpeckers and bluebirds while I ran the dogs in the opposite direction. In the afternoons, we sat in our folding chairs, Ryan engrossed in Arthur Schopenhauer's *The World as Will and Idea* while I read from the stacks of books required for my doctoral exams. Every few days, we drove to Reno for supplies and a shower in the university gym.

In the third week of our exile, I had the forest to myself while Ryan drove the truck to Sacramento for a teachers' conference. By day four, when I needed more than a sponge bath in gas-station water, I loaded the dogs, Inyo, and Lupe into Hanna and we rolled to town in the coolness of early morning. Over a cup of coffee, I browsed the rental ads in the *Big Nickel*. Amid want ads for brothel memorabilia, naughty playmates, and firearms training, I found an ad for a rental house that allowed dogs—not "small dogs only," or "pets on approval," just "dogs okay." I borrowed the café phone and sat down, hands shaking. Perched on my shoulder, Lupe burbled in my ear. For good luck, I lifted my feet off the floor and plugged my nose, the magic I'd used as a kid to keep trains from hitting my mother and me as we drove across the railroad tracks.

A man answered the phone sounding tipsy, lingering a little too long on the *r* in rent. He said the place was still available, a two-bedroom, one-bath house on a fenced quarter acre of land with a pond and two apple trees, $650 a month plus deposit. I could barely contain myself, asking to see the place that morning. In a slight country drawl he said, "Name's Darryl. C'mon round. I'm here."

It was all I could do not to shriek into the phone, "We'll take it!" Showering at the university, I stuffed my clothes smelling of campfire and mountain dust into a plastic bag, glossed my lips, smoothed my hair, and drove toward a place called Panther Valley. I glanced down at the directions on a piece of paper: Right on Panther Drive. Left on Lariat Lane. Then go straight, and when it looks like you're about to drive off the edge of the world, turn right on Jack Rabbit Road.

Pulling up a steep gravel driveway past a jumble of jagged red boulders and a cinder-block cellar built into the side of the hill, I parked in front of an open garage with a vintage Coke machine at the entrance. Antique farming equipment, including a sickle grinder and a wood-frame corn sheller, lay strewn around the gravel yard. A cast-iron woodstove sat on one side of the house, and several rusted handsaws decorated the property's perimeter fence. A second seven-foot fence enclosed a large backyard.

Darryl, a stocky middle-aged man with graying hair, stepped out of the garage into the sunlight holding a can of Coors Light. He introduced himself and offered me a "pop." His tan face was leathered from ranching red poll cattle on the North Dakota prairie, and when he smiled, the skin around his eyes creased. He told me that he came to Reno once a year to gamble and to do repairs on the house. He didn't hesitate when I said my husband and I had three dogs and a parrot.

Turned out the rental house was actually a 1980 Fairmont single-wide mobile home that had been sliced open lengthwise to allow the addition of stick-built rooms. Vinyl siding covered the old shiplap pre-finished aluminum. The brown carpet in the living room was stained, but clean. The main bedroom overlooked the backyard with its dry pond of poured concrete and a chicken coop of torn and rusted wire. Noticing my gaze lingering on the coop, Darryl said, "Last tenant tried to have chickens, but the coyotes got in there. Those chickens were about as safe as a cow in the stockyards."

The bathroom had a cameo pink toilet with matching tub and sink nestled in a glittery Formica countertop. The carpeted kitchen was a leftover from the single-wide—bouncy floor, low smoke-stained ceiling, and counter trim peeling away. Its window looked out on a gutted 1976 Airstream trailer, an AmeriGas propane tank, a rusted-out 1930s Ford pickup, and a twenty-foot-tall wheel-mounted crane with telescoping boom. Looking at this place, someone else might have seen a junkyard. I saw a jungle gym for Inyo. Even better, immediately beyond the property line lay at least two hundred acres of undeveloped sagebrush steppe where we could run. When I asked Darryl if he was sure about the dogs, he took a sip of his Coors and said, "Aw, sure, I love dogs. Long as they don't tear the place up."

I imagined the rake of Inyo's teeth on window ledges and doors. But what the hell—for fifty bucks I could replace all the trimmings on this rent-a-wreck with its single-pane windows framed in plywood. "That won't be a problem," I said.

Darryl didn't ask to do a background check and didn't need references from previous landlords. He just wanted to know when we planned to move in so he could get back to North Dakota. I wrote a check for the deposit and toured my new neighborhood. Ceramic deer decorated the flower beds and plastic sunflowers spun in the dusty breeze blowing off the hills at the end of the world. One neighbor, whose porch was falling off the front of his house, had hung a twenty-foot banner on his fence: Kill the Terrorists. A fellow at the end of Collins Circle tossed hay out for the three cows in his backyard, a large pig wandering among them. I heard the *kak-kak-kak* of a peregrine falcon and slowed Hanna, coasting in second gear past a hacking pen, a mesh enclosure for exercising birds of prey that stretched the length of a front yard.

When I swung by the house on Jack Rabbit Road to take one more look, a barefoot old woman in a nightgown and shower cap ran in front of Hanna waving her arms. I slammed on the brakes and she ran to my open window. "I'm Rose. My son beats me," she cried. "He's trying to kill me!" She pointed to the mobile home across the street from my new rental house. "I live there, but I'm leaving home," she said, breathing heavily, her hands wrinkled and shaking. Inyo howled, and the dogs crowded the window, smelling her distress. I pulled over and walked Rose home. Her son answered my knock and told me she'd been experiencing dementia. The night before last he'd found her wandering Lariat Lane barefoot in her nightgown. I left Rose in his care and drove away with the rental agreement in my lap.

When Ryan returned from Sacramento, I took him to see our new house, uncomfortably aware that he was staring at the water heater that leaned through a rip in the trailer's siding. "This is a shit hole," he said.

"Yeah, but it's *our* shit hole! Isn't it perfect?"

Darryl had told me that the kitchen disposal occasionally backed up, but it usually cleared with a little Liquid-Plumr. I didn't mention that to Ryan, and after sleeping and showering in a hotel room with access to free Internet, he thought anything looked better than the national forest, especially when I told him he could have the second bedroom for his office.

We prepared to break camp—and just in time. Someone had reported a wolf in Dog Valley, and the ranger who strode into the campsite looked skeptical when I swore up and down that Inyo was not a wolf. He asked how long we planned to stay. Thank God I could reply with all truthfulness that at the end of the week we were heading home.

CHAPTER NINETEEN

Beautiful Day
for a Neighbor

For the animal shall not be measured by man. . . . They
are not brethren, they are not underlings; they are other
Nations, caught with ourselves in the net of life and time.
—Henry Beston, *The Outermost House*

A map of Reno showed an empty grid behind our house on Jack Rabbit Road. Brushy acres stretched in all directions between Panther and Golden Valleys, and Inyo and I could run and explore on the way to nowhere in particular. But sometimes, to tire us both to foot-dragging exhaustion, I aimed us up a steep dirt track to the radio towers on a nearby hill. Leaning into the grade, we climbed toward the summit overlooking Panther Valley and downtown Reno, my quads screaming.

Afterward, we'd plunge downhill into the dry washes filled with bullet-riddled cars blackened by fire, our only company a tribe of chattering black-billed magpies that scolded us from the juniper trees. Occasionally we'd see a coyote, and Inyo, in a burst of speed, sprinted after it, but unable to close the distance, she would eventually give up and circle back.

Each week the burned red soil and sagebrush thickets bloomed with new bags of kitchen garbage, bathtubs, dresser drawers stuffed with old clothes, couches missing cushions. I often brought certain treasures home for Inyo's jungle gym—a Sealy box spring, a wooden cable spool for a perch, a section of PVC pipe for her to crawl through, a sack of cotton bath towels for games of tug-of-war between her and the dogs, and oodles of smelly treats like a sun-dried pig's head, a deer's front leg, a pile of horse poop. Whatever I couldn't bag, drag, or roll, I retrieved with the pickup, pitching along the pitted roads in first gear.

Then fall turned to winter and frosty air seeped through the single-pane windows and blew through cracks in the doors. One afternoon, when clouds had dumped a foot of powder on the high desert, Inyo and I jogged uphill to the radio towers. Kicking the snow off my sneakers with each stride, the laces frozen stiff in their bows, I lifted my knees and plunged forward through the drift. Like a satellite, Inyo orbited me, keeping a steady distance, but traveling her own trajectory, stopping occasionally to cock her head and turn an ear to the world under the snow where the mice lived. She dug furiously to find the source of the tiny animal noises lost to my ears. The snow came down fast and sideways; the temperature dropped, and the contours of the road to the tower softened and disappeared. Flakes stuck to my glasses, and my lungs burned with the cold. When we reached the towers, the city had vanished in a whiteout. Even the flashing red lights of the tower above had disappeared. Inyo and I took long draws of cold air, our breath mingling, the only sound the crinkling of snowflakes as they landed.

With no clear path to follow down and the snow coming hard, we trekked for an hour, picking our way toward the house. Shivering and sweaty, I turned Inyo out with Thelma and Argos, and each one retreated to a private corner with a fresh marrowbone. Sure she'd be too tired to challenge the fence (which I'd reinforced with four strands of taut 14-gauge wire delivering 5,000 volts), I jumped in the shower. Five minutes later, as I stood on a stack of cinder blocks, potato skins from the backed-up disposal swirling around my feet, the phone rang. A woman shrieked into my ear, "Your wolf is stalking my goats!"

I wrapped myself in a towel and dashed out the door in my flip-flops, half-running, half-hopping along Jack Rabbit Road toward the goat pen two houses away. "She'll kill them!" the woman shouted when she saw me. The hair had started to freeze on my head as I clambered up the woman's driveway and cut through the front yard toward the goat pen, a rectangular section of the yard surrounded by field-fencing stretched tight with two-by-four planks.

"Inyo!" I called, almost losing the grip on my towel as I slipped on a bouquet of plastic pink and purple flowers sticking up through the snow. I dodged a birdhouse made out of an old mailbox and ducked under a frozen clothesline. "Inyo, come!" She ignored me as she circled the goats, advancing through the hunting sequence: stalk, rush, chase. Unlike the moose or elk that might hold its ground against a wolf, the domestic goats bolted to the other side of the pen. Triggered to chase when the goats fled, Inyo gave a kid a sharp nip on the rump, and it cried out, leaping into the crowd of other goats wide-eyed and pressed together.

"Hurry! She's gonna kill my babies!"

I scurried through the pen gate, my bare shoulder grazing the electric wire, feet sinking into half-frozen mud, and grabbed hold of Inyo's collar to pull her away.

The woman checked the goat Inyo had nipped. There were no wounds, only mussed goat hair and wolfdog slobber. She clutched the neck of her dingy peach bathrobe, her hair in tight curlers flecked with snowflakes, feet stuffed into heavy rubber boots. "That thing was gonna kill one of them."

"I'm so sorry. It won't happen again," I said, glancing down at my own feet, brown from mud and gray from the cold. They looked like a couple of dead smelt. Clutching the towel with one hand, gripping Inyo's collar with the other, I hobbled home. When I slammed the door against the cold, I heard water running. In my panic to get Inyo, I'd left the shower on, and the tub had overflowed. Argos pounced on carrot chunks as they floated down the hallway.

I lay towels down to soak up the water while Inyo nudged open the refrigerator door to rifle through the crisper. When I shooed her from the kitchen, she settled in a corner of the living room, content to lick goat scent from her paws. The ends of my hair, which had turned to icicles, began to thaw, sending rivulets of cold water down my back. With shaking hands, I lit the gas stove and slumped to the floor. Argos sat beside me, a tan paw resting on my shoulder. Thelma dragged her rug from the bedroom to lie down next to us. With knees tucked under my chin, I rocked back and forth against the cold. Inyo and I were supposed to be partners. She would protect me from people who wanted to hurt me and be the loyal companion I relied on to stick close. But Inyo could not be my guardian. Instead I was hers. Not only did I have to shield her from the world, I had to shield the world from her. Until that moment, I'd never allowed myself to think that I couldn't do it, and even as the thought entered my mind I shoved it away. Plan better. Work harder. No room for mistakes. I dressed and went out to the yard to inspect the fence. Chunks of red plastic floated in the icy pond. Inyo had disabled the hotwire by pulling the control box off the mounting brackets and gnawing it to bits.

If Inyo had killed one of my neighbor's goats that day, the headline in the *Reno Gazette-Journal* might have read: "Wolf Kills Local Livestock." The fine print clarifying her identity would have done nothing to slow the tidal wave of resistance to the idea of wolves repopulating their historic ranges in the West. In fact, other wolfdogs and captive-bred wolves have made wild wolves look bad. Years after the incident with my goat-owning neighbor, I read about a "mystery predator" killing sheep in eastern Montana. Ranchers who found their pregnant ewes disemboweled insisted that the predator was a wild wolf, but forensic analysis showed only that a canine of *some* kind had bitten the sheep over their entire bodies, behavior characteristic of a dog, captive-bred wolf, or wolfdog acting on prey drive but without the knowledge to kill efficiently. (Wolf pups learn to hunt from their parents, so wolves orphaned before they learned to hunt might also have been responsible.)

The animal killed for ten months, taking out 120 sheep before federal wildlife officials shot it from an airplane and sent the carcass to the Clark R. Bavin National Fish and Wildlife Forensics Laboratory in Ashland, Oregon, the only facility in the world dedicated to solving wildlife crimes. A few months after the phantom was killed, I visited Dyan Straughan, a forensic scientist specializing in wolf casework. She met me in the lobby full of Igloo coolers containing the latest evidence in animal carcasses and body parts, and guided me toward the genetics lab.

Biometric security scanned Straughan's fingerprint, the door buzzed open, and we entered the room where Straughan had analyzed the mystery predator's DNA. With access to 700 to 800 mitochondrial DNA profiles of wild North American wolves, as well as to nuclear DNA samples unique to wolves of the Great Lakes region, Straughan and her lab mate, BioRobot 8000, an automated workstation that handles DNA material, could discern which wolf populations the animal belonged to. The evidence told her that the "phantom livestock killer" contained DNA from Wisconsin and Alaskan wolf populations. Although wolves do disperse and travel great distances, "that kind of mating just doesn't happen in nature," she said, meaning that the animal had been a captive-bred wolf that had either escaped its home or been dumped by its owner.

Although genetics played a major part in determining the ancestry of the sheep-killing wolf, Straughan emphasized the partnership between genetics and morphology, sending me down the hall to meet morphologist Margaret "Cookie" Elizabeth Sims. Passing the dermestid bug room, I watched as half-inch beetles swarmed over the skulls of fresh specimens, eating the connective tissue and performing a service for investigators by thoroughly cleaning the bones. (Construction workers remodeling the lab joked that the lab was not a place to take a nap.)

Crammed with skeletal parts, the morphology lab served as a reference library of bones. Sims pulled out several drawers containing wolf, dog, and wolf-hybrid skulls. When scientists question the identity of a canine, morphologists like Sims examine the animal's skull and jaw shape, as well as its tympanic bullae, which house the inner ear. The rounded bullae of wolves contrast markedly with dogs' flattened bullae, whereas hybrid bullae might appear round, flat, or anywhere in between. When I told Sims that many people believe that German shepherds, Siberian huskies, and Alaskan malamutes are more closely related to wolves than other breeds, she laughed. "Strip off the fat and fur," she said. "Then you'll see the skull measurement differences." Sims also examines an animal's paws and teeth to determine identity. The mystery predator had small paws, its long claws typical of a captive animal, not a wolf traversing varied terrain, which acts as a natural nail file. Estimated at about four years old, the animal's teeth were also too perfect for a wild wolf—not a chip anywhere.

Identity matters. If forensics had identified the mystery predator as a wild wolf, ranchers who'd lost sheep would have been eligible for compensation from Defenders of Wildlife and the federal government, but because the animal was a captive-bred wolf, they got nothing.[1] Many ranchers who'd experienced losses didn't accept the scientific explanation. One rancher was quoted as saying, "There's no doubt it was a wolf. It's a matter of trying to evade the burden of damage." Many have continued to view wild wolves as bloodthirsty, wasteful predators that threaten their livelihood, instead of large carnivores trying to eke out an existence in a world full of people. I thought of Inyo and what my goat-owning neighbor had said: "Your *wolf* is stalking my goats!" And sure enough, in the weeks after the attack, my neighbor used the word *wolf* every time she told the story, feeding the already widespread contempt for wild wolves.[2]

CHAPTER TWENTY

Alphabet Soup

A alligators all around
B bursting balloons
C catching colds . . .
—Maurice Sendak,
Alligators All Around an Alphabet

News had spread about "the wolf" attacking goats, and when Inyo and I took our training walks, neighbors gave us sour looks. Clem, one of our neighbors, scowled. "I swear to Jesus if she hurts my cat, you'll have one less animal to worry about." I comforted myself with the fact that a week had passed since the incident, and with a new hotbox mounted out of Inyo's reach, the hotwire system seemed to work once again. To keep her jungle gym interesting, I added a portable metal stairway I found behind Darryl's garage. Parked in the center of the yard so Inyo couldn't use it to leap out, the fifteen-foot stairway with standing platform gave her a 360-degree view of the valley. From my desk tucked into a corner of the bedroom, I could keep an eye on her and even climb out the large sliding window to give her treats.

Well into our second week with no escapes, I came rumbling home from school in Hanna, a bag of bones from the Virginia Street butcher on the front seat. Argos shrieked as usual, then burrowed his head into my shins, while Thelma greeted me with *arruuh!* and a paw wave. But Inyo had bolted again, slipping her collar and digging out of a weak section of fence behind the chicken coop.

Pulling on a pair of fleece pants, a heavy coat, and boots, I marched down the road to the goat pen and ducked under the clothesline to peer inside. No Inyo and no dead goats. I circled the neighborhood and scanned the desert behind the house. With a recent rabbit kill out there, Inyo had shown me that she knew her way home, having trotted a mile back to the house with the carcass in her mouth, and as I retraced my steps to phone animal control, I hoped she might be waiting outside the door. She wasn't, and the shelter dispatch told me that an animal matching Inyo's description had been picked up in Panther Valley. So Inyo was in the can again, but fortunately she hadn't hurt the goats, and I could spring her the next morning.

With Inyo's collar and tags in my coat pocket along with proof of her rabies vaccination, I drove to the shelter. When the receptionist asked if my dog had been in the pound before, I paused before answering. If I gave Inyo's real name and showed her license, the woman would find a record of impoundments, and the fee would be yet another $100. And if Inyo ever got into trouble with the goats, a long history of escapes wouldn't help her case. Here was a chance to wipe the slate clean. "Her name's Carla," I said. "She hasn't been here before." The woman asked for proof of "Carla's" rabies vaccination, and I said I'd left it in the car and would come right back. Rummaging through my schoolbag for a bottle of Wite-Out, I doctored the vet certificate, penning "Carla" in neat script under "Patient ID." This would be the first of many names, from Carla to Pepper, I would give to animal control. After this incident I kept Inyo's license at home, buying a new one every time she ended up in the slammer.

Lately, Ryan had been in the habit of stopping at the market in Panther Valley RV Park on his way home from work to buy a 40-ouncer of Miller High Life and a bag of Mac's Pork Cracklins. Sometimes I saw him from the Laundromat next door where I shared the folding table with a skinny, white-haired woman in curlers and bunny slippers who sipped black coffee from a Styrofoam cup, squinting through the steam to watch *Days of Our Lives*. I could see Ryan browsing the beer cooler as if he might choose something different that day, but he always reached for Miller, and the woman who ran the register, chain-smoking between customers, rang him up.

Ryan kicked off his evenings and most weekend mornings with Miller. When he began locking himself in his office, I tugged the hair out of my head and spent hours organizing the refrigerator shelves with all labels facing outward. I told Ryan about the debt collector who'd called and threatened, "We'll take your vehicle, your house, whatever he owns we'll seize," and described the website of his collection agency—shark silhouettes swimming across the screen. Ryan twisted the cap off a bottle still in its brown paper sack, took a long drink, and announced, "Better that land thing didn't work out. We don't want to live in Nevada anyway. We should move to Mexico."

Not long after that pronouncement, Ryan quit moving at all. He locked himself in his office for an entire weekend, and when Monday morning came he refused to come out and go to work. "I'm in a hole I can't get out of," he said through the door. "I can't live like this." He told me he'd quit taking the Prozac. "It wasn't helping anyway."

God, what if he hurts himself? What if he's got a knife in there? I was shaking, but got stone-cold bossy to deal with my fear. "Listen," I said. "That stuff only works if you take it. Now open the door."

"You live with a sick person."

"Open this door."

"I'm totally lost."

I found a spare key and unlocked the door. "Get your shoes on!"

I phoned Ryan's boss and told him that Ryan had the flu, then I ordered Ryan into the car. "We're going to the hospital," I said.

He didn't fight me. On the way to the emergency room he squeezed my hand. "Please don't leave me."

"I won't leave you."

The truth was I had thought about leaving, more than once, but somehow I convinced myself that I just hadn't figured out the magic formula to make him a reliable husband. To call it quits would mean I'd failed, not him. And now that Ryan had finally hit bottom, I thought, he'd get the help he really needed.

After checking Ryan in, I drove home relieved that someone else would keep an eye on him awhile, but trembling so badly that I stalled the truck twice when my foot slipped the clutch.

Thelma and Argos greeted me at the door. Inyo was nosing through the crisper. I poured myself a stiff drink to quiet the shaking, and got after some business on the computer to make myself feel better. Thelma dragged her rug into the living room and curled up at my feet. Argos rested his chin on my knee. Inyo finally settled down to gnaw a marrowbone in the corner while I surfed the websites of debt rehab companies, warnings covering the screen:

Defaulted student loan garnishment will ruin your life!
Defaulted student loans will haunt you for years!

Then I saw words of hope:

Don't let defaulted student loans keep you from your dream home.

I quit tugging the hair out of my head and started making a new plan. One morning, while Ryan was still in the hospital, I dialed the 1-888 number and waited, staring out the bedroom window where Inyo stood looking back at me, tethered on the chain I'd vowed would be only temporary. She'd been in the hoosegow twice more since the goat incident, twice more since I'd reinforced the weak sections of fence. She'd brave that hotwire no matter what, so until I got the credit straightened out and could buy a large parcel of land where I'd build a better enclosure, my choice was to keep her on a chain or start packing again. I told myself that at least she had the shade of birch and apple trees, her own pond, a cable-spool perch, and access to two of her favorite hidey-holes. She was off the chain more than she was on it, and got daily off-lead runs in the desert, as well as backpacking and rock-climbing adventures. Anything to justify the chain to myself.

When an automated voice said, "All of our representatives are currently helping other customers . . . " my knee bounced and made the window rattle. What if my plan didn't work? What if I got caught? I should just hang up right now and forget it. But then the customer-service rep answered and I deepened my voice. "Yeah, uh, I wanna see about gettin' my loans outta default." For some reason, trying to sound like a guy made my voice take on a country twang.

The rep said I'd called the right place, and which loans were we looking at today? I'd rummaged through Ryan's office to find all the loan information buried under a plate of moldy pizza crusts. My voice cracked once and rose in pitch as I recited Ryan's birth date and address, but the rep said nothing. Did other wives do what I was doing? I tried not to talk too much, lots of "Yep," "Nope," and "Uh-huh."

When we finished the application for consolidating the debt, she told me she'd get back to me with the terms of the agreement and the monthly payment amount. "Yeah, uh, listen, don't call the house," I said. "My wife doesn't know about this yet. I wanna get it all set up first before I tell her. She's been hounding me about this for a while, and uh, I wanna surprise her."

"That's not a problem, sir. This is completely confidential."

The sound of breaking glass woke me one night and I leaped out of bed to check on Inyo. Peering into the kitchen, I found the refrigerator door ajar, spilling light onto the floor. My heels pounded the hallway to Ryan's office where the screen saver on his computer shot out blue stars. When I flipped on the light, mice scurried back to their nests in the walls, leaving turds and urine sprinkled on the crusty dinner plates stacked next to the computer. His students' Shakespeare essays, Cap'n Crunch boxes, and empty bottles of Miller littered the floor. When a cold wind whipped my nightgown around my knees, I switched on the hall light and saw a pile of glass on the carpet. Luckily I hadn't stepped in it. Inyo had likely pawed the single-pane window until it cracked and shattered, then she'd jumped through.

Ryan and I had developed a routine for chasing Inyo down. We kept the keys in the truck, and within two minutes of realizing that she'd gone AWOL, we'd pulled on pants, laced shoes, and hit the pavement—Ryan behind the wheel, me on foot. Sometimes we didn't even bother getting dressed, like the time Inyo took it on the lam at 5 a.m. with Ryan on her heels in his boxer shorts. Under the pale pink light of a streetlamp on Sagehen Lane, we'd found her tipping garbage cans. Playing the slow-down, speed-up game with the truck, we'd caught her and made tracks back to bed.

But tonight, with Ryan still in the hospital, I had to catch Inyo alone. I headed for the desert behind the house, where a couple guys had trained their pickup lights on a row of beer bottles, happily popping away with their rifles. Inyo's eyes flashed orange in their headlights. "Don't shoot!" I screamed. "That's my dog!" I darted in front of their gun barrels in a T-shirt and underpants while Inyo veered through the sagebrush a hundred yards out.

"Oh hell, lady," one said. "We coulda shot you. We thought that thing was a coyote."

After that incident I tied a bright orange and purple scarf around Inyo's neck so no one would mistake her for a coyote and shoot her.

Inyo wasn't the only one vanishing. When Ryan first came home from the hospital, he drifted through the house pale and quiet, but told me that the therapy had seemed to help. A week later, when he planned a tabletop game of Warhammer at Crystal's house, I felt encouraged because he'd be socializing with real people instead of cyber friends. But then Crystal's fiancé, Mike, called the house to tell me he hadn't shown up. An hour passed, then two. Mike and Crystal made phone calls to mutual friends. Nobody had seen Ryan. After three hours of waiting, I freaked. No way he'd miss a game of Warhammer unless he'd taken a dive off One Hand Clapping, a sketchy crack climb on Donner Summit, or kicked off a game of Inquisitor at Heroes Games & Hobbies and forgot the time.

I rang every game shop in town, but Ryan wasn't there. When I'd called all the hospitals and no one matching Ryan's description had been brought in, I phoned the police to file a missing person's report. More hours passed. An officer came to the house around one in the morning. As we sat filling out the form, tires crunched on the gravel drive and headlights splashed against the kitchen wall. A door slammed and Ryan staggered in, his arm around the shoulder of Sandy, a teacher I recognized from faculty parties. When she slipped out from under Ryan's arm, I noticed her loose braid and rumpled shirt. She took one look at the cop and beat it.

Ryan scoffed. "I went to a party. What's the big deal?"

I told him that everyone had been worried, that he was supposed to be at Mike and Crystal's.

"I changed my mind," he said, sliding to the floor.

The officer stood and pointed a finger in Ryan's face. "If she yells at you, you let her."

"I just went to a party," Ryan said, and passed out.

As the officer gathered his clipboard and keys, he said, "Leave him on the floor. Let him learn." But I couldn't do it. Once the officer left, I put Ryan's arm around my shoulder and dragged him to bed. He lay there a moment, then rolled over and threw up on my dissertation research.

CHAPTER TWENTY-ONE

With or Without You

To look into the eyes of a wolf is to see your own soul—hope you like what you see.

—Aldo Leopold

When he woke the next morning, Ryan sat at the kitchen table with his head in his hands. "I feel sick," he said. "Honey, I'm so sorry."

"Did you quit taking your medicine again?"

"Makes my head fuzzy. I can't wake up."

"Damn it, you have to take your meds," I said.

Ryan's remorse turned to anger. "You know, if you mind your own business you'll stay busy all the time."

But as Mrs. Busybody, I decided to count his pills and make an appointment with a marriage counselor. "I'd rather have a root canal," Ryan said, but finally agreed to go.

A few nights later, his escapade forgotten by everyone but me, a horrible scream woke us at two in the morning. I flipped on the porch light while Ryan grabbed his headlamp and shone the beam across the backyard. Inyo's eyes flashed like ball lightning as she stared back at us, guarding a mat of pulsing fur.

"What is it?" Ryan said, shooing Inyo away, his light on a tangle of glistening entrails.

I recognized the tortoiseshell pattern—it was Clem's cat, Harley.

"No vet can sew this cat back together. Get Inyo out of here!"

I dragged Inyo into the bedroom with Thelma and Argos and shut the door. Ryan came out of the kitchen with a black plastic bag and grabbed a shovel leaning against the side of the house. "Hold it open," he said, thrusting the bag at me.

"What are you doing?"

"We can't let him suffer." He slid Harley into the bag. "Now don't look," he said, and I heard him crying as he brought the shovel down on Harley's skull.

"Oh my God, what are we going to tell Clem?"

"We're not telling him anything!" Ryan said. "Bastard's just crazy enough to kill Inyo for this."

While I waited for the debt consolidation materials to arrive, the collection agencies called two and three times a day. They'd continued to garnish Ryan's wages. Next they'd probably seize the truck. After work Ryan would come out of his office just long enough to pluck another Miller from the fridge, and when I'd tap on his door to ask what he wanted for dinner, he'd say, "Let's just forage." I knew his job wore him out. He'd assigned his ten o'clock lit class to read *Macbeth*, required sophomore reading, but when the students shot rubber bands at one another and played with their iPods, he realized most of them couldn't read worth a damn. He told them the story and asked them to illustrate it by cutting out magazine glossies of knives, angry women, and ads for laundry detergent.

One day the television vanished. Turned out Ryan had pawned it for cash to buy a new video game, *Cutthroats: Terror on the High Seas.* "We don't watch it anyway," he said.

I couldn't play the name game with animal control much longer, so when Ryan's consolidation paperwork finally showed up in the mail, I made his favorite dinner—linguine with clam sauce—and set out the nice dishes. "Don't you want to eat together?" I squeaked, when he heaped his plate with noodles, grabbed a Miller, and headed for his office.

"We're starting a game at six," he called over his shoulder. "A bunch of guys from Japan and the Netherlands. I can't miss it." His door slammed shut.

At the kitchen table, twining noodles with my fork and staring out the window, I glimpsed Argos creeping close. He'd developed a new ploy, one I should have nipped but found irresistible. Approaching the dinner table innocent as a peach, *Hi, how ya doin'?* he sneezed, a little cover for the sudden presence on my plate of a big black nose, now covered in shavings of Parmesan. "You bozo," I said, "get away from the table." But his company eased my loneliness and I slipped him a noodle.

By ten o'clock, when Ryan still hadn't come out, I paced the living room and the hallway, clutching the loan papers. What could he have been doing all this time? I stood on a kitchen chair to peek through the slats in the vent above his office door. I saw the back of his dark head haloed in light from the monitor. At his elbow a mouse nibbled a linguine noodle. Then, ever curious, Inyo stood on her hind legs and pawed me. I lost my balance and pitched into the door. It banged open, the mouse scurried off, and I tumbled onto a pile of pizza boxes.

Flicking a piece of pepperoni off my elbow, I showed Ryan his loan repayment papers. If he signed now, I could mail them the next day. He scanned the figures and thrust the forms back. "Forget it. It's cheaper to let them garnish."

I told him we didn't have much time left before Inyo killed one of the neighbor's goats. I wanted us to have a place of our own, someplace remote.

"What you want and what you get are two different things," he said and adjusted his headphones, swiveling around to face the computer screen.

I burned the loan contract in the kitchen sink, the corners turning yellow, then black and shriveled. Thelma pawed my shin and bunny-hopped around the room. Usually, she was long asleep by now, accustomed to early bedtimes and early mornings. But that night she tugged a leash from the corner basket where I kept the dog supplies, and dropped it at my feet. *Hey, how's about it?*

"Okay," I said. "Let's cheer up." We looped around the block in the darkness before crawling into bed.

That night I dreamed animal control took Inyo because she'd killed a goat. They told me I'd had all the chances in the world to keep her safe, and I'd failed. Now they would gas her.

"No!" I shouted, and sat up. Tears had pooled inside my ears.

"What's the matter?" Ryan flipped on the light.

I took a deep breath and dried my ears with the bedsheet. "Inyo can't live with us," I said. "We don't have the right kind of place for her, and I don't know what to do."

"Time to do a dyno, honey." He meant the move of a climber abandoning all contact with the rock to leap for a higher hold.

I hated him in that moment. I'd been counting his pills and knew he'd been skipping doses. I wanted to turn and kick him and kick him until he fell out of bed. Instead I just said, "I hate this. If we can't get a place for ourselves, then at least Inyo needs one, someplace with acreage and no goats or cats."

"It's your decision. You're on the sharp end."

"I'm always on the fucking sharp end!" I threw off the covers. It was 3 a.m., a warmish June morning. I took Inyo running in the desert, the two of us like a couple of white dwarf stars drawing too much mass from each other and about to explode from the pressure. Gazing upward into that unpeopled sky-country, Inyo orbiting me in the dark, I saw us as specks in all that celestial acreage where she and I could never run. Along the rutted dirt track we picked up the pace toward the radio towers. Faster now, we sprinted uphill until my lungs ached and I fell on my knees. Pressing my palms into the dirt, I realized how close I'd come to having our lives figured out. But close wasn't good enough. I had to find Inyo a new home.

Wolfdog needs acreage to run.
You must be athletic, outdoorsy.
No cats or livestock.
Strict contract.

Calls poured in when the ad appeared. "Did you get her from a den?" one man asked. "Does she hunt her own food?" He sounded deflated when I told him she ate kibble with turkey mash and raw bones from the butcher. "I'm looking for a *wild* wolf," he said.

I asked all the callers why they wanted a wolfdog. One woman who lived in a Sacramento town house told me she'd been robbed at knifepoint and heard that wolfdogs made the best guard dogs. A construction worker from Carson City wanted a wolf he could take to work.

Wolves are so family-oriented.
I love their wildness.
They're endangered. If I have one, that's helping the species, right?

A few days later, a woman named Jackie phoned from the Virginia City Highlands. She lived on twenty acres far from any highway and twelve miles from downtown Virginia City. "I've had wolfdogs before," she said. "I know how they are." The urge hit me to pack a few clothes and some Clif Bars, and disappear with Inyo into the Black Rock Desert again. But I couldn't. If the place checked out, taking Inyo to live with Jackie was the right thing to do.

Jackie, a tall cowgirl, shared her ranch with a husband, two dogs, and three feral mustangs adopted from the Bureau of Land Management. When I told her that Inyo might chase the horses, she waved away my concern. "Those desert rats can fend for themselves," she said. "They've lived with coyotes."

"Inyo likes to be outside," I said, "but she might get lonely and want in."

"She can come and go as she pleases. There's a dog door."

Inyo would chew anything she could get her mouth on, I warned, but Jackie had an answer for everything.

"The animals have the run of the house," she said. "As far as I'm concerned, *they* own *me,* not the other way around."

"She might dig under your house."

"No problem."

I also explained that Jackie had to keep a brightly colored scarf on Inyo to mark her as belonging to a person so no one would shoot her for a coyote. She also had to continue Inyo's diet of kibble with plenty of cooked vegetables and meats, and to supply her with fresh marrow-bones, beef bones, and pork hocks.

A two-week trial-period contract outlined Inyo's needs and stipulated that if for *any* reason Jackie couldn't keep her, Inyo would come back to me, no questions asked.

I carried Inyo's cedar bed into the cabin, and when I returned for the kibble bag and tub of turkey mash, I found her crouched on Hanna's backseat, shivering. Ears laid flat against her head, she'd curled into a ball, making herself small. *Stay with you. No trouble. Good good.*

Sucking in a breath, I took her by the collar, my voice cracking as I invited her to come out. "Let's get a bone!" Together we walked into Jackie's kitchen, where I busted open a package of knucklebones, gave one to Inyo, and slipped out the back door of the cabin. Driving down Geiger Grade, a knot in my belly, I pulled over twice to throw up.

That same week Ryan and I saw Jennifer, the marriage counselor. After several sessions she diagnosed Ryan with ADD and told me to take my bossiness down a notch. Advising me to read Karen Pryor's book *Don't Shoot the Dog!*, she claimed couples could turn around their troubled marriages by practicing a few of Pryor's behavioral training methods. I paid particular attention to the section on cooperation without coercion. Instead of scolding when Ryan came home late, or crabby and quiet with his hand choked up the neck of a 40-ouncer, I ignored his mood and the bottle. On the days he came home at a reasonable hour and didn't immediately retreat into gaming, I tried what Pryor called "a cheerful demeanor" and a "positive reinforcer." "Thanks for coming home on time, honey. Good job!"

"I'm not a dog," he would say, and grump into his office.

Sometimes regretful, he left a note or poem on the kitchen table. "You are my love and you inspire me. I feel blessed and lucky to be with you."

Luck was something we needed more of. Three days after I'd taken Inyo to Jackie's, I got a call from a woman named Cora who ran an unofficial animal shelter out of her house in Virginia City. Inyo had spent the night in one of her kennels. I left a message for Jackie and wound up Geiger Grade once more. Cora turned out to be a tiny woman with wispy white hair and hands knotted by arthritis. She plodded around in a pair of oversize rubber boots, her spine bowed as she hosed down a set of outdoor kennels. "Boy, that creature loves you," she said, when I told her that Inyo was supposed to be twelve miles away at Jackie's house.

When we pulled up to Jackie's, she said she hadn't wanted to worry me. Inyo had harassed the horses in the pasture, eventually biting one on the flank. When Jackie locked Inyo in one of the stalls in the barn so she could dress the horse's bite wound, Inyo had scaled the wall and run off.

"She's beautiful and sweet," Jackie said. "I really want to keep her if she'll just leave my horses alone."

The phone continued to ring.

Wolves are magnificent and free.

I've always wanted to own a wolf.

I'm part Native American, and the wolf is my totem animal.

If she can have puppies, I'll pay you.

Then Jackie called to tell me that Inyo had bitten another horse just behind the knee, exposing a tendon. "You have to come and get her," she said. "Today." Including her stay with Cora, Inyo had lived with Jackie only five days.

Inyo howled when I pulled into the driveway, circling Hanna and pawing the driver's door. She balanced her front paws on my shoulders to nibble and lick my mouth. *You!*

When we got home Ryan told me that a man from Silver City had called, a Vietnam vet named Max who lived with his Irish wolfhound in a converted school bus on eighty rambling acres in the Highlands.

"She'll love it here," Max said on the phone. "There's so much room."

I asked Max if he had goats, horses, or cows.

"None of the above," he said.

When I explained the failed re-homing attempt at Jackie's place he said, "I ain't worried."

I told him he could take her for a trial period, adding that I had a contract for him to sign.

"Works for me."

Ryan and I drove Inyo to the Highlands in the pickup, rolling along Main Street through Virginia City, passing the Comstock Lodge and the Gold Hill Hotel. Eight miles farther on, we wound up Max's gravel drive and parked inside a one-acre compound enclosed by a twelve-foot cyclone fence. Mounted on the back of a school bus, American and POW/MIA Never Forget flags snapped in the breeze. "She's gorgeous!" Max said, stepping from the bus into bright sunlight. A stocky, gray-haired man with a tattoo of a wolfhound on his forearm, Max gave Inyo a scratch behind the ears when she sidled up to lick his hands. Max's wolfhound, Riley, sniffed the air, keeping his head low and his eyes averted from Inyo. He looked well cared for, but the thought of leaving Inyo with another stranger made me nauseated again. I handed Max the contract and sat in the dirt beside the school bus with my head between my knees.

"She's emotional," Ryan said.

Inyo crawled into the shade under the bus, peering at her new surroundings—old oil drums and tractors, lawn furniture, and a barbecue set up in the dusty yard—just like the house on Jack Rabbit Road but with eighty acres of private land attached. I gave Max the rundown on Inyo's diet, her temperament, and tendencies to chew and roam. "She can roam all she wants," Max said.

I got to my feet. "Let's just go, Ryan."

As we rolled down the driveway I glanced in the rearview mirror. "It's okay. It's okay," I said, scratching my scalp. "Just drive." Then I saw a grayish-blond streak kicking up dust and making straight for the compound fence. I braked and the truck skidded to a stop. Inyo sprang onto the chain link, toes flexed and gripping the wire, the muscles of her hindquarters tight as she climbed to the top and vaulted to the other side, barely breaking stride as she raced after the truck.

I banged the steering wheel. "I can't do this!"

"We're doing the right thing," Ryan said.

"Shut up. Just shut up! If it weren't for your stupid credit, we wouldn't be in this mess." I walked Inyo back to the compound, and this time Max put her inside the school bus until we'd disappeared.

The next morning the phone rang. When I answered, a woman yelled, "I have your wolf in my kitchen! She's standing on the counter eating bacon out of the frying pan!"

Inyo had gnawed through her screen door to get in and the woman had been able to get close enough to read the collar tag. I told the bacon lady that I'd pay for the door, and then called Max, still sleeping and unaware that Inyo was missing.

"Guess she can smell pretty good," he said, chuckling.

But that night, Max wasn't laughing. He left a message on my voice mail: "Come get your wolf. That thing got Riley killed. If it weren't for that contract, I'd have shot her."

A feral mustang herd that roved across the Virginia City Highlands must have wandered onto Max's land and Inyo caught the scent. Riley had followed on Inyo's heels as she stalked the horses. When the two didn't return, Max hiked into the brush with a flashlight to look for them. Maybe those mustangs held their ground the way elk and moose sometimes do when wolves rush them. Inyo, somehow adept at dodging hoof and horn, escaped the horses' swift kicks, but Max found Riley lying under a clump of sagebrush with his skull crushed. Lurking in the brush, her muzzle glazed with dried horse blood, Inyo slunk out when Max called her. Unable to stand the sight of her, Max called his neighbor Tom, who put Inyo on a chain in his yard until I could pick her up the next morning. Her stay with Max had lasted only one night.

When I came to get her, Inyo whined and licked and smelled every inch of me. "Riley's death has Max real tore up," Tom said. "No offense to you, but that girl's a hell-raiser."

There had to be someone who could help me figure out what to do. I stumbled on to the website of the United States American Wolfdog Association, with its banner of red, white, and blue and wolf silhouettes running across the screen. On the page about ownership, I read the statement in bold red and blue letters over and over: "Don't forget—your wolfdog is your responsibility. Be a responsible owner!" Underneath there was a number to call in case of an emergency: (412) 229-PACK. When I punched it in, a woman's voice came on the line: "You have reached a nonworking number."

CHAPTER TWENTY-TWO

The Things We Do
for Love

It is foolish to tear one's hair in grief, as though sorrow would be made less by baldness.

—Cicero

I'd wanted to be Inyo's anchor in the world, and I got what I wanted. *I* was "home" to her. Pat Tucker and Bruce Weide of Montana's Wild Sentry point out that wolves and wolfdogs often cannot adapt to a new environment and a new owner, even if those surroundings might seem like paradise in terms of space. I had believed that Jackie and Max, with their remote acreage and tolerant personalities, would make Inyo happy. Looking back now, I realize that even with the best intentions I'd only managed to make her situation worse by putting her through the trauma of separation. At the time though, I convinced myself that if the acreage had been only my own, Inyo would have stuck around because she was living with me and not some stranger. But the fact is, Inyo was acting on drives I couldn't control. Like a wolf, she always had to roam.

Years later, Kathy Bennett, one of the wolf caretakers at Colorado's Mission: Wolf, explained to me that, raised in captivity, wolves and wolfdogs may sometimes act like dogs, enjoying the company of their people, but they have wolfy instincts driving them to wild behaviors they can neither suppress nor fulfill. Many of them get severely upset, she told me—they pace, chew on themselves, or develop a short flight response to strangers. Out of sheer frustration some perpetually escape

187

their enclosures or become socially aggressive with their people.[1] Jill Moore of Indiana's Wolf Park once remarked, "You can have your wolf's or wolfdog's adoration, but it can change and fast. They are not dogs—they have stronger instincts, which can be easier to trigger and harder to shut off, and a far greater intensity in most of what they do than even 'harder' dog breeds."[2]

I couldn't bear to think about the disastrous rehoming effort, so I opted for evasive action—a backpack trip to Washington State's Glacier Peak Wilderness. With a little cajoling, Ryan agreed to go. "Whatever, yeah, I guess."

Except for snatching a peanut butter sandwich from the hand of another backpacker who then cussed us out and hurled a rock at the blond thief, Inyo was a stellar companion in the wilderness and didn't kill any wildlife. When I nudged and then prodded Ryan toward more outings before the school year started, he blew a gasket, called me pushy, and disappeared night after night to play Warcraft on his office computer until two or three in the morning.

Then his wedding ring disappeared. He'd hocked it to buy Warhammer Fantasy Beasts of Chaos. "Don't make such a big deal out of it, I'll get it back," he said, and shut his office door.

I replenished my food sacks and took Inyo backpacking alone, leaving the dogs with Ryan while I devised a new plan. I still had one more year to go for my Ph.D., but I figured I'd take a shot at the job market early and see what I could get. Meantime, I'd open a separate savings account and put a little money aside from each of my paychecks for a down payment on land.

While I plotted, a developer bulldozed the desert behind our rental, slapping up houses and paving streets with flashy new signs for Fire Opal Lane, Opal Glen Way, and Opal Star Drive. When we'd first moved to Jack Rabbit Road, Inyo and I rarely saw others on our runs—only the cock-a-doodle-doos using beer bottles for target practice or lonely men idling their pickups with the latest issue of *Penthouse*. I missed my uninhabited Eden of waste. Now we encountered at least one respectable citizen with her dog every time we ventured out.

One August afternoon as Inyo and I ran up the dusty road, sunlight gleaming off the new street signs, I heard a sound like a riding lawn mower in the sky and glanced up to see a single-engine Cessna trailing a banner: BLM = CATTLE RUSTLERS. Distracted by the plane, I hadn't noticed a woman and her dog approaching. By the time I spotted them, Inyo had dashed ahead of me, hackles pricked from her neck to the base of her tail, as if someone had plugged her into a wall socket. "Inyo!" I called, sprinting to catch up. She'd always shown a playful interest in strange dogs, inviting them to chase her, but this time she gave the collie a fixed stare as the dog averted its gaze and looked to its owner for direction. "Sadie, come!" the woman said, but Inyo had closed the distance and lifted her flues to show her teeth. With a throaty growl, she sprang on Sadie, pinning her to the dirt. Sadie squirmed under her. "Stop it! Stop it!" the woman shrieked. I dove on Inyo, yoking her barrel with my arms, and hauled her backward, the two of us landing on a bag of fresh kitchen garbage. She panted, her muzzle smeared with Sadie's blood. She'd torn off a large flap of skin from the dog's muzzle and bitten the tip off her left ear.

"I'm so sorry," I said. "She's never done that before."

"She's a wolf, isn't she?" the woman said. "I knew it the second I saw her. She's vicious."

"She's not, I swear. I don't know why she got crazy like that." I sounded pathetic and stupid, and offered to pay Sadie's vet bill.

"You bet you'll pay," the woman said, as Sadie whimpered, the blood clotting on her muzzle.

Later that week I charged the $700 vet bill to my Visa card and received a visit from Officer Steve. "We take complaints about dangerous dogs seriously," he said, adding that Sadie's owner thought Inyo would attack her next. He informed me that Inyo would be deemed a "dangerous dog" if without provocation she attacked or killed another person's domestic animal. A judge would take action to impound her, while charging me with "harboring a dangerous or vicious dog."

Inyo never threatened the woman, I told him. She would never bite a person. I'd paid Sadie's vet bill, and since both our dogs had been off leash, the woman shared some responsibility. He wrote me a warning, citing Washoe County Code Chapter 55.

In case we met Sadie again or encountered another strange dog, I leashed Inyo when we ran in the desert behind the house. She tugged and fought as I tried to control her. "Heel. Good girl. Heel. Good girl." Broken record.

Our desert shrank overnight. Driveways had been framed and concrete poured. U-Haul vans groaned up Chisholm Trail with couches, televisions, and bunk-bed kits from IKEA. People moved in, erected mailboxes, rolled sod, and planted rose bushes. But I figured if we ran between five and six in the morning, we wouldn't meet anyone.

One morning at the fork where a school bus had been gutted and dumped, we veered straight into a woman coming over the crest of the hill with her Weimaraner. Too late to turn Inyo around and run the other way, I hopped over a clump of woody-rooted aster with its bunched white flowers and parked Inyo behind a stand of scraggy rabbitbrush. As the slender gray body of the Weimaraner streaked toward us through the desert scrub, ears flapping, his owner called, "Don't worry. He's friendly."

I wanted to yell back, "Friendly and dead!" The dog screeched to a halt in front of Inyo, and in the time it took for me to inhale, she morphed into Cujo. She strained and growled, but the leash held and the dog turned tail.

Inyo hadn't done any damage—this time. But our early morning runs got earlier. I set the alarm for 3 a.m., and for three weeks the whole Panther Valley neighborhood was ours and I let Inyo run off leash. Then a family moved into the house on the corner—the corner we had to pass to get to the open desert—and they owned a dog Inyo hated instantly. One day, while taking a leash walk, Inyo and I encountered the new occupants out for a stroll with their springer spaniel. We met traveling on opposite sides of the street, and as we passed, Inyo suddenly lunged across me, teeth bared, growling and straining to reach the other dog. Choking up on the leash, I held her as tightly as I could. The little boy walking the dog looked wide-eyed with fear. "C'mon, Polly!" he said and tugged on her leash. Suddenly I felt a warm liquid sensation inside my pant leg and looked down. My jeans were ripped at the shin and stained dark all the way to my shoe.

I managed to restrain Inyo until Polly and her people disappeared around the corner, their mouths agape. Blood seeped through my fingers as I examined the gash in my leg. Hobbling back to the house,

I poured peroxide on the wound and watched it fizz like pink seltzer water. No way Inyo had meant to bite me, I thought. And even if she had (but of course she hadn't), she didn't bite me as badly as she could have. I groped around in my backpack for the first aid kit and wrapped the wound in gauze.

Kept chained in the front yard day and night, Polly became Inyo's target, even at three in the morning. When I tried leashing her just until we rounded the corner past Polly's house where the desert opened up, she would crane her neck and sniff the air, uttering an almost inaudible growl. I couldn't let her loose. As a solution, I rummaged in Darryl's garage for a pair of wire cutters and snipped a "door" in the chain-link fence just large enough to crawl through. He'd never notice a flap that could be opened and closed, and Inyo and I could get to the desert without passing Polly's house.

By 3:10 every morning, Inyo, the dogs, and I shot out the door to crawl through the opening. With my headlamp lighting the path, we made our daily loop around the desert. And as long as we avoided Polly's house, Inyo and I could still take our leash walks during normal daylight hours—at least until she added Jake the Australian shepherd to her hit list. He lived at the opposite end of Jack Rabbit Road from Polly, and one afternoon, as Inyo and I passed his house, she took umbrage at Jake, who was taking an afternoon siesta in his own yard. Straining toward him, hackles pricked and quivering, she growled and snapped. When I put my hand on her collar and uttered a sharp "No!" she pinched my wrist and hand between her teeth.

Eight wrist bones. Five palm bones. Fourteen finger bones. I felt the skin on the back of my hand tear and the blood-flow to my fingers pinch off. Instead of pulling away and possibly making the situation worse, I let my arm flop and warbled a few lines from a cheesy song.

Ooh, you made me love you

A screen door banged. Jake's owner called: "Need some help?"
"All set," I chirped, waving my free hand.

You think you're gonna break up—

He frowned and shook his head, leading Jake into the house. As soon as Jake disappeared, Inyo returned to cheery-beery-bee and released me. Wriggling my fingers, I felt the blood-flow return and my hand zing with scattershot itching. At home, I poured peroxide on the bite and wondered what the hell had just happened. Watching the pink bubbles sparkle and pop, I recalled something the vet had said when I'd taken Inyo for her rabies vaccination so long ago. "She's a sweet pup, but you don't know how she'll turn out."[3]

The peroxide ran in pink rivers down my hand. My finger tracing the bite marks, I glanced in the mirror, my hair choppy and uneven where I'd tried to hide the missing chunks by trimming. I'd held thatches of hair to the light, some strands parched from desert heat and stiff as cat whiskers. Snip, snip.

When Ryan came home, he found me perched on the bathroom counter staring at the pink bubbles in the sink, raking my scalp with my fingernails.

"What happened to you?"

I hadn't told Ryan about my fall in Desolation, the day Inyo stood on my back with her teeth on my neck, and I wasn't going to make a big deal out of this. I told him about Jake, that Inyo hadn't realized what she was doing. "Everything happened so fast," I said, "I can't even be sure myself. It's a surface scratch. Hardly anything."

"Hardly anything? Are you crazy? What if some neighbor kid is walking the family dog and Inyo goes postal? It won't matter whether she *meant* to bite the kid or not. Inyo will be dead and we'll be in jail."

I told him that would never happen. Inyo would never bite a child. But I'd completely forgotten about ten-year-old Vivian and her little brother Paulo who knocked on the door every afternoon asking to walk "the wolf." Sometimes I caught them trying to climb over the fence to see her and had to remind them about the electric wire. I let them pet her when I was home, but what if they sneaked into the yard while I was at school?

"Listen to me," Ryan said. "Call Leda. She made Inyo. She should know what to do."

192

CHAPTER TWENTY-THREE

Everything We've Worked For

You will beget wolves on earth.
You'll teach them to wag their tails.
And if, later, you have to pay the price,
So be it; that will be later.
　　　—Alexander Galich, from "One More
　　　Time About the Devil"

I punched in Leda's number and waited. She had told me to call if I needed help—maybe she could house Inyo for a short time, just until I figured things out. I'd drive Inyo to Tucson, stay a few days, help her adjust. Two rings and then a woman's voice: "You have reached a number that has been disconnected or is no longer in service."

Had I punched in the right numbers? I tried again. Same message. Flipping through my address book, I found numbers of mutual friends and left messages, including a frantic plea to Heather who'd introduced me to Leda three years earlier.

More often than not, breeders can't help, and refuse to take problem animals back, though they go all out to advertise the merits of their puppies. Several I met represented their puppies as "wolfdogs," but from the evidence they were really mixed-breed dogs, not wolfdogs at all. Others inflated the percent of wolf in the litters they sold and often attached their bloodlines to wolfdogs used in movies. In Idaho, a breeder named Nancy introduced me to Nitro and claimed he was 95% wolf. "I just call him a 'malamutt,' " she said with a wink, dragging him off the back porch, his tow chain clanking. "People around here get itchy if you say 'wolf.' " Nitro's wolfiness was evident—large cheek tufts, yellow-green eyes, long legs with paws pointed slightly outward so that his elbows nearly touched. Shy and fearful of strangers, he hid his face behind Nancy's legs. "Don't be such a baby," she said, rubbing him behind the ears. "He was abused," she explained. "My daughter rescued him and gave him to me. His daddy is the wolfdog in *Air Buddies*." When Nancy let go of Nitro's collar, he darted up the porch steps to cower behind the white plastic lawn furniture.

Leading me across the yard, Nancy opened a shed door and hauled out a Doberman-rottweiler mix she identified as 80% wolf. The dog stared me in the eyes and growled. "She's not good with strangers," Nancy said, choking up on the dog's collar. "Wolves are very protective."

A few of the four-week-old pups, housed in an adjacent shed of corrugated fiberglass, huddled on a blanket, while others tussled in the mud of an adjoining pen enclosed with chicken wire. Several of the puppies wore collars of plastic zip ties marked with red ink to indicate they'd been sold, the new owners having guaranteed their purchase with a $50 deposit.

When I asked Nancy if she did home inspections or required buyers to sign a contract, she shook her head. "Don't see the point. If a person is willing to drive two or three hours just to see these guys and then pay three hundred dollars for a pup, the animal is going to a good home." Backing into a cat's cradle of tie-out cables crisscrossing the yard, I asked her if she accepted returns if a buyer had trouble with one of her puppies. "Heavens no!" she said. "Once the sale is made, the animal is theirs. Besides, why on earth would someone want to return one of my puppies? These guys just want to hug you all the time."

Good dog breeders screen their buyers carefully and require a contract, which includes provisions for returning an animal. Not that anyone would want to return a puppy to the likes of some wolfdog breeders. I visited one cramped kennel after another, diamonds of chain link warped by the teeth of frustrated creatures who'd twisted and pulled. Ammonia fumes stung my eyes as I stroked the bellies of friendly mommas, my fingers finding a rash of bleeding sores that had erupted around their teats and been left untended. I held puppies whelped in dark barns surrounded by old logging equipment baking in its own oily mud. Slits between the boards let in scant light, enough for my eyes to make out buckets of dirty water where mosquitoes had laid their eggs, enough to see some pups so frightened by my presence that they hid their heads in a hole in the wall where a horse's hoof had busted through. The breeders, hovering somewhere in the gloom, encouraged me to buy: "They're going like hotcakes!"

A year after my visit with Nancy, she posted another ad in the paper. I called anonymously, and from her descriptions of the sire and dam, I knew they were the same parents I'd met, though this time Nancy claimed the sire was a pure wolf, and the price of the puppies had jumped to $1,200. When I mentioned that she needed a USDA permit to own a pure wolf because wolves were an endangered species, she said, "Who the hell are you? I don't need no permit," and hung up.[1]

Traveling around the country to meet active wolfdog breeders, I also met those who'd quit. At her California home, former breeder Terry Jenkins told me that she had loved the wolfdog's fierce independence, its wolfy aloofness. She'd valued the challenge of earning the animal's affection and trust. But producing such animals had come at too high a price. She invited me to walk the sunlit pasture around her house and meet Moe, Larry, and Curly, her goats. Dutifully shepherded by Nester and Bart, two of Terry's five dogs, the sociable goats pressed close to be petted. I scratched Moe's head and waited for Jenkins to tell me what had happened to her wolfdogs. Smoke from a recent rash of wildfires had settled in the Sacramento Valley, the air thickening as we strolled under a canopy of oaks, yellow summer grasses brushing our shins. Many of the puppies she produced had ended up neglected or caged for the rest of their lives, she said, or passed from one person to the next, each home another failure. When others ended up dead after mangling children's arms and legs, Terry pulled the plug. She'd done her best to be responsible in striving for her goal: to produce an animal that looked like a wolf but behaved like a dog. It simply hadn't worked.

After meeting Terry, a question nagged: Were there any breeders of true wolfdogs who not only took responsibility for the puppies they produced but whose breeding program had been successful? Another former breeder, Gail Whitford, who managed a website of wolfdog stories and information for the Wolf Is At The Door, Inc., urged me to contact Dora Simpson of Cottonwood Kennels in Texas. "She's the *only* breeder out there, in my opinion, who has a real goal for her breeding program and who comes close to being truly responsible," Whitford said.[2]

Everything we've worked for!
12-generation pedigree
OFA on Parents, all Grandparents

I flew to the Lone Star State and met Dora and her family at the Longhorn Café, probably the only place left in America where a full-plate breakfast costs less than the Sunday paper, and if you're down on your luck, you can write the owner an IOU.

Like Terry Jenkins, Dora had tried to produce an animal that looked like a wolf but was as tractable as a dog. While the fifty-year fox experiment had employed 10,500 fox parents to produce another 50,000 offspring tested for tameness, Dora had been breeding for fifteen years, produced between 25 and 30 animals, and claimed to have accomplished a similar goal. "People told me I couldn't produce a tractable, sociable wolfdog you could just load up in the car and go. Well, I've done it! When someone tells me I can't do something, I set out to prove them wrong. I push things. I like a challenge." She told me she bred for temperament *and* appearance. "My animals still look very wolfy," she said. "You'll see."[3]

After breakfast, I followed Dora back to the hundred acres she shared with her husband, Jason, and six-year-old daughter, Jessica, just outside a small north Texas town where the marquee outside a little Baptist church read "No one can serve two masters." She offered me a 7UP and we sat in the grass behind her house, slapping on vanilla extract to keep away the bull gnats. Three of the five newest wolfdog puppies, born in April, climbed gently into my lap to nibble my chin and lick my teeth. Those puppies were some of the wolfiest-looking wolfdogs I'd ever seen, and some of the most docile.[4] Jessica, looking just like her mom—same jeans and bright yellow T-shirt, hair tied up in a high blond ponytail—sidled up to me. "Do you know how to do a cartwheel?"

R.J., whom the family called "Uncle R.J." because he was tolerant as a wild wolf of small pups, yawned and blinked sleepily as the puppies climbed on him, pulled his ruff, and bit his ears with their needle teeth. He had an easygoing attitude with people too, which Dora hoped he would pass on to the puppies in his care.[5]

R.J. made hospice visits, greeting cancer patients who stroked his head and thought they were touching a wolf. According to Dora, he also occasionally helped the sheriff and game warden by locating deer that hunters had wounded but not killed. "He's really good at it," Dora said, adding that his reward was a piece of meat cut from the carcass. "R.J. is fail-safe. He'll never do anything to tarnish my reputation."

Dora's criteria for temperament were specific. She pointed to one puppy who kept his distance from us, peering out from the safety of his den. "Now he may come around and be more social with people as he matures," she said. "Puppies go through stages. But if he doesn't, I won't breed him. I'll neuter him. They have to be sociable."[6] When I met the sire, a wolfdog named Hat, I saw where the pup's shyness came from. Hat usually warmed to strangers after some time had passed, Dora told me, but that day he kept his distance. Dora had euthanized only one wolfdog, a male named Iceman she had purchased from another breeder. He tried to pull her through the fence the same way he'd tugged a miniature goat through the fence and eaten it. "I won't put up with that," she said. "I've got children." I looked over at Jessica who hugged one of the puppies to her. Dora hoped to breed one of her wolfdogs to a pure wolf whose temperament met her specifications and who was one of the last remaining pure wolves from the well-known Gabe Davidson line. She would not divulge the name of the wolf's owner, she said, because the person didn't have the necessary permits to own a pure wolf. When I asked her how someone without a permit got her hands on a pure wolf, Dora gave me a stern look. "There are *a lot* of pures out there. People know people, and that's all I'm gonna say about it."

We went inside to escape the Texas heat, and I asked Dora how she evaluated potential buyers. Jessica snuggled next to me on the living-room couch as close as she could get without sitting on my lap. "Give her some room, Jessica," Dora said. "Quit crowding." From a thick stack of three-ring binders containing her animals' pedigrees as well as the names and biographies of breeders, she pulled out a preapplication application with questions about criminal records and sexual attraction to animals, designed to screen out the irresponsibles and weirdos. If she approved of an applicant's intentions and facilities, then the applicant could get one of Dora's puppies after reading and signing an additional six-page contract with return policies and stipulations for minimum care and space requirements (a twenty-five-by-twenty-five-foot enclosure of 9-gauge chain-link fencing with dig guard, lean-in, and other precautions against escape). Except for the rare case when a new owner hadn't complied with the terms of her contract and she'd had to repossess a puppy, her contracts had so far been mostly a formality because she'd produced relatively few animals in her fifteen years of breeding, and sold fewer puppies than she'd kept or given away to people she trusted—people like Sue Cranston, owner of Indigo Mountain Nature Center in Colorado, and wolfdog breeder and owner Stormy "Wolf" Renee.[7] Dora had sold one of the pups from the current litter to a local man, whom she described as well intentioned, but a bit of a "nervous Nellie." "He calls me fifty times a day to tell me that the puppy is being aggressive toward him. I don't produce aggressive animals. He's probably trying to pet it while it eats or something." Dora said her trainer, Carla Collins, would help the man with his new puppy. Carla, who'd joined us wearing a bright red shirt that read Sit Means Sit, nodded in agreement.

Later, Dora introduced me to her other wolfdogs. I visited one called Pooh Bear inside his enclosure, but he played tug-of-war with my ponytail and wouldn't let go. As I tried to pull away he tightened his grip, and finally Jason, Dora's husband, had to intervene.

Dora's hard work over the years would be worth it, she told me, if her animals could someday appear in music videos and films, or alongside beautiful models in magazines. I asked her if she ever worried that wolfdog breeding might become illegal in her county. "Who's gonna

legislate me up here?" she said, laughing.[8] Jessica, who'd been pluck-
ing stems of pink musk thistle and yellow chinchweed, presented me
with a bouquet and put a clump of wolfdog fur in my palm. "Nobody
bosses us in Texas," she said.[9]

From what I'd seen, Dora was a rarity in the world of wolfdog
breeding. She didn't produce many animals and took care of the ones
she'd brought into the world. But of all Dora's wolfdogs that I met,
only two—R.J. and Sandman, a chummy fellow who just wanted his
belly rubbed—were as responsive to humans as Belyaev's foxes. The
others were either distrustful, disinterested, or saw me as a plaything to
tug on. To some degree Dora must have recognized a missing element
in her animals' behavior when she said, "You know, someday I'd like
to throw a toy and have one of my wolfdogs retrieve it off leash like a
regular dog. Maybe I'll try it with the puppy we named Reno. If I start
him early enough I just bet I can do it."

There's never any agreement among those in the wolfdog community
about what should be done about the many wolfdogs—and in some
cases, their owners—who end up homeless. At the time of my problems
with Inyo, my own little family was about to join those unfortunates.
If I didn't figure something out we'd all be on the street. Heather hadn't
called from Tucson, and mats of blond hair choked the sink drain.
One day a woman stopped me on Sierra Street where I'd taken Inyo
for a leash walk. When she told me she had a male wolf at home and
wouldn't it be lovely to breed the two, I wanted to wave my bloated
purple hand in her face and shriek, "Don't you see what we've done?"

I left another urgent message for Heather. "Please, please call me
back." A week after my first frantic call, Heather finally phoned. But
instead of my cheerful friend who'd said, "Get ready, we're going to
meet some wolves!" Heather sounded exhausted as she told me that
Leda had had some serious problems. She'd been evicted from the
house in the cul-de-sac and was going through a painful breakup with
her husband.[10]

My heart sank as Heather gave me Leda's number, but I was determined to talk to her. She must have some ideas, and I'd take any help
at all. Cradling the receiver in one hand, I picked my scalp with the
other as I heard Leda's familiar voice, "Hello?"

Waves of relief washed over my body. She'd have something to offer, something I hadn't thought of yet. "I need help," I squeaked.

How could I tell her that Inyo was on her seventh name at animal control, Ryan and I were living in our fourth rental after a long stint in the national forest, and no matter where we moved, the neighbors hated us? How should I explain that Inyo suddenly wanted to kill every strange dog she met, and now she'd bitten me—twice?

"Um . . . I can't seem to control Inyo. Things are getting bad, and I'm scared she might bite a kid. I don't know what to do."

"I've got problems of my own," Leda said, and offered to house Inyo for two weeks, but that was it. "I've only got the one kennel."

I recalled the first day I'd met Loop and Voodoo in their kennel—two strides up, two strides back. I imagined Inyo in that tiny space with her parents. Loop might see her as a strange female, a threat. How could I possibly have thought Inyo could stay with Leda? She was offering two weeks, and Inyo could be dead in that pen within a day. Or she might escape the kennel and run off. I really had lost my mind.

"Thanks. I'll give it some thought," I said, having pulled out another chunk of hair by the time I hung up the phone.

CHAPTER TWENTY-FOUR

Prisoners of Love

There can be no friendships where there is no freedom.
Friendship loves a free air, and will not be fenced up in
straight and narrow enclosures.

—William Penn

Although Harley's owner thought his cat had been hit by a car, I knew the truth and the guilt weighed on me. I also worried about the goats and had bad dreams, like the one of Inyo stalking horses, nipping their ankles to make them run. Two women asked if they could adopt her. "We'll make Inyo very happy." Did they have acreage? They didn't. Did they hike or backpack or rock climb? They didn't. "But we have a nice big pen for her," they said. "A special kind she'll never escape."

One night I woke to the sound of Inyo's teeth splintering the window trim—*Out! Out now!* I fumbled in the dark for my running shoes. Leaving Ryan zonked on the bed with Argos and Thelma, I slipped through the flap in the fence with Inyo. At three in the morning, the bulldozers slumbered in the dirt, but by seven they'd groan awake, scrape-dragging brush from the desert floor to level a new section of valley for tract houses. With no moon to help me keep my balance through the ruts, I jogged slowly, Inyo orbiting me somewhere in the darkness. I'd managed to put aside $200 from my last paycheck. At that rate, in five years I'd have saved enough money to buy a sizable patch of desert scrub, and if I got a full-time job I might cut the waiting time in half. Meanwhile, Officer Steve's warning echoed in my head: "We take complaints about dangerous dogs seriously."

Inyo's dog enemies lived north and south. Sneaking west through Rose's property was out—her son had put her in a nursing home and adopted a Doberman. East, the direction of last resort, would soon be full of homes, dogs, cats, and kids. And just down the road, the goats bleated.

A flier at the local library announced an upcoming presentation about wolfdogs given by the owners of Wolf Spirit, a sanctuary that advertised education, rescue, and adoption assistance.[1] Following their talk, the young couple, Tim and Heidi Erickson, invited me to visit their facility in a remote area outside Reno.[2]

Her wheels spitting dust and gravel, Hanna chugged toward the sanctuary along a dried mud road at the bottom of a slot canyon. Inyo stood on the backseat as we neared the entrance, staring at the wolves and wolfdogs housed in pens around the property. When I hopped out to take a quick look around, I found the enclosures small, but the water buckets looked clean and the animals' waste had been shoveled out. Boulders provided perches for some twenty animals who lay in the shade or paced and woofed at us. Two arctic wolf crosses trotted their fence line, nervous at the arrival of a stranger.

Heidi, her brown bangs framing a gentle moon face, invited me into the house and gave me a glass of lemonade and a handout: "Living with the Wolf: A Guide to Wolf & Wolfdog Stewardship." I took sips of lemonade as I silently read each directive.

If your animal escapes, YOU, as the owner, are held responsible for any trouble it causes. It is likely the animal will be shot, run over, picked up by strangers or animal control . . .

I know.

For the safety of you and your animals, it is ESSENTIAL to have proper containment. The fencing should be heavy-gauge chain link a minimum of 6–7ft. high with ground wire or hotwire to prevent digging . . .

I'd tried, but no matter the height of the fence, no matter the shock of the hotwire, Inyo would climb or dig and escape.

The idea of "lifetime commitment" should be first and foremost in your decision-making process.

It was. It always was. But Inyo and I needed help, and we needed it now. I told Heidi and Tim about Inyo's behavior, sticking to the evictions, the goats, and my failed rehoming attempts. Although I felt ashamed, I didn't mention she'd bitten me, afraid they'd turn us away. They told me their refuge was full, but Tim, scratching his shrubby beard, added that one of the animals might be adopted out, so a space could open up. "Hang in there," they said, and I could see by their drawn faces they were following their own advice.

As I loaded Inyo into Hanna, I watched two wolfdogs, their noses wrinkled, teeth bared, gang up on a third animal until it rolled on its back. If Inyo lived here, would she be the aggressor or the animal on her back?

As I found out years later when I visited other sanctuaries, "enrichment" activities and space are no substitute for freedom. The energies of wolves—normally channeled into cooperative hunting, defense of pack territory, sexual relations, and caregiving behaviors—can turn into social aggression under the stress of confinement.

Kent Weber, cofounder and director of Colorado's Mission: Wolf, keeps the resident animals in pairs to prevent "gang violence." When I arrived for a visit at Weber's sanctuary, it was almost feeding time. Two women volunteers wearing blue rubber gloves and armed with knives sawed through donated frozen meat. They would cook the meat just slightly in a giant pot, mix in vitamins and kibble, and serve the refuge's twenty-nine resident wolves in white five-gallon buckets with each animal's name printed on the side—Nyati, Ned, Merlin, Lily . . .

Kent called these animals "lifers," which for a captive wolf could mean sixteen years or more. He and his wife, Tracy, have dedicated themselves to educating visitors about wolves and hope to see the day when people respect wild wolves for their place in the ecosystem and do not keep them in captivity. "If we do our job we hope to put ourselves out of business," Kent said. To that end, they don't breed resident wolves to produce more lifers (the males have been vasectomized), and they evaluate each rescue animal for its suitability to public education, allowing visitors to greet only those animals comfortable with people. Animals that tolerate travel get to be "ambassadors" and participate in wolf education programs around the country, riding in a converted marine transport bus left over from Desert Storm.

Kent introduced me to some of the animals. Orion's owner had kept him in a cage for years. Kent likened him to a three-year-old human child kept in a closet and let out at eighteen. He had no communication skills and had only recently made play overtures toward his pen mate, Soleil, who'd been owned by a man who'd wanted a fighting dog and kept her chained to a tree for five months.

Daisy, a wolfdog, began to dominate her owner when the woman became pregnant. When the woman attempted to discipline Daisy like a dog, Daisy challenged her and became dangerous. Though she loved and missed the woman who'd raised her, she would have to live out her life at the sanctuary.

Groomed for documentaries, a pure wolf named Baltazar (screen name "Akai") was neurotic, Kent said, attempting wolf suicide by chewing grapefruit-size holes in his legs. But unlike many wolves used in film and television, Baltazar had a story with a happy ending. When he and another wolf named Mera showed interest in each other, Kent put them together. "It was like two people falling in love for the first time at forty-five years old," he said.

Like Mission: Wolf, many sanctuaries I visited are serious about working to end captivity for wolves. They don't breed or buy puppies to attract visitors. They try to take in as many animals as they can, often animals no one else wants—the wolfdog whose eyes were gouged out in a cult ritual, the sockets sutures of pink flesh that have to be rinsed and medicated daily, the wolfdog too doggy for a pure wolf sanctuary, too wolfy for dog rescue—the *zweiweltenkind*, child of two worlds who has no home.

But like Tim and Heidi's Wolf Spirit, these mom-and-pop operations are long on love, short on money. Financial difficulties have caused some to shut their doors permanently, while others limp along for years on the edge of ruin. They survive on donations of money, dog food, a slaughtered dairy cow, and the occasional road-killed deer or elk. All are in need of volunteer labor to maintain enclosures and feed the animals, and each one has a wish list of items to help keep the sanctuary functioning—everything from hotboxes, jumbo-size Greenies, and canned dog food to ATVs, chain saws, and rolls of three-foot wire for dig guards and overhangs.

The people who run these facilities often live in trailers with subflooring and no bathroom because caring for the rescue animals takes all their resources—which they gladly give, working outside jobs to support their efforts. Craig Watson who, with his wife, Paula, runs WolfWood Refuge and Adoption Center near Ignacio, Colorado, wakes early and waters seventy-one animals before going to work at a local coal mine.

He'd just left when I arrived at WolfWood for a tour. Paula Watson met me in a pair of brown work overalls, her gray hair falling over her shoulders. The Watsons had been forced to move their sanctuary from Pagosa Springs to the Ignacio area when noise complaints landed them in court. For a woman who'd been chased by angry neighbors from one town to the next, Paula looked remarkably relaxed, even though she and her husband continued to suffer harassment by neighbors who complained about howling and feared the wolfdogs would get loose and attack their livestock and children. One neighbor threatened physical violence, circling outside the refuge entrance on his four-wheeler and brandishing a rifle. Another neighbor had launched a successful boycott of Purina, a company that had donated excess pet food to animal shelters, including WolfWood, as a tax write-off. When Purina halted its donations to WolfWood, the shelter lost more than $4,000 worth of kibble a month.

But the Watsons ignored the threats and carried on. They were well within their rights, having all the necessary permits to run their facility, and they'd found new sources of donated food. Moving a second time would have been an enormous hardship with seventy-one resident animals in their care. It took four and a half hours for me to meet them all. Paula and I walked uphill among the juniper trees, visiting one enclosure after another—each a chain-link pen reinforced with cattle panel, dig skirts, and overhangs (depending on the animal's climbing and jumping abilities). Some animals lived singly, others in pairs. Some paced from the stress of a stranger's presence or hid inside their donated igloo doghouses, while others whined to be stroked, and longed for human contact.

By now the stories of neglect and abuse had become all too familiar. Titus had been rescued from a man who'd kept upward of forty intact wolfdogs that bred indiscriminately and ran loose, harassing and killing livestock. A few had been shot, others died of parvovirus. Paula had taken in fifteen puppies in 1999 and another fifteen in 2000. The animals' owner had been taken to court, and all but those that Wolf-Wood rescued had been euthanized.

It was eighty-three degrees and dusty. A few wolfdogs rested under pine trees and junipers, or in holes they'd dug into the dry earth. Others paced trenches inside their enclosures or, like Matok, looked for the nearest tree to climb. Matok could scale ten-foot fences with ease, Paula said, and she'd had to reinforce his enclosure with an extrawide lean-in. Another wolfdog, a female, found lean-ins helpful to escape. She could hang from them upside down like a Flying Wallenda before scrabbling over the lip. "For some wolfdogs," Paula said, "not even the world is big enough."

Some animals trotted figure eights until they'd bloodied their paws. But Paula urged me not to paint a sad picture of her sanctuary, not to make the animals' confinement worse than it was. "Yes, the pens are small," she said, "but for some of these animals, that's all right. The world is a scary place, and they feel safe here." I saw her point when I met Cassidy, a wolfdog who'd been chained to a group of animals at a California drug house. She'd arrived at WolfWood unable to lift her head because her neck muscles had atrophied. The wolfdogs were locked in, yes. But the people who'd hurt them and the world that had rejected them were locked out.

Like the Watsons, Patricia and Kelly Reed, owners of Eagle Tail Mountain Wolf Sanctuary in Tonopah, Arizona, also put what money they earn into animal care. Patricia Reed works at the Palo Verde Nuclear Generating Station. Kelly Reed drives the town ambulance and knows everyone at the Tonopah truck stop where I met the Reeds for lunch. "I've run almost everyone in here," he said, waving to the man with leukemia sitting in a corner booth and the waitress who'd had a heart attack the month before. Both the Reeds know how to stay cool under pressure, a trait that serves them well as caretakers of 120 wolves and wolfdogs.

They've found out the hard way that animals experiencing captivity stress will fence fight. During one altercation, a wolfdog had shoved his paw through the chain link separating two of the pens, and the animals in the adjoining enclosure had chewed it off. In the commotion and heightened tension, the animal's own pen mates attacked him from behind. Now he hobbled around on three legs, his foreleg amputated to the shoulder.

The Reeds keep their animals in pairs—male and female (one of them altered to prevent breeding) or a father and son combo—to prevent fights. (An exception is the wolfdog who lives alone because he's killed every companion placed with him.) The Reeds have designed the sanctuary as a cluster of self-contained hexagons, each one composed of six fifty-by-fifty-foot chain-link enclosures with a central feeding station that contains kibble, toys, running water, and maintenance equipment. Concrete poured two feet into the ground and reinforced with an additional three feet of cyclone fencing acts as a dig guard. Three strands of barbed wire line the top of each enclosure fence to prevent the animals from climbing out. Hotwire and mesh skirting run along the base of each connecting enclosure to prevent fence fighting. Although scraggly creosote bushes offer little cover in the Sonoran Desert, Kelly has built lean-tos to shade the animals.

The Humane Society of the United States and the USDA estimate that there are between 100,000 and 300,000 wolfdogs in private ownership in the United States alone. (Other sources suggest a figure closer to 500,000 and more.)[3] Like the owners of all the wolfdog sanctuaries I visited, the Reeds receive daily calls from owners unable (and sometimes unwilling) to care for their animals. "We can't take them all," Kelly said. As we walked from one enclosure to the next, passing bags of unlabeled kibble that had been donated, Kelly pointed out a few mixed-breed dogs misidentified as wolfdogs by their owners and by animal control. "People want to think they have a wolf," he said.[4]

All those years ago I hadn't yet heard the term "enrichment," but I'd believed that my version of a life for Inyo would be perfect if only Wolf

Spirit could temporarily house her. I'd supply all her food and pay a board bill, whatever it took. I told myself she wouldn't bite Tim or Heidi because I'd take her out running, climbing, and backpacking to ease her frustration in confinement. I told myself that soon I'd have my own place like Wolf Spirit, far from people. But I worried. Could I ever get *far enough* from people? Even Tim and Heidi had told me they'd had their share of trouble with distant neighbors fearful the animals might get out of their enclosures and harm someone. As for Inyo, I suspected she *would* get out, determined as she was to go where she wanted to, fences be damned. In the wilderness, we were in constant motion over new terrain, satisfying her need for travel and novelty. On acreage, no matter how remote, we'd be settled. There would always be people and their animals in her travel range, and she'd seek them out.

One night, when I knocked on Ryan's door to talk to him about Inyo, I got no answer, only the clinking of bottles. I knew he was depressed again. The school principal had chewed him out for his messy classroom. Wealthy parents griped that he gave their kids low grades. He was ready with his Spanish skills, but Spanish-speaking parents, working two and three jobs, never showed for parent-teacher conferences. Some of his kids had just stopped coming to class. Every day he came home and locked himself in his office to play Age of Empires, covering the vent above the door with a towel so I couldn't spy. When I heard artillery fire and battle anthems, I knew that at least he was breathing and left him alone.

Two weeks after my visit to Wolf Spirit, I called Tim and Heidi. Would they have a space for Inyo? Waiting for an answer, pressing the phone to my ear, I paced the hallway and scratched a new hole in my scalp. My jaw had been clenched for weeks, crackling when I opened it just enough to slip in a spoonful of yogurt. The picture window in the hall, still broken where Inyo had jumped through, flapped with the heavy plastic sheet I'd stapled to the wood frame. Crumbs of glass sparkled in the carpet where the vacuum hadn't caught them. Finally Tim answered. He'd been outside filling the water buckets. It was a blazing September day and the wolves were hot. He was very sorry but the adoption had fallen through and they weren't able to help me. "I wish I could tell you what to do," he said. "Try to hang in there for another year."

CHAPTER TWENTY-FIVE

When the World
Is Not Enough

*Until one has loved an animal, a part of one's soul remains
unawakened.*

—Anatole France

One night, not long after my disappointment about Wolf Spirit, I
stood in the kitchen filling dog dishes. While Thelma and Argos sat
patiently waiting for their dinner, Inyo put her front paws on the counter and shoved her nose into the pot of turkey mash. When I pushed
her away and uttered a sharp "No!" she leaped up, her teeth raking
my ear, then fastening on my arm just above the elbow. I shrieked and
pulled away, stumbling backward as the pot toppled off the counter.
Inyo stood guard over it, keeping one eye on me as she ate. Thelma and
Argos slunk off to the living room as if they were in trouble.

A bruise budded on my arm. There would be no new home for
Inyo. There would be no sanctuary. I pressed a dish towel to my bloody
ear, feeling sick. I had to face it: Inyo's birth had been the result of a
terrible human error.

Roaming the meat department at Raley's, I scanned various cuts and
settled on two tenderloins, a T-bone, and two boneless rib eyes. When
I unloaded the basket, the clerk asked if I was having a party.

I slid open Hanna's side door and Inyo snatched the tenderloin still
sealed in its package, retreating to the backseat. I peeled the cellophane

from another steak and drained the blood onto the pavement, slipping the raw hunk onto the floor of Hanna.

I wanted to stuff Inyo with steaks for all I couldn't give her. I glanced down at my arm, flesh above the elbow the color of thunder clouds. "It's not her fault," I told friends. "She's a wolf. She's a dog. Both and neither."

When I climbed into the driver's seat and turned the ignition key, the engine revved then died. Hanna had overheated again. Shopping carts wheeled around us, car doors slammed. Mothers ordered their children to sit still. The smell of blood and muscle filled the van. Hanna had been Inyo's safe haven for three years—the movable den whose door slid shut and reopened at the ocean, where she chased lather scudding up the beach; closed and opened again, having magically transported her to Desolation Wilderness or to the slopes of Mount Shasta, Mount Jefferson, or Glacier Peak.

Cellophane and Styrofoam trays littered the seats as Inyo licked the blood from her paws. I waited five minutes and turned the key again. The engine sputtered then started. Now the words I often spoke as we headed into the wilderness: "We're going on an adventure."

I shifted into first.

At Rancho San Rafael Regional Park above downtown Reno, Inyo and I followed the dirt and gravel single-track past the National Monument to the Basque Sheepherder, "Bakardade," meaning "Solitude," and dropped down to Evans Creek, a stream fed by Highland Ditch, where we crossed the wood-plank bridge. Together we'd looped around this wetland of cattails at least twice a week for three years, run up-canyon toward Peavine Peak, past the yellow tailings left over from Reno's mining days, and plunged through waist-high cheatgrass, skirting the grove of ponderosa and Jeffrey pine at 7,000 feet where the coyotes denned.

Inyo slipped into the stream with her belly full of meat, nose glistening with beads of fat. The current rushed into her open jaws and churned around her shoulders. She devoured the world in that moment, the world that had never been enough.

A few evenings before, Ryan had come out of his office to sit next to me in the backyard under the picture window Inyo had shattered. I rolled my toes in the dirt and stroked Inyo where she sat at the end of her chain, calm after two runs that day and a bowl of turkey mash.

"You're solo on this one," he said, swigging from a bottle of Miller.

Solo. I'd been solo before. Three hundred feet in the air on a climbing route called Bear's Reach in Lake Tahoe. I'd been climbing short cracks with a few slab moves, but when I reached the crux of this route and faced leaping for a distant hold, fear of falling pinned me to the granite and I couldn't budge. I scanned the whole of Lover's Leap with its granite spires and rounded humps, then looked down at my feet bound in tight climbing shoes, at the pulsing blue veins that made my ankles thrum. Fingers crimped on a thin ledge, I watched the blood run out and my nails turn blue. If I reached for the next hold and missed, I would lose my footing and possibly take a zipper fall, my weight and the increasing speed of my body ripping each piece of protection from the rock—a cam, a nut plucked out—until I hit the ground. My body strained against the wind and gravity trying to force it into motion, but soon those forces would win. I had to make a move.

Belaying me from below, Ryan had shouted, "Stick it."

I called down that I was afraid to fall. He hollered back that if I spent too much time thinking about it, I *would* fall. I exhaled, clenched my teeth, and made the leap.

Inyo swam farther up Evans Creek and I took her picture. When the shutter clicked, I pressed my fingers to the helix of my left ear, the curved outermost fold where Inyo's tooth had lacerated the tissue. The flesh felt hot and red, glowing like the auroras in the skies above Reno. The sun had hurled charged particles at the planet for several nights running, battering the Earth's magnetic field. The lights in our house flickered. A bulb in the kitchen burst. Every night I'd dreamed that Inyo came when I called her, circling my legs like a cat and rubbing her mantle of gray-blond fur against my thighs. *Open the gate. Open the gate.*

Sitting beside me that evening as I stroked Inyo, Ryan had drained his Miller and said that if he told me what to do and I regretted it, I'd blame him. If I made the decision I'd have only myself to blame. Inyo buried her face in half a watermelon, black seeds sticking to her brow. Truth was, I wanted to blame him—for everything. For his irresponsibility, for his bad credit that kept us from buying our own land, for the decision I now had to make. I'd begged him to backpack one more time in Desolation or climb the domed walls of Green Phantom, but he wouldn't. Too painful, he'd said, and went back to his office.

So Inyo and I had gone alone to run on Peavine Mountain, our old standby. We charged into the creek where I splashed cool water on my ear, then sprinted across the rocky soil of the high desert, leaping over the yellow blooms of hawksbeard. I sprinted uphill on my toes to keep up as she plunged into the washed-out gullies and vaulted over the ruts in the dirt road, their mud banks hardened by the late summer heat. We ran up-canyon until my lungs burned and Inyo's tongue lolled, then circled back to Evans Creek where I kicked off my shoes and waded in after her.

She sniffed among the reeds as the Great Reno Balloon Race began. The pilots fired their burners and cut loose their ballast. A crowd of red and orange balloons lifted off and hovered together like a hundred embers. Inyo climbed out of the creek and shook her ears. Her amber eyes fixed on me for a moment before she trotted through the brush on those long wolf toes that had gripped domed granite walls. I scrambled up the bank after her, and we returned along the dusty path to the parking lot where I gave her another rib eye, this one spiked with the tranquilizer the vet had given me. Heading south on Virginia Street, I drove Hanna in second gear, crawling past the Circus Circus parking lot where we'd slept those first nights in Reno. Taxis rolled past us advertising Fantasy Girls, a strip club on East 4th. A man in a pair of dingy saddle shoes bobbed a sign on the corner: "Have mercy. Too ugly to strip." Across from the Park Lane Mall the proprietor of the Reno Psychic Clinic flipped the window sign to Closed. When I parked outside the vet clinic, the evening was early and still warm, heat radiating off the pavement. The engine ticked as it cooled. Hanna smelled of wet fur as Inyo gnawed the last of a ragged-edged T-bone on the plaid seat. In the rearview mirror the clinic's smokestack belched crematory steam. I got out and circled Hanna in one direction, then turned and circled the other way, curling strands of hair around my index finger and tugging. Bald patches had already appeared behind both ears, and I'd taken to wearing a hat even in the heat.

Ryan pulled the truck in next to Hanna. Maybe he remembered the time he and Inyo had gone into Desolation alone during winter and gotten lost. Inyo had climbed down a frozen waterfall in a whiteout, following Ryan faithfully as he oriented with compass and map to find a way out of the mountains. He'd burst through the door, dropped his pack, and announced, "She's stellar!"

I don't remember if we said a single word to each other in the five minutes we stood in the parking lot, dusk pressing on us. When I slid open Hanna's side door, the steak bones were gone. I leashed Inyo and we climbed the cement steps to the doors of the vet clinic, our image superimposed on the high peaks of the Sierra Nevada reflected in the tinted glass door marked Dogs.

Turn around. Turn around. Turn around. I don't have to do this. I'd leave Ryan, and Inyo and I would live in the mountains and sleep in Hanna. Then I looked down at my arm, the bruise spreading like an outrage.

A blast of air-conditioning rushed through the open door and the smell of bleach and dog hair hit my nose as we entered the waiting room with its coffee table stacked with *Better Homes & Gardens.* Inyo wore her prong collar, but she hardly needed it as the mild dose of tranquilizer calmed her. At the check-in desk the receptionist wore a smock printed with Scooby-Doos, and there was that damn drawing again, the same one I'd seen when Ryan and I carried Panzer in with the snakebite: a little boy and his grinning dog. I wanted to rip it off the wall.

I took Inyo into the bathroom and, flipping the lock, pressed my shoulders against the cool door, then leaned over the toilet and retched. Crouched on the pink tile floor, I stared into a dark corner as if something I hadn't thought of yet would suddenly come out of there. Then I could make a new plan and things would turn out right. Inyo nibbled my chin, then licked the back of my neck where a fever had started. When we came out the receptionist led us to Exam Room 1 and told us to wait.

A dog whined from another room.

We could leave. We could leave right now. We could stuff ourselves with Double-Doubles at In-N-Out Burger and run in the desert all night. But I didn't move.

The vet came in, his face a blur. He looked from my hands stroking Inyo who was already sleepy and lying with her paws crossed, and back to the syringe in his hand. Why did his presence in the room feel like an attack? Did he secretly think that if I were only stronger, I wouldn't be putting down this healthy animal?

"You're doing the right thing," he said.

You don't understand. It was wrong from the beginning.

I'd been so sure that our latest home at the edge of the city, with its undeveloped high desert sprawling for miles, would be a refuge. I'd felt sure we would fit into the Panther Valley neighborhood of working-class, half-country people who couldn't afford to live anywhere else, their half-acre lots sanctuaries for extreme personalities who wished to be left alone as I did. My plan had failed. I hadn't been able to figure out how to keep Inyo safe in this world.

Friends had patted my shoulders, told me I'd tried everything and how could I know. My mother told me she was sorry. "But really, honey, what else can you do?"

I lifted Inyo onto the exam table, her weight pressed against my chest. She'd never been big on hugging, but sleepy from the drugs she let me be close now. The vet shuffled around the room, gave Inyo a shot of sedative. I stroked her, kissed her eyes, and sang "You Are My Sunshine." The vet told me again that I was doing the right thing. *Shut up. Shut up.*

The vet flicked the syringe of blue juice and eased one of Inyo's forepaws toward him, then paused, asking if I was ready. How could I be ready? Inyo and I had climbed mountains together, slept deep in the backcountry in the middle of winter, waking in three feet of snow. We'd survived evictions, camped in a friend's spare bedroom, lived out of Hanna in the national forest.

"She's going to slump toward you," the vet said, sliding in the needle.

Wait, I'm not ready! But no words came out.

I had to let her go where there would be no chains, no pens, no dig guards, no hotwire. Her head lolled and she licked my hand, her tongue resting against my skin. A few seconds passed. I pressed my hand to her chest, felt her heartbeat slow, then stop. Her eyes went glassy. In a whisper, the vet told Ryan we could pick up Inyo's ashes the next afternoon. Then he stepped back, said he'd give us a minute, and slipped out the door.

Just go.

CHAPTER TWENTY-SIX

Chain Link

I've always said that the best wolf habitat resides in the human heart.

—Ed Bangs

After Inyo's death, I drifted through the fall months. I'm sure I paid bills, bought groceries, and walked the dogs, but I don't remember any of it. My fingers in cold dishwater, I often stood at the kitchen sink staring at the desert behind the house. The dogs camped at my feet, Argos resting his chin on my foot, Thelma curled up on her rug. I couldn't remember if I'd just been somewhere or was supposed to be going somewhere. I missed meetings with my dissertation adviser or arrived late, flushed and anxious for approval.

But I wasn't thinking much about my dissertation. I thought of nothing but the dirt track Inyo and I had run together to the radio towers. She'd never been completely happy in her life, kept from roads, animals, neighbors. Kept. But I had glimpsed her joy at the summit, with the red lights of the towers blinking, and in the wilderness, where she'd run completely free, the wild part of her satisfied in those moments, muscles and mind fulfilling their design. Inevitably though, we would have to go home, and there, face her confinement—the fences and hotwire—followed by another escape and a chase.

A wolfdog owner once told me that if I hadn't allowed Inyo to run—hadn't let her out of an enclosure—she would never have developed a lust for roaming. The world would have been terrifying, so she'd have stayed inside the only place she felt safe. I don't believe that, but even if it were true, I'd still choose our nearly four years of wilderness adventures over ten to fifteen in a "containment system" built with eight-foot high-tensile Tightlock game fence stapled to ten-foot wooden posts sunk two feet into the ground, with half a bag of concrete per hole, and a three-foot dig guard battened with hog rings, the whole mess of wire reinforced with electricity buzzing top and bottom.[1]

I longed to see a wild wolf, that part of Inyo wholly embodied and set free to roam. For years that desire nagged at me until finally I gave in, flew to Bozeman and drove from there to Yellowstone, one of the first sites of wolf recovery in the Rocky Mountains. In the mid-1990s, federal biologists had captured wolves in Alberta and British Columbia and released them into Idaho and Yellowstone National Park, where wolves had been exterminated by 1930. My first day I woke at 4 a.m. to join a group of other visitors for a dawn trek into wolf country. The hard winter showed in the bodies of elk, skinny and snowbound. In ten-degree temperatures, a dry wind blowing, we scanned the hills with binoculars.

"Wolf!"

"Bison!"

"Bear!"

"Sorry, guys," said our guide. "It's a boulder."

We kept scanning.

Two hours into our search, we spotted a wolf in a meadow and set up a row of spotting scopes. Our guide told us that the wolf was a yearling male, a member of the Agate Creek Pack. The wolf paced and howled, and our guide explained that he was trying to locate his pack mates. Through the scope, I could see the wolf's tail. It was a real mess, cropped and shaggy, and he limped on one rear leg. Our guide added that he might have been mauled by a neighboring wolf pack during a conflict over territory. The wolf howled again. This time his pack answered from somewhere behind us. He limped toward our group, then stopped and howled once more. The sheer thrill of seeing a wild wolf made us forget how cold we were, that our feet had gone numb. Shutters clicked. A woman from New York whispered, "I've seen wolves and coyotes today. Now I'd really like to throw in a big black bear against the snow, that white snow."

Someone muttered, "Sounds like you're ordering dessert."

Before I left Yellowstone, I tracked down Doug Smith, leader of Yellowstone's Wolf Project, hoping he could tell me more about the yearling wolf. Turns out "he" was a "she" that biologists had named "Half-Tail" because as a pup she'd been hit by a truck and lost half her tail. One rear leg had also been broken. That early morning in the meadow, twenty-eight fellow gawkers and I had formed an obstacle between her and her pack. She'd paced and howled in distress, eventually loping a wide arc around us to get to them.

So much for my fantasy of seeing a wolf wild and totally free. Yellowstone wolves may not be hemmed in by chain link and hotwire, but they suffer a kind of confinement stress nonetheless. Inside the park they're observed by ecotourists, whose visits are encouraged as a way of fostering an educated appreciation for wolves. They're numbered and tracked by biologists collecting information about wolf behavior even as they realize that their methods may be distorting it. Doug Smith explained that when he chases wolves to collar them, "the females really turn on the afterburners—the chopper pilot has to work to keep up." Chased down or trapped, darted with a tranquilizer and collared, wolves are sometimes injured or traumatized in biologists' quest to learn more about them. And although wolves are protected inside the park from predation by humans, they're pressed for space, making fights between packs common. The average life span of a Yellowstone wolf is just 3.4 years—Inyo's age at death.

Waiting for my flight home, I browsed the airport gift shop, its shelves lined with wolf plush toys made in China and little fuzzy cows that mooed when you squeezed them. I realized that wolves must face pressures everywhere, and though I'd done a lot of research about wolf-dogs, I wanted to do something practical to help wild wolves.

In my home state of Oregon, the twenty-some wolves comprising two packs—the Imnaha and the Wenaha—have until recently been protected by the federal Endangered Species Act.[2] But in April 2011 Congress removed federal protection for gray wolves in the eastern part of Oregon and across the entirety of several other western states. The delisting allows states to manage wolves according to their own conservation plans. For now, wolves in Oregon are still protected by the Oregon Endangered Species Act, but the act hasn't changed attitudes. Shortly after a revised version of the Oregon Wolf Conservation and Management Plan was approved, a poacher shot a two-year-old male wolf never involved in a livestock attack. He had been fitted with a GPS collar to help management agencies and ranchers know where his pack was denning and hunting, essential information for protecting livestock. The Oregon Cattlemen's Association condemned the killing and pledged support for a wolf-management plan that protects both wolves and livestock. But frankly, for all the effort put into it, the revised Oregon plan amounts to little more than a playbook for when it's okay to kill wolves and who gets to do it.[3] Though minimizing wolf-livestock conflicts is the only way to assure wolves a safe presence in the state, the plan devotes just a few stray phrases to methods for avoiding conflicts to begin with. And the revised plan has done nothing to curb the name-calling and threats. Environmentalists accuse ranchers of being wolf-hating greedhogs, and ranchers and hunters sport bumper stickers that read WOLVES . . . Smoke a Pack a Day.

I'd heard environmentalists say that ranchers have been getting a free lunch at the expense of American taxpayers, grazing each cow-calf pair on public lands for just $1.35 per month. They fear that if given the legal go-ahead, ranchers will kill wolves with impunity. So I drove to Bend for the annual meeting of the Oregon Cattlemen's Association to listen to what ranchers had to say about running their cows in what may become wolf country. They worry that with less political power than ever, they'll go out of business if environmentalists use the need for wolf recovery to end grazing on public lands. They complain about lack of compensation, not just for direct livestock kills, but for stress-induced weight loss and injuries. There are hard feelings on both sides. As association president Bill Hoyt told me: "There's a whole lot of conflict and not much resolution."

I didn't know how ranchers would receive a city person who likes wolves. When I told those at the meeting that I respected ranchers who used sustainable practices and wanted my students to know where their food came from, I got a big round of applause. My follow-up comment that I also respected wolves as large carnivores with a place in the ecosystem was greeted with a few dark comments. If more teachers drilled the U.S. Constitution into America's young people, one woman said, ranchers could defend themselves against a government that drops wolves in their backyards. If city people wanted wolves so badly, ranchers would gladly round them up and dump them off in the city parks. One person suggested I cuddle a wolf if I thought they were so warm and fuzzy. (I wanted to say, "Done that, know better.") Someone else suggested that since dogs chase cats, wolves would chase cougars and keep the "exploding" population in check, so why not round up the wolves and dump them on the west side of the state where cougars had been sighted near homes? Two people told me that wolves in Oregon were an invasive species from Canada.

I was already familiar with that claim. During a recent trip to Joseph, I'd seen a poster mounted in the window of the Sports Corral announcing CANADIAN WOLF ALERT. Depicting a snarling wolf in full color—yellow eyes blazing, fangs gleaming—the poster charged the U.S. Fish and Wildlife Service with fraud and claimed that wolves now inhabiting Oregon were not native wolves, but a disease-ridden and dangerous invasive species from Canada threatening to swallow livestock and big-game industries. Oregonians for Wolf Free Oregon, the poster's sponsors, had misappropriated the language of invasive species science to make their argument. Yes, gray wolves living in Canada were used to repopulate the northern Rockies, but they are still *Canis lupus*. Wolves don't recognize political or international boundaries, and frankly, scientists don't take the "invasive" charge seriously. In a recent *Oregonian* article, Ed Bangs, the U.S. Fish and Wildlife Service's gray wolf recovery coordinator, joked that wolves living in Oregon and the whole Mountain West were *Canis lupus irregardless.*[4]

Despite comments about tutoring my students in the U.S. Constitution and cuddling wolves, several ranchers shook my hand after the meeting and thanked me for making the drive and caring about them. They also asked some hard questions. One rancher wondered why Oregon needed wolves. "We were doing fine without them," he said, and pointed out that monitoring wolves and then killing problem animals was expensive. Why spend all those taxpayer dollars just to make an ideological point? Another asked, "What good are wolves anyway?"

I wouldn't have known what to say if I hadn't already met Suzanne Fouty, a Forest Service hydrologist in Baker City, and Timmothy Kaminski of the Mountain Livestock Cooperative, who has worked with ranchers in Montana and Alberta to minimize wolf-livestock conflicts. Suzanne, whom I'd met the previous summer while visiting some sheep-rancher friends, invited me to join Kaminski and others on a tour of wolf country and then sit in on Kaminski's public talk about new strategies for reducing livestock losses. A hydrologist, Suzanne understands the connection between wolves and water. As we gathered windfall peaches in her backyard, she explained that we need wolves in the ecosystem to keep elk on the move, preventing herds from over-browsing, putting them at risk for starvation and disease while eroding stream banks and degrading water quality needed to support both livestock and people. Ranchers need to change their grazing patterns, she told me. They need to keep their cattle traveling the way wolves move elk. When ranchers move their cattle away from fragile stream areas, riverbanks suffer less trampling, allowing shaded and cool streams to maintain oxygen levels, which support the salmon population.

Before a crowd at the Eltrym Theater in Baker City, Kaminski admitted that federal management agencies had made some mistakes, and when agencies get their science wrong, people get upset and their positions harden. But simply killing offending wolves and compensating ranchers for losses hasn't worked.

Understanding predator-prey behavior and changing grazing practices is part of the solution. To start the hunt, wolves must goad their prey to bolt from the herd and run. Wild prey animals that stand their ground often live. Cows tend to scatter, and a lone cow is easy prey. On private land where ranchers feed cattle at night so they're huddled together during the wolf's peak hunting hours, the number of livestock kills has gone down, and ranchers are more tolerant of wolves traversing their property. On public land, when range riders move animals in tight groups, ranchers suffer fewer losses. Biologists can provide information about wolf-den sites, and directional telemetry can tell range riders where wolves are so they can herd cattle away.

Management agencies need to rethink their rules. Present grazing allotments are fixed and fenced, but if a rancher grazes cattle on the same allotment at the same time every year, wolves learn the routine and return to places where they found food before, including carcass piles where ranchers dispose of dead stock. We need to bring back the old-fashioned rendering plants or start a mobile rendering service.

The ranchers at the cattlemen's meeting weren't much impressed with the ideas I'd shared. One man who'd lost several calves to wolves wanted to know why he couldn't shoot wolves on his own land. But after the meeting, a young guy approached and stuck out his hand. He wore a big grin, a blazing-white cowboy hat, and a bright red scarf tied around his neck. His hands were thick and calloused from ranch work, his legs bowed from riding. He wanted to connect with urban markets, he said, expressing an interest in "predator-friendly" labeling for beef and lamb, because he thought that city folks would be willing to pay a premium for meat produced with a minimum of wolf deaths. He wanted me to know that there were more ranchers like him, the younger generation open to resolving conflicts and coming to the table with ideas. He gave me his card and told me to bring my students to his ranch. "We can work together," he said. "Make a difference."

"You bet," I said. I'd been living with a whole lot of remorse. Even though Leda would have bred her animals with or without me, I was sorry for the part I played in bringing Inyo into the world, and once she was with me, sorrier still that I couldn't find a way for her. But maybe now I could find a way to help wild wolves survive.

Eagle Cap

*The dog is the most faithful animal, and it might be held
in great worth, if it were not so common.*

—Martin Luther

The following summer, driving the freeway east from Portland, Argos
and I leave the Willamette Valley where we've been living for five years
and follow the Columbia River, its channel markers crowned by osprey
nests. At Hood River, fir forest gives way to grasslands and bare cliffs
of the eastern Columbia River Gorge. Sparks from a freight train have
ignited the yellow grasses on the Washington side of the river, setting
the hills ablaze around the Dalles Dam. Dry heat stales the bread on
my sandwich as I eat it. Sleepy, Argos sighs and rests his chin on my
thigh.

We pass through La Grande on the way to the town of Lostine,
where we turn south on a paved road toward the Lostine River campgrounds. Seven miles in, the road turns to gravel. A few miles farther
it becomes pitted with water-filled dips the size of fishponds. Eighteen
miles from Lostine and six hours from Portland, we finally pull into
Two Pan Campground at the base of Eagle Cap Wilderness in the Wal-
lowa Mountains. An afternoon thunderstorm has dimpled the dust
and left the metallic smell of ozone in the air. I cinch down the straps
on Argos's pack, the one he's always carried, with the yellow reflective
strips sewn to each saddlebag filled with kibble and hot dogs. Ten years
old now, with white hairs misting his muzzle and pips, the Big Man
still backpacks in the mountains with me, and year-round he runs the

223

miles-long trails that snake through the woods near our home, leaping easily over maples and Doug firs downed by winter windstorms.

With enough food inside for our four-day trek, I heft on my pack, tightening the belt to lift the weight off my shoulders and open my stride as we head into Eagle Cap along the west fork of the Lostine River. A steady pace keeps the August mosquitoes in our wake.

A year ago Thelma's right foreleg shattered when she tripped in a shallow ditch, a simple misstep another dog wouldn't blink at. A freak accident, I thought. It was cancer. The vet amputated the foreleg, even removing her shoulder bone. One hind leg required a pin and a cast and couldn't bear weight. She adjusted with unyielding grit to a two-legged life, my brindle girl with those cauliflower ears, souvenirs of Inyo. When I came home from work, she tried to wave at me as she always had, though her leg was missing. She still wanted to go along when I went to the barn across the road to feed my old thorough-bred jumper. Feeding the horse and retrieving the mail had been her daily jobs, and she wouldn't give them up. Like a bicycle, as long as Thelma kept forward momentum on those two legs she could stay upright. Digging out her favorite sleeping hole at the base of a cedar tree, she would balance on her one good hind leg, using the pinned leg as an occasional kickstand, and dig with her single forepaw. When she couldn't get much earth moved, she wrenched hunks of soil with her jaws until she got the hole just the right size to lie down in. Although she was nine years old, I still called her Little Pup, and she allowed me to carry her down flights of stairs in my arms. Leaving Argos at home, I gave Thelma a boost into the back of the car, and she settled on her cedar bed for surround-sound tours of the city, Mozart or Beethoven piping through the speakers as I ran errands. On the way home, we'd sail through the Burgerville drive-thru for her favorite—a double beef cheeseburger.

Argos and Thelma had lived with me aboard my old sailboat, though Thelma thought living on a boat was unseemly and hated the constant motion. She was relieved to visit my mother's real house, her tail spinning like a propeller when we pulled into the driveway. *This is where we're supposed to live!* But still, she would go wherever I asked her to. Always polite and gentle, she needed coaxing to take a treat from my hand, and even then she was careful to avoid scraping my skin with her teeth. Self-possessed, calm, and friendly with everyone, she was a dog motivated by praise and duty, and she had my unwavering devotion.

When a starburst tumor bloomed above her previously healthy left knee, the vet showed me X-rays, pointing to black holes where her other leg bones had turned to pumice. He said, "Spoil the heck out of her."

Thelma's mind had been sound, but her bones had crumbled—a genetic fault maybe, or just bad luck. Argos, on the other hand, has a sturdy body, but a troubled mind. He still has occasional shrieking fits when I come home from work, but mostly he just whines with excitement—*Thank God you're here!* He surfs the kitchen counter the second my back is turned, shamelessly noses strangers' butts, and screams bloody murder when getting his nails clipped, but food and squirrels are the only things rivaling his loyalty to me, and I can hardly hold that against him. His teeth are as white as a puppy's, and his bones are thick. He heels beautifully off lead and comes when I call him, as Thelma did. Argos, whose DNA test revealed that he's a purebred American street dog—a little Samoyed, a little rottweiler, and a whole lot of who-knows-what—wants to take direction, go where I go, do what I do. I can cuddle him and he hugs me back. I don't know if there's a heaven for people, but there's definitely a heaven for dogs.

No, dogs aren't perfect. They're a miracle. They're eager to do what we breed and train them for—hunting, herding, guarding, assistance, and therapy, and simply being our friends. We admire the well-trained dog and love our favorite breeds and the breeders who produce high quality animals, but we tend to forget the driving force that makes the human-dog partnership possible: thousands of years of domestication that have made dogs, in all their variety, uniquely suited to living with people. Dogs want to get along with us so much that they watch all the time to see what we'll do next. If I lace up my sneakers, Argos leaps around and scrambles for the door. *Those* shoes mean a run in the woods. If I slip on my teaching shoes, he flops on his bed with a sigh. He's staying home. If I pull a carrot out of the fridge, he heads straight for the barn because he knows it's time to feed the horse. He also understands my speech and hand signals, and during walks when I point and say, "That way!" he follows my finger and changes direction.

We dog owners tend to take for granted the abilities reflected in the cute little anecdotes we tell one another about doggy cleverness, because most of us have had no experience with wild or part-wild canines, nothing to contrast our domestic dogs to. Wolf intelligence has been shaped by the need to survive in the wilderness. Wolves do not need or want our intimacy, and in fact their survival often depends on avoiding us and our livestock. On the other hand, having lived with a creature both dog and wolf, I now see how much dog intelligence is devoted to reading people, including our moods. Their survival depends on it.

Though I'd believed that no dog could keep up with me in the wilderness, Thelma and Argos had always been able trekkers, and after Inyo's death, an overnight trip to the Sierras proved once and for all how wrong I'd been. By that time Ryan had lost all appetite for backpacking and would have preferred to stay home and play World of Warcraft, but I needed the backcountry and persuaded him to go. Our preparations were halfhearted and disorganized, but we skied into the mountains expecting to find a cabin we'd stayed in the season before, a wooden shack often used as an emergency shelter. But we couldn't find it. We traversed the slope where it was supposed to be, shouting to each other and pointing at any dark smudge on the landscape. In late afternoon, with darkness coming fast and a blizzard pelting the mountains, we couldn't backtrack. When clouds spit ice needles at our cheeks, Ryan dug a snow cave with our one shovel, while I scooped with a cook pot. Argos and Thelma watched as we scraped and jabbed, our sweat reeking of dread. We'd taken our last pull from the water bottles, and our gear, including the backup lighter we relied on to melt snow for drinking water, was soaked. We couldn't nibble ice without lowering core body temperature, so we went thirsty, huddled in the cave with the dogs to wait out the weather.

But I couldn't wait. I hadn't been eating regularly since Inyo's death, picking at the food on my plate or skipping meals altogether, and with little body fat to warm me, my clothes soaked by ice and sweat, I told

Ryan we should strap on our skis to look for a way out of the mountains. He said we were more likely to die outside the cave than in, which would normally be true, but I had to circulate my blood or I'd die frozen to the cave wall. Grumbling that leaving our only shelter was a terrible idea, he slipped on headlamp and skis. Certain he knew the route, he hadn't bothered to bring a compass. So driven to get out the door and get away, I hadn't checked. Now we were without even the simplest tools to help us navigate.

In that whiteout, with no visible landmarks, we set forth, blasted by sleet blowing sideways, our feet heavy as cinder blocks. We took short rest breaks every few minutes, hunkering out of the wind in a clump of trees, each of us hugging a dog for warmth. Their aliveness reminded us of our own as their hot breath warmed our chapped lips and cheeks, and we stood again and trudged on, peering through the sheeting snow to read the land for any familiar sign.

With his thick coat and large paws, Argos had been better prepared for those conditions than Thelma, who, although well muscled, had a thin coat and smallish paws. Yet she trooped forward. When I tumbled ass over teakettle into a frozen creek, she licked my face and ears, whining for me to get up. If Ryan and I drifted too far apart in the blizzard, she herded us closer together. But after several hours slogging upslope and down and fording creeks with no clue where we were, our wills slackened. Ryan sat under a pine so weighted with snow the branches disappeared underground. "We're not gonna make it out of here."

"Get up," I said, tears freezing on my face. "Get up!" Argos nudged him, licking his cheeks, and we started out again, morning light cutting through the snow showers. After nineteen hours we stumbled onto a familiar drainage that led us out. Without the body warmth and unflappable cheer of the dogs, Ryan and I wouldn't have kept going. Just hugging them kept us alive.

"If we can make it through this," Ryan said, his eyes on a plowed road ahead of us, "we can make it through anything." But our marriage was already over, I just hadn't admitted it yet.

After Inyo's death, it took two more years to untangle my life from Ryan's. I've always wished I were one of those people who could say, "You know what? We're really not that great for each other. In fact, we were a terrible idea to begin with, and I'm leaving." But I'm not one of those people, and I cheered as Ryan made stabs at helping himself with counseling and took his meds more regularly.

But always, just as I started to get hopeful, he'd slip back into old habits.

Everyone has her own last straw. Mine came after we'd moved to California for my first university teaching job. With two dogs and a parrot, the only dwelling space we could afford was a slip in Ventura Harbor, a giant parking lot for boats, where people of little means lived cheek by jowl aboard sailboats in various stages of decay and shared a bathroom at the end of the docks. Our vessel, a 1964 Spencer sloop purchased with a loan from my mother and stepdad, was the closest Ryan and I would ever come to owning a home together. Despite its age, that blue-water sailboat was a beauty with its navy hull and white boot-stripe. But Ryan's drinking worsened after the thrill of our new life wore off. One morning at 2 a.m., with a storm kicking up the waves in the Santa Barbara Channel, he stumbled into the boat's cockpit, having glugged down homemade hooch with some poker-playing sailors, and grabbed the ignition key. I'd long been asleep in the V-berth, the sleeping quarters in the bow, and by the time I woke, Ryan had the boat in reverse. "Huevos, get on deck!" he shouted.

Wind gusted through the cockpit as I scrambled through the companionway. "What are you doing?" I yelled over the growl and sputter of the engine.

"Sailing!" he bellowed, and shoved the tiller hard right to avoid smashing into the boat next to us.

By this time our neighbors had poured out of their hatches in pajamas and bathrobes, flooding the dock with flashlights.

"Fend off!" Ryan ordered, meaning I should push off whatever object—the pier, a jetty, rocks, or in this case our neighbor Hank's boat—we were about to ram. Too late. A thud, then the scrape of fiberglass as our port side struck the stern of Hank's Catalina. I grasped a wire shroud to keep from being knocked into the drink by the impact. Ryan cut the engine. Stubbing my toe on a chain plate, I groped for the bowline and tossed the end to another neighbor, who helped guide our boat back into the slip.

When everyone had shuffled back to bed and I'd promised Hank I'd contact the insurance company first thing, Ryan hollered, "You're a horrible first mate!" and threw a wine bottle at the cabin wall next to my head.

But not even the bottle was my last straw. The next morning, while Ryan snored off the sauce, I rowed the dingy to Hank's boat and told him some cockamamie story about how Ryan had been trying to surprise me with a romantic cruise to the Channel Islands.

"You looked pretty silly running around the bow in your underpants," Hank joked. He could tell that Ryan had been lit the night before, but he also knew we'd be evicted from the marina if management found out what Ryan had done. With nowhere else to go, we'd be forced to anchor offshore with all the other homeless people in their leaky tubs. The compassion in Hank's eyes told me he'd keep quiet, but I knew in that moment I couldn't tell one more lie to keep us safe.

I'd gotten off track, forgotten my own lesson—about being like the jay and avoiding poison. But I've learned that in order to avoid poison I need to pay attention to what I see with my own eyes, and then probe deeper, ask questions, do research. After all, research is what I'd been trained for, so why didn't I explore the meaning of the Cap'n Crunch and the missing telephone service? Why did I accept Leda's rhapsodizing about wolfdogs instead of taking it as my cue to look for other sources of information? I was stuck in the belief that by sheer will I could make any relationship work. But sometimes will is not enough. And it was never fair or reasonable for me to expect that a creature like Inyo could be my guardian and constant companion. I'd based that expectation on flimsy mythologies rather than science.

Argos and I traverse a subalpine meadow where crystalline tributaries snake toward the Lostine River, feeding the yellow blossoms of columbine and the buttery heads of Cusick's paintbrush that glint like signal fires. The scent of wild onion tickles my nose. By dusk we reach Minam Lake, six miles in, where I set up the orange Hubba tent and fire the one-burner for mac 'n' cheese. When I finish eating, Argos, ever the hungry pup even when full to the gills with kibble and hot dogs, scours my cook pot and bowl to store-shelf new, leaving no cheesy smell to attract bears. Lassoing the branch of a wind-shorn fir by tying nylon cord to a stone and aiming high, I hoist the food sacks out of bears' swiping range. Darkness has pressed in by the time I crawl into the Hubba heavy-lidded, Argos curled beside me.

The next morning, cocooned in my sleeping bag, Argos pressed close, I'm stirred by the hollow thump of waves pounding granite boulders. Wind buffets the lake surface to chop. Argos trots out to pee among the limber pines while I balance between two boulders at the shoreline to filter drinking water with my hand pump. Inyo would have liked this wilderness of icebound lakes and granite peaks, so much like Desolation. When I drove to the clinic to collect her ashes, I breathed her scent in the van, gusts through the open window wheeling tufts of her wooly undercoat around me. Back at home, I locked Hanna's doors and didn't unlock them until I sold her two years later.

After a mug of cowboy coffee, I bury the leftover grounds and fold the Hubba. Saddled with our packs, Argos and I ascend the steep incline toward the mountain pass. As I rest-step through snowmelt rippling across the path, making the plainest pebble blaze like a garnet, he rolls on a stubborn patch of last year's freeze, shoving his black nose through the icy powder. At Carson Pass we shed our packs and gnaw strips of jerky. Two hikers crest the trail and spot Argos perched on a granite slab overlooking Mirror and Upper Lakes. One says, "He looks just like a wolf sitting there."

"He's all dog," I say, recalling Lyudmila Trut's expression when I'd told her that American taxonomists had reclassified the dog as a subspecies of gray wolf. Her mouth had tightened and she'd shaken her head, asking Anastāsiya to translate again, certain she'd misunderstood me. Maybe in Russia there's a cultural reluctance to link wolves and dogs because of old stories about wolf packs hunting people. On the other hand, because Americans are a dog-loony bunch, wolf advocates here want to link wolves and dogs as closely as possible: *If you love your dog, you should love wolves because your dog is basically a domesticated wolf.* Wolves and dogs have been helped and harmed by this crude coupling. When the science gets oversimplified, people start improvising, feeding their dogs based on faulty notions of the way wolves eat, developing dog-training methods based on captive wolf behavior, and, of course, breeding wolves with dogs because isn't the wolf just a raw, more intense version of a dog anyway?

Dogs are not wolves. Wolves are not dogs. Evolution and domestication have seen to it.

Although I'm not likely to see a wolf out here, or even to hear one howl, it's enough to know that the Imnaha Pack—at least ten animals including some half-grown pups—is going about its wolfy business nearby. The hikers take a picture of Argos and me, my arm slung over his back. To love dogs is to keep them close. To love wolves is to leave them wild.

Just a few miles from Minam, at the base of Eagle Cap peak, Argos and I make camp at Mirror Lake in a grove of fir, our site edged with wood betony and penstemon. The wind spins dirt and fir needles into whirligigs that batter the tent walls. I stake down the Hubba and zip a fleece jacket to my chin. Enough light remains for Argos and me to climb the steep summit trail to 9,595-foot Eagle Cap, but we get only as far as Horton Pass when thunderclouds muscle in, obscuring the sun. In the chill and wet we hotfoot back to camp for all we're worth and hole up in the tent until the storm passes. It's a welcome shelter, like my new marriage to a man I knew even before Eddie, a good friend I should have married in the first place. A builder and an artist, Lonnie restores old cars as artfully as he paints canvasses. He built the house we live in, including my rooftop studio, a light-box modeled after an old forest-service lookout. He's my partner in adventure—sailing the San Juan Islands and climbing Mount Hood—and a reliable companion at home, a man I can trust to pay the bills on time. He even washes more than his fair share of dishes.

By evening, when the firs drip the last of the rain and slanted sunlight reddens the bark of limber pines, I suit up for bugs, pulling on a hat, pants, and camp shoes, and build a campfire just large enough to subdue the clouds of gnats and bullheaded mosquitoes that drill through my socks. A group of hikers passes by searching for a site, and Argos barks a warning, guarding the territory we've claimed for the night. When the hikers' voices fall away, their scent disappearing down the trail, he sprawls out next to me, his chin on my foot, bandit mask illuminated by the firelight. Sipping tea, I whistle over the steam into the darkness.

Some people find this love between human and dog too easy. Like me at one time, they can't accept love freely offered. They can only value love they have to "earn," striving to win the heart of a part-wild creature that lives at odds with its dual nature. I think of Sandman, one of Texas breeder Dora Simpson's wolfdogs. She dismissed him as too "doggy" because he just wanted to be petted and loved on. Too doggy? I thought he was lovely.

Even Leda seems to have figured out that the "too easy" love of a dog is worth something. The last time I heard from her, she was living in Vienna and didn't have wolfdogs anymore. She had an English setter–greyhound cross she described as "the nicest, easiest animal on earth." She told me: "Wolves just aren't an option in the city."

Where would they be an "option"? Where and with whom would these animals live the kind of life that satisfied *them*? Even Jan Koler-Matznick, who'd studied canid behavior, worked with captive coyotes, and had a long career as a dog trainer, could not successfully raise a wolfdog. "I was more of an expert than the average person," she told me. "I felt competent to keep a wolfdog, understanding its natural instincts. And even with all that, I failed. I did my best, but my best wasn't good enough." But as Terry Jenkins explained, no matter what you tell people about wolfdogs, there are always some who think their experience will be different. "It's those people who fall the hardest when things don't work out. Either they blame the animal and go on as if nothing ever happened, or they never get over it for the rest of their lives—like you and me."

Even now I tap and circle, but a lot less and never in the backcountry. My hair has grown back, and I still have my teeth. Yet I'm tormented by the question of how I could have kept Inyo safe without the misery of confinement. In any case, she would have found a way out of any pen I could have built. As one wolfdog owner put it, "For these animals, there's no such thing as an escape-proof enclosure."

I'd have needed that nonexistent escape-proof lockup even if I'd bought remote acreage bordering public land because people are everywhere and they would still complain. As for my fantasy about living in a national forest, the place where Inyo and I were the best partners, I could have done that, moving camp every fourteen days to stay legal. But without keeping Inyo chained I'd have had to tolerate her killing of wildlife, including threatened species. Impossible. And the national forests and wilderness areas are patrolled by rangers. Eventually we would have been run off.

I still hurt over Inyo, as Terry Jenkins still grieves for Blue whom she shot when he became so unpredictable she couldn't go inside his pen. Jan Koler-Matznick grieves for her wolfdog Cody. When he slipped through the backyard fence and bit three-year-old Michael Landers who was riding his Big Wheel in the alley behind the house, she couldn't believe Cody meant to hurt the boy. "He was the biggest baby in the world—afraid of everything outside that fence."

Euthanasia. Beheading. Rabies testing. No second chances.

"Tell my story," Jan said. "Tell yours."

Some authors have suggested that it is "universally acknowledged" that however great the love between a person and a wolf or wolfdog, the animal can "turn" against its owner. Not only does this explanation overlook the frustration resulting from animals' unmet genetic drives, but it is simply not true that the difficulties and ethical problems of keeping wolves and wolfdogs are "universally acknowledged." I've met owners who claim that keeping wolfdogs does wild wolves a service by preserving the bloodlines of a threatened species and helping dispel the myth of the "big, bad wolf." Some people say their Native American heritage gives them a special kinship with wolves and the right to own wolfdogs or even pure wolves without permits or regard for laws. Others—men and women alike—view the world as a hostile place that does not welcome them, and view their wolfdogs as outlaw animals that mirror their own alienation from society. Owning a large predator gives them bragging rights, while displaying control over such a creature shows how tough they are. These people behave as if their wolfdogs lend them a power and menace of the same kind they'd get by waving around a loaded gun. The society that has wounded and rejected them gets the message loud and clear: "It's me and my wolfdog against the world. Don't mess with us!" A few even find power in the word "wolf" itself, adopting it as part of their own names. They may claim to be part of their wolfdogs' "pack," but theirs is not a pack at all—it's a group of animals artificially assembled and held captive, and the owners don't live in the pen with the animals—they drop in and out as they please.

Recently, a woman asked me about wolfdogs because her son was "hell-bent" on buying one. When I advised against it, I never heard from her again. Maybe I didn't tell her what she wanted to hear.

Of course, not all wolfdogs turn out like Blue and Cody and Inyo. A few owners have temperamentally stable adult wolfdogs—*real* wolfdogs, not mixed-breed dogs—that don't require a maximum-security enclosure. I'm glad for them—really. Those wolfdogs won the genetic crapshoot. But what about their littermates? I contacted Heidi, who'd run Wolf Spirit sanctuary where I'd tried to place Inyo. She told me she'd quit rescue work. It had been too disheartening: "There was always another animal who needed to be rescued, and another, and another, and another."

I remembered a wolfdog who'd been left tied outside a rescue's gate in the middle of the night, a note stuffed into its collar: "Please teach me to hunt and set me free."

Our third day in the eastern Oregon wilderness, mountain sorrel and heather guide our trek toward the summit of Eagle Cap. Usually just behind or beside me when we hike, Argos spurts ahead to wallow in an old snowdrift saddling Horten Pass. Buttercups and pussytoes gleam in the alpine exposure as I shadow him across the watermelon snow—patches reddened by algae—and roll pink fastballs for him to chase. We climb past wind-shorn whitebark pine and subalpine fir, their needles soft to the touch, not prickly as I'd expected, Argos panting beside me, his pack swishing with each stride. Clouds clenched with thunder loom, and my own breath comes hard as I keep a strong pace, heart pressing against the chest strap on my pack. We should turn around, get off this peak before the storm rolls over the top of us, but this time I can't. I have to keep going, get to the summit to do what I came here for.

When we finally reach the summit with its views of the East Lostine River Valley and Hurricane Divide, I slide the pack off my shoulders and watch as chimneys of sunlight brighten Matterhorn summit to the north, then fade and light up Aneroid Mountain to the east. Thunderclouds seem to move faster at this elevation. A nippy wind pipes through the brush, and Argos and I take refuge behind a boulder. I fill his collapsible water dish and he rests, chin on paws, while I slip a poncho over my head, hair matted with pitch where I'd napped against a leaking pine. Through the poncho the granite feels cold against my shoulder blades. Terry Jenkins says that animals have souls like we do. If we've wronged them and are truly sorry for what we've done, she believes they'll forgive us.

Cradling the bag of dust and silvery bone-flakes I've kept for so many years, I carry Inyo's ashes to the edge of the summit overlooking Glacier and Pocket Lakes. Argos sits next to me on a shelf of granite—rock Inyo had once so skillfully gripped with her toes, clawing to heights I was often afraid to shin up. I still had to haul myself up the rock, just as I alone had to repair all that was broken inside me. But I was braver for witnessing Inyo's grace.

I expect the breeze to carry her ashes over the mountains. Instead, as bone chips and ash slip through my fingers, a sudden wind gusts the chalky grains into my hair and eyes, powdering Argos's nose. He sneezes. My poncho whips around my thighs as I sweep traces of Inyo across my damp cheeks and laugh. I've done it again—so sure that if I plan carefully even the winds will cooperate. Besides, how could I forget? Inyo will go where she wants to, even in death.

Rain pits the dust, muddying Inyo's ashes with this mountain dirt, soil wild wolves now walk on. My jaws clack from cold as I see the first lightning strike in the distance. Argos and I head down the mountain toward camp, and that night he sleeps with his head buried in my chest, one giant paw thrown over my neck.

And I'm so grateful.

Acknowledgments

I couldn't have written this book without the generous contributions of so many people who shared their time and expertise with me. I am deeply grateful to Bridgett vonHoldt, Robert K. Wayne, Dyan Straughan, Lyudmila Trut, Anastāsiya Kharlamova, Brian Hare, Ádám Miklósi, Michael W. Fox, Jennifer Leonard, Elena Jazin, Elaine Ostrander, Kerstin-Lindblad-Toh, and Charles Kunert for their dedication to unraveling the mysteries of genetics and behavior; to Margaret "Cookie" Elizabeth Sims for her indispensable work in morphology; to Paula and Craig Watson, Patricia and Kelly Reed, Kent Weber, Tracy Brooks, Kathy Bennett, Jill Lute, Lois Tulleners, Beth Duman, Pat Tucker and Bruce Weide, Wendy Spencer, Jess Edberg, Sherrie and Charlie LaBat, Jeremy Heft, Pat Goodman, Gale Motter, Monty Sloan, Lori Schmidt, and Gail Whitford for the work they do on behalf of captive wolves and wolfdogs and for the many hours they spent with me; to Janice Koler-Matznick, Terry Jenkins, Elaine Gower, and many others for their powerful and moving stories; to L. David Mech, Timmothy Kaminski, Russ Morgan, Suzanne Fouty, Wally Sykes, and Carolyn Sime for their vital work to make a way for wild wolves. I thank Riley Woodford and other staff members of the Alaska Department of Fish and Game, Donna Gatewood at the USDA Center for Veterinary Biologics, D'Anna Jensen of the U.S. Department of Agriculture, and Ed Bangs of the U.S. Fish and Wildlife Service for taking time out of their hectic days to answer my questions. I deeply appreciate Dora Simpson for spending a full day in the Texas sun with me and for her honesty and care of the animals she produces. I thank

Crystal and Mike Atamian for their compassionate friendship and patience with my family and me as difficult guests. I thank Snezhana Rudakova for translating the Alexander Galich poem, Rick Hallwyler of Graphic Arts Center, Lisa Metzger, Scott Erickson, and Lonnie Kinser for assisting with photos. Thanks once more and love to my husband, Lonnie Kinser, whose art and wit kept me hopeful and laughing; to my stepdad, Ken St. Thomas, who provided the support that made many research trips possible; and to my aunt Alice, uncle Larry, and cousin Liz for buying the plane ticket that allowed me to go home. I'm deeply grateful to my mother, Kathryn St. Thomas, my first reader and editor, who endured draft after draft and sometimes five phone calls a day. Thanks also to Debra Gwartney, my mentor at Summer Fishtrap. Noted author Sallie Tisdale's kindness to this beginning writer provided an introduction to Kimberly Witherspoon who became my agent. She and William Callahan at Inkwell Management have been real champions of this book. Even now, I can scarcely believe my luck. Add to my champions the peerless Alexis Gargagliano, my editor at Scribner, whose warmth and encouragement, keen-eyed reading, and thoughtful notes have made this a better book. I simply couldn't finish without sending some hugs and ear rubs to all our companion dogs, especially those behind chain link at the animal shelters, who want to be our friends even when we may not deserve it. To Argos and Thelma: I hope I deserve it. And how could I forget wild wolves who go about their wolfy business largely unseen by most of us, and yet just by their presence make our world a little richer. Finally, thank you to Inyo who taught me so much about wildness in her short time on earth.

Notes

CHAPTER TWO: YEARNINGS

1. Pinkola Estes, Clarissa. "La Loba, The Wolf Woman," in *Women Who Run with the Wolves* (New York: Ballantine Books, 1992), 21–27.

CHAPTER THREE: VOODOO

1. The Mackenzie Valley wolf (*Canis lupus occidentalis*) is one of five recognized subspecies of gray wolf in North America. This subspecies, which inhabits western Canada and all of Alaska, numbers between thirty and forty thousand despite legal hunts in most of its range. The other four subspecies include the arctic wolf (*Canis lupus arctos*), Eastern timber wolf (*Canis lupus lycaon*), Great Plains wolf (*Canis lupus nubilus*), and the Mexican gray wolf (*Canis lupus baileyi*). The red wolf (*Canis rufus*) of the southeastern United States is considered a separate species because of its distinct genetic profile.
2. Located in the far north of Canada, above the Arctic Circle, remote Ellesmere Island is characterized by ice fields and low temperatures, and it's difficult to get there. The breeder who sold Kid to Leda may have invented his lineage to get more money for him, but at some point in the past the ancestors of *all* captive wolves alive today were stolen from the wild. Den thievery and subsequent captive breeding to produce gray wolves for the fur industry, for zoos, and for the pet trade occurred widely prior to passage of the Endangered Species Act and other wildlife protections.
3. According to researchers Todd K. Fuller, L. David Mech, and Jean Fitts Cochrane, the earliest known breeding age of wild wolves is two years. However, in captivity wolves have been known to breed as early as nine or ten months of age.
4. Some wolfdog enthusiasts cite dog breeds created by backcrossing dogs to

wolves as evidence of the wolfdog's legitimacy as a breed. While some of these claims have merit, others are unsupported. The German shepherd, a breed developed by Captain Max von Stephanitz, who selectively bred German sheepdogs (collie bloodlines were later introduced), was not created by breeding a wolf to a dog. Likewise, fans of the "American tundra/timber shepherd" claim that this dog was the result of crossing a German shepherd with a gray wolf for the U.S. Army Veterinary Corps Super Dog Project during the Vietnam War. Veterinarian Michael W. Fox refuted that claim: "I initiated the Super Dog Project as an unpaid consultant to the army during the Vietnam War when I was an assistant professor of Biology and Psychology at Washington University in St. Louis. . . . The army's Super Dog Project involved German shepherds only. Wolf hybrids were never used." The "American tundra/timber shepherd" remains unrecognized by any national kennel club.

5. Robert K. Wayne's studies show that mitochondrial DNA differs by not more than 0.2% in wolves and dogs, but those studies are limited in what they can tell us about dog origins. Wayne himself told me that nuclear gene information will provide a more complete ancestral picture. Bridgett vonHoldt, in the Department of Ecology and Evolutionary Biology at the University of California, Los Angeles, predicts that with the recent mapping of the dog genome, she and others will be able to take a closer look at genome locations and identify "candidate genes" responsible for the differences between dogs and wolves on a behavioral, phenotypic, and physiological level. The result, according to vonHoldt, will confirm that dogs and wolves are of two distinct species. Regarding species-defining formulas, she believes that applying a combination of formulas is more helpful than relying on just one.

6. Ádám Miklósi is head of the Department of Ethology at the Eötvös University in Budapest.

7. In her paper "The Origin of the Dog Revisited," Koler-Matznick argues that the dog probably descended from a generalist canid—a medium-size, compact animal with a short, dense coat, curly tail, short muzzle, and upright ears. When we met at her southern Oregon home, she told me, "When Don E. Wilson and DeeAnn M. Reeder came out with their unsupported revision of the nomenclature, that was a great boon to the wolfdog people, because then they could say the dog is nothing but a wolf anyway. Well, the difference [between wolf and dog] is about 40,000 years of selection."

8. There are plausible explanations for why the coyote and the wolf, though distinct species, produce fertile offspring. It's possible that not enough time has passed on the evolutionary clock to reproductively isolate the coyote from the wolf. In any case, when given their druthers and healthy populations of their own species, wolves and coyotes would rather not mate with

each other or with dogs. Some biologists contend that cross-matings have occurred primarily in areas where predator-control programs and habitat loss have radically depleted wolf populations, making potential mates scarce. There is, after all, no Internet dating service for wolves.

CHAPTER FOUR: VOODOO CHILD

1. There is no USDA-approved rabies vaccine for wolves or wolfdogs. In 1999, the USDA considered amending the Virus-Serum-Toxin Act to allow vaccines recommended for use in dogs to be recommended for use in wolves and wolfdogs. Proponents of the amendment, which included the National Wolfdog Alliance and the Wolf Dog Coalition, cited Title 9 of the USDA's Code of Federal Regulations as it pertained to the Animal Welfare Act. Title 9 designates crosses between dogs and wolves as domestic animals and defines *dog* to mean "any live or dead dog (*Canis familiaris*) or any dog-hybrid cross." Advocates for the proposed amendment reminded the USDA that because the dog had been reclassified by the Smithsonian Institute and the American Society of Mammalogists as *Canis lupus familiaris,* a subspecies of gray wolf, wolves and dogs were essentially the same species, and thus, the rabies vaccine should be approved for use in wolfdogs.

But according to Dr. Donna Gatewood, Section Leader of Virology at the USDA Center for Veterinary Biologics, they didn't succeed in convincing the USDA, which withdrew the proposed amendment in 2001 after opponents argued that it would have a negative effect on public health by eliminating the USDA's own requirement of a *direct virus challenge* to prove the vaccine's effectiveness—a test that every other species authorized to receive the vaccine has had to undergo. Vaccinated wolves and wolfdogs would be injected with the live rabies virus and observed for signs of infection or immunity. Eventually all the animals would be euthanized and their lymph nodes, brains, salivary glands, and kidneys carefully examined for signs of the virus.

Gatewood added that although the Center for Veterinary Biologics is not in the business of taxonomic classification, it views wolves as a distinct species from dogs. Yes, the two species are closely related, but their immune systems don't necessarily behave the same way, she said. "We know how long dogs shed the virus through their saliva, and we've been able to determine an appropriate quarantine period," she told me. "But no such data exists for wolves or wolfdogs."

On the other hand, to err on the side of caution, many zoos and wolf research facilities vaccinate wolves against rabies even though inoculating them is considered off-label use of the vaccine. Gale Motter of Indiana's Wolf Park, a research and education center, told me, "There's no reason to think that wolves would not be equally protected by the rabies vaccine. We and our vet feel it's better to protect the wolves." At the International Wolf Center in Minnesota, the wolves receive the vaccine annually rather than every three years—the routine schedule for dogs. According to curator Lori Schmidt, the wolves' titer levels indicate that the vaccine is present.

2. I wondered then why Cochise, with his established identity as a wolfdog and his history of biting, had been held for his owner instead of being immediately euthanized. At this writing, identification of an animal as a wolfdog remains at the owner's discretion in several states, counties, and municipalities. However, if an animal is involved in a biting incident and is suspected of being a wolfdog, the courts may bring in experts to determine the animal's identity.

CHAPTER EIGHT: ON THE TRAIL

1. Conservation groups offered a $5,000 reward for information leading to the arrest and conviction of the person who shot "the Ukiah wolf."

    Over the last decade several other wolves have migrated into Oregon with varying success:

    - A radio-collared female entered Oregon from Idaho after dispersing from her birth pack. Concerned that she wouldn't find a mate in Oregon, biologists returned her to Idaho. (1999)
    - Another radio-collared wolf was struck by a car and killed on I-84, south of Baker City. (2000)
    - A female wolf was shot dead in Union County. (2007)
    - Biologists tracked a radio-collared female (B-300F) in the Wallowa-Whitman National Forest near the Eagle Cap Wilderness. This female is still alive. (2008)
    - Biologists confirmed the presence of Oregon's first reproducing pack of wild wolves, dubbed "the Wenaha-Tucannon Wilderness pack." (2008)
    - Collared female (B-300) observed with a large, black male wolf and two pups. (2009)
    - Video shows B-300's pack of at least ten wolves living in the Imnaha Unit of eastern Oregon. This pack dubbed "the Imnaha pack." (2009)
    - Oregon Department of Fish and Wildlife authorized USDA APHIS Wildlife Services to kill two wolves involved in livestock kills in Keating Valley. (2009)
    - Yearling female born in Oregon disperses naturally to Washington State. (2010)
    - New wolf pack detected in the Walla Walla Unit east of Milton-

Freewater. This pack may use territory in both Oregon and Washington. (2011)

2. The wolf is listed as "threatened" rather than "endangered" in Minnesota where populations are thriving.
3. In the summer of 2010, poachers shot three Mexican gray wolves in Arizona and New Mexico.

CHAPTER NINE: LIMBOLAND

1. In fact, geneticists can determine the presence of wolf DNA in an animal by comparing it to a database of mitochondrial and nuclear DNA samples taken from several wolf populations.

   Wolfdog owners have expressed concern that mandatory DNA testing may accompany laws prohibiting wolfdog ownership. One owner posted this response to an online discussion list: "With genetic testing we won't be able to hide behind 'malamute mix' and 'husky mix' anymore. It's downright scary. It's going to give the antis more ammo against us and our animals."

   The DNA of mixed-breed dogs can also be analyzed and breed assignments made—with varying degrees of accuracy. As recently as 2007, private companies like Mars Veterinary and MMI Genomics have launched their own patented tests to detect the genetic signatures of breeds recognized by the American Kennel Club (AKC). (The list of AKC breeds available for comparison continues to expand.) Within a few weeks, owners of mixed-breed dogs receive a detailed account of the purebred ancestors in their dog's background, including breed characteristics.

CHAPTER TEN: WOLF WHISPERER

1. According to wolf-behavior specialist and educator and dog trainer Beth Duman, dark pigmentation on the roof of the mouth and along the gum line is one of many diagnostic features of a native wolf. By contrast she points to the piebald gums of an Alaskan malamute.

CHAPTER ELEVEN: IN YO FACE

1. But even though training techniques like the alpha roll have been largely discredited, here's the rub according to Duman: Now everywhere a dog owner looks she sees evidence that her dog is trying to take over her life and

challenge her position as leader in the relationship: "My dog shouldn't eat before I do because the alpha wolf always eats first." "I should go through the door before my dog does, otherwise he'll think he's dominant over me."

"Get real," Duman says. "It's okay to let your dog eat before you have your pizza."

2. These lines are from Pablo Neruda's poem "Your Laughter."

CHAPTER TWELVE: PINK SLIP

1. I met Ed Bangs while attending a public hearing in Pendleton, Oregon, regarding removal of the Rocky Mountain wolf population from the Endangered Species List.

2. The International Union for the Conservation of Nature, Wolf Specialist Group, of which L. David Mech is chair, published the following resolution statement on wolf hybrids, passed April 24, 1990:

> Wolf-dog hybrid regulation: WHEREAS hybridization between wolves and dogs and the keeping of these hybrids as pets is becoming increasingly common in various countries, and especially in the United States and Canada; WHEREAS most wolf-dog hybrids are poorly adapted to be pets, and there have been numerous fatal and non-fatal attacks on people and domestic animals which, in addition to being tragic and avoidable, detract from the public perception of wild wolves; and WHEREAS the perpetuation of these hybrids has no scientific or educational value; and WHEREAS the ease with which escaped or unwanted hybrids can interbreed with wild wolves threatens the genetic integrity of wild populations, now therefore be it resolved that the IUCN-SSC Wolf Specialist Group views the existence and expansion of wolf-dog hybrids as a threat to wolf conservation and recommends that governments and appropriate regulatory agencies prohibit or at least strictly regulate interbreeding between wolves and dogs and the keeping of these animals as pets.

3. I would learn later that animal-control officers have been given guidelines for identifying hybrids, although they sometimes misidentify mixed-breed dogs as wolfdogs. In the September/October 1991 issue of *National Animal Control Association News,* officers were advised that the best indicator of a wolf hybrid is the owner's own claim. Owners "are often proud of the fact that their animals are part wolf." Other than the owner's identification, the issue offers a series of physical characteristics to aid officers in identifying wolfdog hybrids:

> Generally, wolves and hybrids are longer—overall—than dogs. The head is large, but not boxy, with a long, slender face. The neck

and tail are long and supple. The back, loin, and especially legs, are long. Even the toes are long and bony looking. Wolves and high content hybrids have disproportionately large feet . . . conical-shaped ears, with more hair inside the ears than dogs. A German shepherd's ears are taller, flatter, and lack interior hair. Wolves' and hybrids' tails hang down, except to display dominance, and do not curl . . . Gums, lips, and eye rims are black . . .

The coat is usually a grizzled gray with cream underparts, frequently with cinnamon tinges at the back of the ears. Grizzling is created by bands of color on each guard hair; wolves tend to have 5 bands, dogs 2 or 3, giving dogs a more even color. Colors range from pure white to black. There are no spotted wolves, and spotted hybrids are rare. In wolves, the gradation from gray to cream on face and legs is very subtle, but in hybrids it can be more distinct as in malamutes and huskies, and some hybrids will even have a mask. Wolves and wolflike hybrids have a heavy ruff of fur around the neck and over the shoulders, which extends to the sides of the head, framing the face with prominent tufts . . .

But animal-control officers make mistakes, and there are dog breeds with well-furred ears and tails that hang to their hocks. In fact, according to the Kennel Club (United Kingdom), the Fédération Cynologique Internationale (FCI), and the American Kennel Club, dog tails can be described as plumed, proud, curled, cropped, feathered or fringed, gay, straight, kinked or twisted, hairless, hooked, sickled (arching) or scimitar, otter (down and flat), whipped, ringed, cranked, screwed, or snapped. Sounds like a night in Amsterdam. Frankly, identifying a hybrid is tricky business. Proper identification requires taking into account a whole host of behavioral as well as physical characteristics.

CHAPTER THIRTEEN:
THE WOLF AND THE HOUSEDOG

1. The researchers acknowledge that crossbreeding with East Asian wolf populations likely occurred later, which would account for the genomic similarities between dogs and East Asian wolves. Bridgett vonHoldt and her team published the results of their study in the journal *Nature*.

2. Even the ancient Greeks believed that some dog breeds, those they considered superior, contained a little wild blood. In his *Historia Animalium* Aristotle wrote that the Laconian hound was a fox-dog cross, and the Indian dog was a tiger-bitch cross. But Aristotle had a wry sense of humor and suggested that when the bitch was tied to a tree awaiting her tiger suitor, "If the tiger be in an amorous mood he will pair with her; if not he will eat

her up . . . " (Taken from Steven Lonsdale's fascinating study, "Attitudes Towards Animals in Ancient Greece," *Greece & Rome,* Cambridge University Press.)

Notions of our dogs' wild parentage have persisted long after the Greeks, including stories about Native American peoples in Alaska and Canada tying their bitches out to be mated by wolves in order to produce sled dogs with "hybrid vigor" (possessing strengths of both parents and few to none of the weaknesses). Although mating happens occasionally, a wolf would sooner kill a dog than mate with it.

Geneticist Jennifer Leonard's work indicates that contrary to popular belief, Native Americans did not domesticate North American wolves and turn them into dogs. In fact, Leonard asserts that dogs were already domesticated and crossed the Bering Strait with migrating humans.

3. Fear, particularly of people, keeps a wild animal hyperalert to any changes in its environment that may be a threat. The animal that avoids danger stays alive to reproduce. If captive wolf pups aren't consistently exposed to positive interactions with people, their tendency to recoil from humans often increases as they mature. Only constant exposure to people works against their genetic wildness. Even then, fear may govern their reactions. In 1967, behavioral geneticists Jerome Woolpy and Benson Ginsburg, of the Behavior Genetics Laboratory at the University of Chicago, published their paper "Wolf Socialization: A Study of Temperament in a Wild Social Species." They wanted to understand how captive-raised wolves move from a state of fear in the presence of humans to a state of friendliness.

They observed and described four stages in the reactions of captive-born wolves during socialization: *Escape,* the earliest stage in which the wolf tries to escape its pen when the researcher enters, may be accompanied by shaking, urinating, and other physiological signs of distress; *avoidance,* in which the wolf no longer tries to flee and exhibits fewer signs of obvious stress but continues to keep as much physical distance between itself and the human researcher as its pen allows; *approach-oral investigative,* in which the wolf may approach the researcher and tug on his clothing. (Woolpy and Ginsburg wanted the wolf to come close enough to be touched, but not allow its teeth to do unintentional harm. However, they discovered that if the person retreated from contact or pushed the wolf away, the animal sometimes became fearful or aggressive.)

In the final stage of socialization, *approach-friendly greeting,* the wolf shows eagerness when a familiar person approaches the run, wagging its tail and standing on its hind legs with front paws on the gate in anticipation of contact. "This is also the stage at which the wolf will attempt to hold the experimenter with his paws and to greet him by placing his jaws around the chin and lower face in much the same way that he would place his mouth around the muzzle of another wolf in a wolf–wolf greeting ceremony."

Woolpy and Ginsburg noted that if, during any of the four stages, the researchers attempted to dominate the wolf, particularly physically, as one might do in asserting an "alpha" position, the animal might attack or regress to the avoidance or escape stages of the socialization process.

4. Domestication, according to zoologist E. O. Price (1984), is "that process by which a population of animals becomes adapted to man and to the captive environment by genetic changes occurring over generations, and *environmentally induced developmental events reoccurring during each generation.*" (Italics mine).

5. For more knowledge about the heritability of behavior and about behavioral differences between offspring and parent generations, Lyudmila Trut and her colleagues crossbred "extreme representatives" from genetically tame and genetically aggressive fox populations. Progeny of the tame-aggressive crosses exhibited tameness and aggression ranging between their parents' extremes, but in no way representing the average—results that disprove the belief in a happy medium. After that first generation, when researchers backcrossed those progeny to genetically tame foxes, the resulting offspring were even more diverse and unpredictable in their behavior. In fact, Trut and her team described the foxes' behavior as "fragmented."

6. Farmed foxes are sometimes referred to as "silver" foxes. However, the silver coloration is merely a color variant of the red fox *Vulpes vulpes*. I also met rats and minks who'd undergone the same selection process with a similar loss of pigmentation. Belyaev had wanted to demonstrate that genetic tameness, with all its attendant changes, was not limited to foxes but would also occur in other taxonomic groups.

7. Trut told me about one fox who'd been sterilized and placed in a home in Moscow. He hadn't stuck around. He'd found himself a wild fox girlfriend whom he occasionally brought around for dinner—but stayed only long enough to eat a bit of meat and then left again, less like a pet than a roommate. While many of the genetically tame foxes exhibited the effects of long-term institutionalization, identifying their cages as the only safe place because it was all they'd ever known, others tried to push past me when I opened their cage doors, as eager as the Moscow fox to see a bit of the world.

8. Some wolfdogs living in sanctuaries around the country are the offspring of zoo animals sold to the public, some by Folsom City Zoo Sanctuary in California, which was originally founded as a breeding zoo in 1963. Folsom had been one of many zoos that supplied wolf stock to private breeders, but in the 1980s Folsom became a sanctuary and now exists solely as a refuge, the management having taken a stand against breeding, selling, and trading animals (still a common practice in many conventional zoos).

NOTES

CHAPTER FOURTEEN: HAPPY HORMONES

1. I asked Miklósi why the team terminated the experiment when the wolves reached two years old. He told me that they ran out of money and couldn't afford to build the kind of secure facility needed to work safely with adult wolves. Mature wolves have very different needs and drives than wolf puppies, and the team didn't want to put working students at risk. The wolves went to what Miklósi referred to as a "wolf farm," where they work for their living participating in films. The dogs in the experiment went home with some of the students they'd bonded with.

2. When Goodman made a pointing gesture, rather than following the invisible line from her fingertip to the site as a dog would, the wolf remained focused on her fingers because that's where the food came from. Goodman had to position her hand over the physical site where she wanted the wolf to go. The wolf, for its part, moved toward the hand to obtain the food. Its behavior was consistent with the behavior of the wolves in the rope-tugging experiment, with its focus on the food rather than on human signals. However, it should be noted that a team of researchers led by Monique A. R. Udell from the University of Florida disputes the idea that domestication is a requirement for canids to follow human social cues. They fault the earlier studies, arguing the results were skewed due to unequal testing conditions. Domestic dogs were tested indoors, whereas wolves in the experiments were tested outside. After conducting tests with wolves at Wolf Park and comparing them to domestic dogs, Udell and her team decided that the wolves in the study followed human social cues better than dogs. The dispute continues.

CHAPTER FIFTEEN: CRAPSHOOT

1. Though genes actually appear as clusters, I find it helpful to think of them as strings of lights. Some stay lit from birth onward, while others remain dark for the duration of an animal's life. Others, lit at first, blink off at maturity, while others suddenly blink on, and those awakened genes express by releasing high levels of particular hormones into the hypothalamus, that ancient brain structure regulating an animal's behavior and emotional state. This flood of hormones may in turn produce startling and unexpected behavioral changes in the animal.

   According to geneticist Charles Kunert of Concordia University, "The key to understanding genes and their activity is to understand that genes are differentially regulated in time, tissue, and sex. Not only are genes turned off in the adolescent while others are turned on, they are turned off and on in different tissues (cells) at different times. Genes also express differently in males and females. Sex hormones regulate the expression of specific genes. For example, testosterone enters cells of the body from the blood stream, binds to testosterone receptor proteins in the cytoplasm of specific cells, and the bound hormone/receptor complex moves into the nucleus where it binds to regions near genes and either turns them on or off."

2. We're now beginning to understand that some changes in gene expression are programmed into the DNA, while others are triggered by the environment. Some expression changes may even skip a generation. (Epigenetics is a whole field devoted to the study of gene expression changes caused by environmental factors and passed to successive generations.)

3. Krushinsky's observations are still valid, but scientists today understand that genes themselves don't dictate an animal's behavior. Instead, gene-expression patterns control hormone levels in the brain that in turn influence behavior.

4. Veterinarian Michael W. Fox would call this a recipe for disaster. Between 1967 and 1974, while a professor at Washington University in St. Louis, Fox investigated the behavior and development of wolfdog crosses that had been hand-raised and identically socialized as puppies. While Fox admitted to me that there are "magnificent and temperamentally stable hybrids alive today," his observations of social aggression (as distinct from prey drive) and excessive shyness in the many wolfdogs he worked with make him worry that people are producing some emotionally unstable and potentially dangerous animals.

CHAPTER NINETEEN:
BEAUTIFUL DAY FOR A NEIGHBOR

1. In September 2010, Defenders of Wildlife ended its twenty-three-year compensation program, allowing state-run compensation programs to take over. In Oregon, Colorado, and Utah, and on Apache tribal lands in Arizona, where compensation programs do not yet exist, Defenders will continue to pay compensation until September 2011.

2. While attending the 20th Annual North American Wolf Conference in Montana, I spoke with Wally Sykes, a former wolfdog breeder, who told me he'd received a call from a woman frantic that her wolfdog would be confiscated or shot because it had killed her neighbors' goat. The neighbors had watched while the hybrid crushed their goat's windpipe and dragged the carcass down the road. Sykes didn't know the fate of the wolfdog, but it was likely that the woman's neighbors focused on the "wolf" part of "wolfdog," concluding from the hybrid's behavior that *wolves* must be savage killers.

NOTES

CHAPTER TWENTY-TWO:
THE THINGS WE DO FOR LOVE

1. As recent news stories make clear, wolves and wolfdogs aren't the only animals to experience captivity stress and temperament changes when they reach sexual maturity. According to April Truitt, the executive director of the Primate Rescue Center in Nicholasville, Kentucky, once primates reach maturity, their behavior can become unpredictable. "An adult chimp has seven times the strength of a man . . . but even a twenty-four-pound monkey has the reflexes and agility to take down a man," Truitt remarked. "These animals have to be removed at birth from the mother, put in diapers, put on a bottle, and sold before they start depreciating—which they do, quicker than a Cadillac . . . By the age of three, maybe five or seven, they reach adolescence and their hormones are telling them to do anything but take commands from humans. They are interested in dominating whatever social group they find themselves in. If it's a human home, they often go after children first, then teenagers, then mom, and by the time they get to dad, we usually get the call."

2. According to the Centers for Disease Control, between 1979 (the first year for which records were kept) and 1998, a nineteen-year period, *captive* wolves and wolfdogs were responsible for 43 severe attacks upon humans (38 by wolfdogs, 5 by captive wolves) and 14 killings of humans (13 by wolfdogs, 1 by a captive wolf). However, such figures are problematic. The CDC's records of dog attacks are incomplete and based largely on media accounts that may misidentify breeds or distort or omit other facts in a case.

    Wolfdog owners get very angry when wolfdogs are singled out and called such things as "ticking time bombs," "loaded guns," and "genetic monsters." They argue that pit bull terriers are more likely to bite a person than wolfdogs are. They're correct in the sense that there are more pit bulls in private ownership in the United States than there are wolves and wolfdogs. (In total, 4.8 million pit bull terriers are registered with the American Kennel Club, the United Kennel Club, and the American Dog Breeders Association.)

    However, Pat Tucker and Bruce Weide, codirectors of Montana's Wild Sentry, point out that "the estimated 300,000 hybrids and captive wolves in the USA killed 13 people between 1986 and 1996 (about 1.3 deaths/year/300,000 hybrids) and injured many more. In contrast, the 50 million dogs in the USA kill an average of 11 people per year (about 0.07 deaths/year/300,000 dogs). According to these statistics captive wolves and hybrids are 19 times more likely to fatally maul a human than a dog is." Of course it's hardly fair to lump dachshunds and Pomeranians in with pit bulls and German shepherds when compiling statistics on fatal maulings.

In the first comprehensive report of attacks by wild wolves in North America, Asia, and Europe published in 2002, John Linnell and an international team of researchers estimate there are 60,000 wild wolves in North America, and yet, between 1950 and 2000, only 11 attacks upon humans and *no kills* by wild wolves had been documented.

In 2005, twenty-two-year-old geological engineering student Kenton Joel Carnegie was killed at Points North Landing, a remote mining camp in Saskatchewan, Canada. The debate continues over whether a pack of wolves or an American black bear was responsible. In 2007 after hearing expert testimony, a six-person jury ruled that Carnegie had been killed by a pack of four wolves habituated to humans as a result of an illegal garbage dump located at the mining camp.

Whether or not wolves were responsible for Carnegie's death, they are officially blamed for it, making it the first documented case of a fatality caused by a wild wolf in North America.

Several points emerge from this data:

1. There are more wolves and wolfdogs in captivity in the United States than there are wild wolves in all of North America.
2. Wild wolves *not habituated to humans or their garbage* have a natural shyness of people and do not suffer the confinement stress that many captive wolves and wolfdogs do, which may help to explain the low number of negative *wild* wolf–human encounters in North America compared to the relatively high number of negative *captive* wolf and wolfdog–human encounters.
3. The incident at the garbage dump runs counter to the popular theory that the dog's ancestor was a wolf who had less fear of people and lived on village trash, eventually evolving into the friendly village dog. Wolves' dependency on human garbage is a recipe for territoriality and aggression, not friendliness.

The second documented case of a fatality caused by a wild wolf in North America occurred in 2010. Candice Berner, a thirty-two-year-old special education teacher, was killed by wolves while jogging outside a rural Alaskan village.

3. Sandra Piovesan, a wolfdog owner who lived thirty miles east of Pittsburgh, hadn't understood the consequences of her animals' severe confinement stress, and she ended up dead. Her daughter found her mauled body. Piovesan's femoral artery had been severed and she'd bled to death.

In the 1960s wildlife photographer Lois Crisler also experienced the consequences of captivity stress when she and her husband transported five pure wolves from the tundra of Alaska to their mountain property in Colorado where they began breeding wolfdogs. Like Piovesan, they kept some of the puppies and gave others away to locals, many of whom dumped the puppies when frustrated by their destructive behaviors. Kuskokwim and Katmai, two of the animals Crisler kept, became aggressive toward her when they reached maturity, circling behind her and backing her into corners. In her book *Captive Wild,* Crisler wondered if confinement stress played a part in the wolfdogs' aggression: "Perhaps our pens, big and varied as they were, had a psychological carrying capacity as well as a physical one." Crisler described ending the lives of all the wolves and wolfdogs in her charge by using sleeping pills followed by a "coup de grâce . . . a bullet to the center of the furry foreheads."

CHAPTER TWENTY-THREE:
EVERYTHING WE'VE WORKED FOR

1. Although Nancy's sire was not likely a pure wolf, I wanted to know which agency was charged with regulating the breeding and selling or exhibiting of gray wolves. I called the U.S. Fish and Wildlife Service (FWS) Division of Information Resources and Technology Management in Arlington, Virginia, and a federal agent redirected me to the United States Department of Agriculture (USDA). After I'd made seven calls and talked to twelve different people, a clerk in Fort Collins, Colorado, had the answer: Wild animal dealers (businesses or individuals who breed and exhibit or sell animals from mink and armadillo to fox and wolf) must be licensed by the USDA's Animal and Plant Health Inspection Service (APHIS).

   As long as a person acquires a USDA-APHIS-AC (Animal Care) license, he can breed, exhibit, sell, and ship wolves to the moon, with one small caveat: gray wolves must be *captive-bred,* not wild-caught gray wolves belonging to a population under the protection of the Endangered Species Act.

2. The United States American Wolfdog Association outlines the basic criteria for a responsible breeder:

   - Produces a litter only if those offspring will "improve, or at the very least, compliment the breed"
   - Is knowledgeable about the background of his own particular lines
   - Provides the potential buyer with honest information about the positives and negatives of wolfdogs
   - Will refuse a sale if the potential buyer is not suited to wolfdog ownership
   - Keeps her animals in clean and well-maintained enclosures
   - Maintains health records on the parents and is able to show the purchaser of a puppy that the parents have an Orthopedic Foundation for Animals (OFA) certificate, rating an animal's propensity toward hip dysplasia

- May require a home visit
- Requires the buyer to sign a strict contract

3. Dora prefers to identify her animals as being "of wolf heritage" and has created her own breed name for them: "northern timber dogs." She reasons that this name more accurately represents her animals because although they look like pure wolves, up to this point she's bred only wolfdog to wolfdog.

4. Dora spays or neuters any animal that comes into season before age two and/or has more than one heat cycle per year, because she believes that wolfdogs that have retained the reproductive cycle of a wild wolf (coming into season only once each year) will throw more wolfy-looking puppies.

5. A common practice when socializing captive pure-wolf puppies is to place them with an adult wolf other than the mother, an animal that feels comfortable with people, so the puppies have the best possible chance of developing into adults that will tolerate human handling during routine veterinary exams and medical emergencies.

6. Dora refers to her culling method as the "American version," which means that instead of euthanizing animals unsuitable for breeding (as in the fox experiments) she spays or neuters those that don't pass the temperament and appearance tests, as well as the preliminary OFA test. In the past she spayed or neutered a litter of puppies that she describes as suffering from "asshole-itis." "They weren't mean," she says. "They just had no interest in pleasing people."

7. Later I discovered that breeders often trade animals, borrow one another's animals for breed-stock, and occasionally make use of a proxy buyer when a breeder refuses to sell an animal to a particular individual. Sometimes the breeder finds out about the trickery, other times not. One thing is clear: Once an animal leaves the breeder's hands, there is no guarantee where the animal will end up, regardless of signed contracts.

8. Wolf-behavior specialist and educator and dog trainer Beth Duman was instrumental in passing legislation against wolfdog breeding in Michigan following several wolfdog attacks on children. She volunteered to help distinguish between wolfdogs and mixed-breed dogs for animal-control personnel, visiting one backyard after another with their "jigsaw puzzles of animal cages." As a consequence, she received death threats from wolfdog owners and breeders who felt their personal rights were being violated.

9. Nobody bosses wolfdog breeders no matter where they live—not even other breeders. When I asked Dora Simpson about breed standards for wolfdogs, she told me that she, along with a few other breeders and owners, had made an attempt to develop a list of wolfdog breed standards, but the group could not overcome personality clashes and differences of opinion about acceptable wolfdog temperament and appearance. Neither could they agree on the appropriate size of a wolfdog's enclosure. The group gave up their effort at a standard, and now, as Dora put it, "People just do their own thing."

10. In a later conversation, Heather would tell me that Loop had become more aggressive, and Leda had stopped taking her out of the pen. "It was really just awful," Heather would say. "I tried to take Voodoo out when I could, but Loop was so aggressive I couldn't do anything with her. Leda never walked them or let them out of that cage. It was totally inhumane." It seems that even for Leda wolfdogs had become too much.

CHAPTER TWENTY-FOUR:
PRISONERS OF LOVE

1. At the request of the owners, I've changed their names and the name of their sanctuary.
2. To their presentation, Tim and Heidi had brought an "ambassador wolf," an animal able to interact sociably with strangers, tolerate travel to new places, and present no threat to children, the primary audience for the evening's presentation. An ambassador wolf is supposed to help dispel the myth of the "big, bad wolf" and encourage respect for wild wolves and their right to occupy their historic ranges without persecution. But the main point Tim and Heidi drove home was that wolves belonged in the wild and wolfdogs didn't make good pets.
3. According to D'Anna Jensen of the U.S. Department of Agriculture, Animal Welfare Information Center, it's difficult to determine the exact number: "These sorts of stats are very hard to come by because no one keeps these records," she said. "Wolfdogs are not well regulated."
4. The Humane Society does not accept wolfdogs. The policy of many animal adoption agencies changed radically in 1991 when "Chief," a five-year-old neutered wolf-husky mix, was featured as "Pet of the Week—Gentle Giant—Well-behaved" in an adoption ad posted by the Panhandle Animal Welfare Society (PAWS) in Florida. Chief had been passed from one owner to another, living on a chain at Eglin Air Force Base and then with a couple and their two small children who surrendered him to PAWS when they moved. The day that Chief was adopted for the last time, he jumped a fence and tore the throat out of a four-year-old boy. He was shot by a sheriff's deputy and PAWS paid $425,000 to the boy's family.

   "The HSUS Adoption Policy Regarding Hybrid Animals" reads: "The HSUS believes that wolf hybrids and other hybrids of wild and domestic canids should not be placed for adoption by shelters due to their special physical, emotional, and veterinary requirements and their frequently unpredictable and unstable nature. We recommend that such animals be euthanized or placed with appropriate wildlife sanctuaries."

NOTES

CHAPTER TWENTY-SIX: CHAIN LINK

1. A highly motivated wolf or wolfdog can escape from just about any enclosure. During a visit to the Wolf Education & Research Center in Winchester, Idaho, home to a captive-born assembly of wolves known as the Sawtooth Pack, resident biologist Jeremy Heft told me about Chemukh ("Black" in Nez Perce), a low-status wolf that other wolves had attacked and wounded several times. One day, desperately hungry, she filched a few scraps ignored by the other wolves and when the pack went after her again, she found a way, against all odds, to escape. The twenty-acre enclosure, mostly double-fenced, had a weakness, a single-fenced thirty-foot section where staff entered with food for the animals. As an added safeguard, this section had been electrified and reinforced with a lean-in of taut wires. But Chemukh didn't let anything stop her, even when one of the caretakers tried to pull her off the fence. She clung to wires pulsing with 5,000 volts of electricity and clambered to the top of the thirteen-foot fence where she squeezed her body between the wires. With no second barrier to stop her, she took off and never came back.

   "It was sheer will." Heft shook his head as he told me the story. To see how she could possibly have gotten through, he'd applied all his strength to pry apart the wires, but managed to create only a three-inch gap. As a captive-bred, human-socialized wolf, Chemukh didn't know how to hunt large game and would not likely have survived.
2. In the spring of 2011 biologists are planning a capture-and-collar effort to fit at least one Walla Walla pack member with a GPS collar.
3. To read the Oregon Wolf Conservation and Management Plan go to http://www.dfw.state.or.us/Wolves/management_plan.asp.
4. For updates on wolves in Oregon, visit the Oregon Department of Fish and Wildlife website: http://www.dfw.state.or.us/wolves/.

Bibliography

"A Case History of Wolf-Human Encounters in Alaska and Canada." *Alaska Department of Fish and Game Wildlife Technical Bulletin.* Retrieved on February 4, 2009. http://www.wildlife.alaska.gov/pubs/techpubs/research_pdfs/techb13p1.pdf.

Adams, J. R., J. A. Leonard, and L. P. Waits. "Widespread Occurrence of a Domestic Dog Mitochondrial DNA Haplotype in Southeastern U.S. Coyotes." *Molecular Ecology* 12 (2003): 541–546.

American Veterinary Medical Association. "Position on Canine Hybrids." *Directory and Resource Manual* (2002): 88–89.

————."Private Ownership of Wild Animals." AVMA policy, November 2006. http://www.avma.org/issues/policy/wild_animal_ownership.asp (accessed December 6, 2007).

American Veterinary Society of Animal Behavior (AVSAB). "Myths about Dominance and Wolf Behavior as It Relates to Dogs." November 11, 2008. http://www.avsabonline.org/avsabonline/images/stories/Position_Statements/dominance%20statement.pdf (accessed June 21, 2009).

————. "Position Statement on the Use of Dominance Theory in Behavior Modification of Animals." November 11, 2008. http://www.avsabonline.org/avsabonline/images/stories/Position_Statements/dominance%20statement.pdf (accessed June 21, 2009).

Animal and Plant Health Inspection Service, United States Department of Agriculture. "Animal Welfare Act and Animal Welfare Regulations." http://www.aphis.usda.gov/animal_welfare/awa_info.shtml (accessed November 2005).

Ardelean, Captain Jeff. Division of Law Enforcement. "Mock Case." E-mail to the author. June 12, 2009.

Associated Press. "Indiana Judge Appoints Attorney for Canine." *New York Times,* May 21, 2004. http://lists.envirolink.org/pipermail/ar-news/Week-of-Mon-20040517/025219.html (accessed May 24, 2004).

BIBLIOGRAPHY

Ayad, Moustafa. "Woman's Body Found in Pen of 9 Hybrid Wolves." *Pittsburgh Post-Gazette,* July 18, 2006.

Bangs, Ed. Interview by Ceiridwen Terrill. March 7, 2007.

Bannasch, D. L., et al. "Recent Advances in Small Animal Genetics." *Veterinary Clinics of North America: Small Animal Practice* 36, no. 3 (2006): 461–474.

Belyaev, D. K. "Destabilizing selection as a factor in domestication." *Journal of Heredity* 70 (1978): 301–308.

———. "Domestication of Animals." *Science Journal* 5 (1969): 47–52.

Belyaev, D. K., et al. "Domestication in the Silver Fox (*Vulpes fulvus*): Changes in Physiological Boundaries of the Sensitive Period of Primary Socialization." *Applied Animal Behavior Science* 13 (1985): 359–370.

Bender, Skie. Wolf Haven International. "Captive Breeding." E-mail to the author. February 12, 2009.

———. "Rabies Vaccinations." E-mail to the author. January 26, 2009.

Bennett, Kathy. Interview by Ceiridwen Terrill. August 7, 2008.

Bernstein, I. S. "Dominance: The Baby and the Bathwater." *Journal of Behavioral and Brain Sciences* 4 (1981): 419–457.

Björnerfeldt, S., M. T. Webster, and C. Vilà. "Relaxation of Selective Constraint on Dog Mitochondrial DNA Following Domestication." *Genome Research* 16 (2006): 990–994.

Blumenauer, Rep. Earl [D-OR3]. Natural Resources Committee. "H.R. 80: Captive Primate Safety Act." January 6, 2009. http://www.govtrack.us/congress/billtext.xpd?bill=h111–80 (accessed February 27, 2009).

Boissy, Alain. "Fear and Fearfulness in Determining Behavior." In *Genetics and the Behavior of Domestic Animals*, edited by Temple Grandin (San Diego: Academic Press, 1998), 67–112.

Boitani, Luigi, Francesco Francisci, Paolo Ciucci, and Giorgio Andreoli. "Population Biology and Ecology of Feral Dogs in Central Italy." In *The Domestic Dog: Its Evolution, Behaviour, and Interactions with People*, edited by J. Serpell (Cambridge: Cambridge University Press, 1995), 217–244.

Brisbin, I. L. Jr. "The Domestication of the Dog." *Purebred Dogs: American Kennel Club Gazette* 93 (1976): 22–29.

Bromen, Nicholas. Wolf Haven International, Tenino, WA. "Howling Differentiation between North American Gray Wolves." April 10, 2008. North American Wolf Conference, Chico Hot Springs, Montana, April 7–10, 2008.

Buffetaut, Eric. "Mad Dogs and Frenchmen." *Cryptozoology* 7 (1988): 120–121.

Busch, Robert. *The Wolf Almanac, New and Revised: A Celebration of Wolves and Their World* (Guilford, Connecticut: Lyons Press, 2007).

———. *Wolf Songs* (San Francisco: Sierra Club Books, 1994).

BIBLIOGRAPHY

Carney, Patrick. Lois Bates Acheson Veterinary Teaching Hospital. Oregon State University College of Veterinary Medicine. Telephone interview by Ceiridwen Terrill. March 10, 2009.

Chenoweth, Peter J., and Antonio J. Landaeta-Hernández. "Maternal and Reproductive Behavior of Livestock." In *Genetics and the Behavior of Domestic Animals*, edited by Temple Grandin (San Diego: Academic Press, 1998), 145–166.

Clark, Kate M. "Neolithic Dogs: A Reappraisal Based on Evidence from the Remains of a Large Canid Deposited in a Ritual Feature." *International Journal of Osteoarchaeology* 6 (1996): 211–219.

Clarke, C. H. D. "The Beast of Gévaudan." *Natural History* 80, no. 4 (1971): 44–51, 66–73.

Clutton-Brock, J. "Origins of the Dog: Domestication and Early History." In *The Domestic Dog: Its Evolution, Behaviour and Interactions with People*, edited by J. Serpell (Cambridge: Cambridge University Press, 1995), 7–20.

———. "Man-made Dogs." *Science* 197 (1977): 1340–1342.

Cockle, Richard. "Wolves Roam, Trouble Follows." *The Oregonian*, September 22, 2009, B6.

Cohn, J. "How Wild Wolves Became Domestic Dogs." *BioScience* 47 (1997): 725–728.

Coppinger, Ray, and Lorna Coppinger. *Dogs: A New Understanding of Canine Origin, Behavior, and Evolution* (Chicago: University of Chicago Press, 2001).

———. "Differences in the Behavior of Dog Breeds." In *Genetics and the Behavior of Domestic Animals*, edited by Temple Grandin (San Diego: Academic Press, 1998), 167–202.

Cranston, Sue. Indigo Mountain Nature Center. "Wolfdogs." E-mail to the author. January 14, 2009.

———. Telephone interview by Ceiridwen Terrill. January 13, 2009.

———. Telephone interview by Ceiridwen Terrill. January 2, 2009.

Crisler, Lois. *Captive Wild* (New York: Lyons Press, 2000. First published in 1968 by Harper & Row, Publishers).

Davis, Simon J. M., and François R. Valla. "Evidence for the Domestication of the Dog 12,000 Years Ago in the Natufian of Israel." *Nature* 276 (1978): 608–610.

Delise, Karen. *Fatal Dog Attacks: The Stories Behind the Statistics* (Manorville, New York: Anubis Press, 2002).

Dobney, K., and G. Larson. "Genetics and Animal Domestication: New Windows on an Elusive Process." *Journal of Zoology* 269 (2006): 261–271.

"Domestic Wolf Responsible for Eastern Montana Livestock Killings." Montana Fish, Wildlife and Parks. February 28, 2007.

BIBLIOGRAPHY

Drews, C. "The Concept and Definition of Dominance Behavior." *Behaviour* 125 (1993): 284–313.

Duman, Beth. *Differentiating Great Lakes Area Native Wild Wolves from Dogs and Wolf-Dog Hybrids* (Michigan: Earth Voices, LLC, 2001).

———. Telephone interview by Ceiridwen Terrill. May 20, 2009.

———. "Wolfdog Question." E-mail to the author. April 19, 2009.

Ebsen, Bob. Wildlife Science Center. Interview by Ceiridwen Terrill. October 22, 2007.

Edberg, Jess. Information Services Director. International Wolf Center, Ely, Minnesota. "IWC Wolves." E-mail to the author. January 21, 2009.

———. "Rabies Vaccinations." E-mail to the author. January 26, 2009.

Electronic Code of Federal Regulations. Title 9 "Animals and Animal Products." http://ecfr.gpoaccess.gov/cgi/t/text/text-idx?c=ecfr&tpl=%2Findex.tpl (accessed April 24, 2009).

Feddersen-Petersen, Dorit U. "Social Behaviour of Dogs and Related Canids." In *Behavioural Biology of Dogs,* edited by P. Jensen (Wallingford, UK: CABI, 2007), 105–119.

Federoff, Nicholas E. "Antibody Response to Rabies Vaccination in Captive and Free-Ranging Wolves (*Canis Lupus*)." *Journal of Zoo and Wildlife Medicine* 32, no. 1 (2001): 127–129.

Fentress, John C. "Observations on the Behavioral Development of a Hand-reared Male Timber Wolf." *American Zoologist* 7 (1967): 339–351.

Fox, Michael W. *Behaviour of Wolves, Dogs and Related Canids* (New York: Harper & Row, Publishers, 1972).

———. *The Dog: Its Domestication and Behavior* (New York: Garland STPM Press, 1978).

———. "Inbreeding." E-mail to the author. June 11, 2009.

———. *Integrative Development of Brain and Behavior in the Dog* (Chicago: University of Chicago Press, 1971).

———. "Individual Differences in Wolf Litters." E-mail to the author. June 2, 2008.

———. "Superdog Project." E-mail to the author. May 25, 2009.

———. "Socio-Ecological Implications of Individual Differences in Wolf Litters: A Developmental and Evolutionary Perspective." *Behaviour* 41 (1972): 298–313.

———. *Understanding Your Dog: Everything You Want to Know About Your Dog but Haven't Been Able to Ask Him*. Revised edition (New York: St. Martin's Griffin, 1992).

———. "Unstable Hybrids." E-mail to the author. June 1, 2009.

———. *The Wild Canids: Their Systematics, Behavioral Ecology and Evolution* (New York: Litton Educational Publishing, Inc., 1975).

———. "Wolfdogs." E-mail to the author. May 11, 2008.

———. "Wolf Dog Hybrids." http://tedeboy.tripod.com/drmichaelwfox/id28 .html (accessed September 29, 2007).

Fox, Michael W., and R. V. Andrews. "Physiological and Biochemical Correlates of Individual Differences in Behavior of Wolf Cubs." *Behaviour* 46 (1973): 129–140.

Frank, Harry, ed. *Man and Wolf: Advances, Issues, and Problems in Captive Wolf Research* (Dordrecht, The Netherlands: Dr. W. Junk Publishers, 1987).

Frank, Harry, and Martha Frank. "Inhibition Training in Wolves and Dogs." *Behavioural Processes* 8 (1983): 363–377.

———. "On the Effects of Domestication on Canine Social Development and Behavior." *Applied Animal Ethology* 8 (1982): 507–525.

———. "Comparison of Problem Solving Performance in Six-Week-Old Wolves and Dogs." *Animal Behaviour* 30 (1982): 95–98.

Frank, Harry, et al. "Motivation and Insight in Wolf (*Canis lupus*) and Alaskan Malamute (*Canis familiaris*): Visual Discrimination and Learning." *Bulletin of the Psychonomic Society* 27, no. 5 (1989): 455–458.

Frisbee, Tyler. Office of Democratic Representative Earl Blumenauer. Washington, D.C. Telephone Interview by Ceiridwen Terrill. March 6, 2009.

Fuller, Todd K., L. David Mech, and Jean Fitts Cochrane. "Wolf Population Dynamics." In *Wolves: Behavior, Ecology, and Conservation*, edited by L. David Mech and Luigi Boitani (Chicago: University of Chicago Press, 2003), 161–191.

Gácsi, Márta, et al. "Are Readers of Our Face Readers of Our Minds? Dogs (*Canis familiaris*) Show Situation-dependent Recognition of Human's Attention." *Animal Cognition* 7 (2004): 144–153.

———. "Species-Specific Differences and Similarities in Behavior of Hand-Raised Dog and Wolf Pups in Social Situations with Humans." *Developmental Psychobiology* 47 (2005): 111–122.

Galich, Aleksandr, and Vasiliĭ Betaki. *Stikhotvorenii'a` I poėmy* (Sankt-Peterburg: Akademicheskiĭ proėkt, 2006), 103.

Gatewood, Donna. USDA-APHIS Center for Veterinary Biologics (CVB). Telephone interview by Ceiridwen Terrill. May 25, 2007.

Gibson, Nancy. "Sensational Geographic." *International Wolf* 18, no.1 (2008): 10–13.

Gogoleva, S. S., et al. "To Bark or Not to Bark? Vocalization in Red Foxes Selected for Tameness or Aggressiveness Toward Humans." *Bioacoustics* 18, no. 2 (2008): 99–132.

Goldfarb, Adam. Issues Specialist, Companion Animals. The Humane Society of the United States. "Wolf Hybrids." E-mail to the author. June 6, 2008.

Goodman, Pat. Research Associate at Indiana's Wolf Park. "Man and Wolf." E-mail to the author. June 12, 2008.

————. Interview by Ceiridwen Terrill. October 4, 2008.

Goodwin, Deborah, et al. "Paedomorphism Affects Agonistic Visual Signals of Domestic Dogs." *Animal Behavior* 53 (1997): 297–304.

————. "♀+♀+♀=☺." *Wolf Park News.* The Quarterly Newsletter of the North American Wildlife Park Foundation 27, no. 1 (2000): 4–5.

Gower, Elaine. Somerset County Humane Officer. Telephone interview by Ceiridwen Terrill. December 31, 2008, January 2, 2009.

Graettinger, Diana. "Man Admits Owning Dangerous Wolfdog. Hybrid Animals Attacked Pets, Bit Neighbor." *Bangor Daily News.* November 11, 2002, B3.

Grandin, Temple. "Behavioral Aspects of Animal Domestication." *Quarterly Review of Biology* 59 (1984): 1–32.

————. "Behavioral Genetics and the Process of Animal Domestication." Ed. *Genetics and the Behavior of Domestic Animals* (San Diego: Academic Press, 1998), 31–66.

Grandin, Temple, and Mark J. Deesing. "Behavioral Genetics and Animal Science." In *Genetics and the Behavior of Domestic Animals,* edited by Temple Grandin (San Diego: Academic Press, 1998), 1–30.

Gross, Edie. "Reputation of Wolf Hybrids at Issue in Wake of Attack." *Largo Times.* May 17, 1999, 1.

Gulevich, R. G., et al. "Effect of Selection for Behavior on Pituitary-Adrenal Axis and Proopiomelanocortin Gene Expression in Silver Foxes (*Vulpes vulpes*)." *Psychology & Behavior* 82 (2004): 513–518.

Haatvedt, Barry. *Wolfzone1.* 2008. http://www.wolfzone1.com/ (accessed June 18, 2009).

Hahn, Martin E., and John C. Wright. "The Influence of Genes on the Social Behavior of Dogs." In *Genetics and the Behavior of Domestic Animals,* edited by Temple Grandin (San Diego: Academic Press, 1998), 299–318.

Hare, B., M. Brown, C. Williamson, and M. Tomasello. "The Domestication of Social Cognition in Dogs." *Science* 298 (2002): 1634–1636.

Hare, Brian. "Wolfdogs." E-mail to the author. December 29, 2006.

Hare, Brian, and Michael Tomasello. "Behavioral Genetics of Dog Cognition: Human-like Social Skills in Dogs Are Heritable and Derived." In *The Dog and Its Genome,* edited by Elaine A. Ostrander, Urs Giger, and Kerstin Lindblad-Toh (New York: Cold Spring Harbor Laboratory, 2006), 497–514.

————. "Human-like Social Skills in Dogs?" *Trends in Cognitive Sciences* 9, no. 9 (2005): 439–444.

Hare, Brian, et al. "Communication of Food Location Between Human and Dog (*Canis familiaris*)." *Evolution of Communication* 2 (1998): 137–159.

————. "Social Cognitive Evolution in Captive Foxes Is a Correlated

By-Product of Experimental Domestication." *Current Biology* 15 (2005): 226–230.

Harri, M., et al. "Behavioural and Physiological Differences Between Silver Foxes Selected and Not Selected for Domestic Behaviour." *Animal Welfare* 12 (2003): 305–314.

Harrington, Fred H., and Cheryl S. Asa. "Wolf Communication." In *Wolves: Behavior, Ecology, and Conservation*, edited by L. David Mech and Luigi Boitani (Chicago: University of Chicago Press, 2003), 66–103.

Heft, Jeremy. Wolf Education & Research Center. "Captive Wolves." E-mail to the author. February 17, 2009.

———. Interview by Ceiridwen Terrill. March 29, 2007.

———. Interview by Ceiridwen Terrill. April 8, 2008.

Horowitz, Alexandra. *Inside of a Dog: What Dogs See, Smell, and Know* (New York: Scribner, 2009).

Hu, R. M., et al. "Gene Expression Profiling in the Human Hypothalamus-Pituitary-Adrenal Axis and Full-Length cDNA Cloning." *Proceedings of the National Academy of Sciences of the United States of America* 97, no. 17 (2000): 9543–9548.

Humane Society of the United States. "Fact Sheet: Wolf Hybrids." 1992. http://www.humanesociety.org/ (accessed December 3, 2003).

———. "Wild Animals: Should They Be Kept as Pets?" September 25, 2009. http://www.humanesociety.org/issues/exotic_pets/facts/ (accessed October 5, 2009).

Humbert, Jonathan. "Pahrump Woman Dies After Attack by 8 Wolf Hybrids." October 5, 2007. www.lasvegasnow.com.

Humphreys, John M. Investigator. Florida Fish & Wildlife Conservation Commission. Summary Narrative. Report #06 SR 43 4851 E, 2006.

Jay, M. T., et al. "Rabies in a Vaccinated Wolf-dog Hybrid." *Journal of the American Veterinary Medical Association* 205, no. 12 (1994): 1729–1732.

Jazin, Elena. "Behaviour Genetics in Canids." In *The Behavioural Biology of Dogs*, edited by P. Jensen (Wallingford, UK: CABI, 2007), 76–90.

———. Interview by Ceiridwen Terrill. 10th Annual Genes, Brains and Behavior Meeting of the International Behavioural and Neural Genetics Society (IBANGS), Portland, Oregon, May 5–9, 2008.

Jenkins, Terry. "Fact Check." E-mail to the author. June 1, 2009.

———. "How High the Price?" *Humane Society of the United States News* (Winter 1991): 18–21.

———. Interview by Ceiridwen Terrill. July 7, 2008.

———. "The Wolfdog Question." E-mail to the author. April 30, 2009.

Jensen, D'Anna. U.S. Department of Agriculture. Animal Welfare Information Center, USDA, ARS, National Agricultural Library. "Number of Wolfdog Hybrids in U.S." E-mail to the author. January 12, 2009.

Jhala, Yadvendradev, and Dinesh Kumar Sharma. "The Ancient Wolves of India." *International Wolf* (2004): 15–18.

Keeler, C., et al. "Melanin, Adrenalin and the Legacy of Fear." *Journal of Heredity* 61 (1970): 81–88.

Kirkness, E. F., et al. "The Dog Genome: Survey Sequencing and Comparative Analysis." *Science* 301 (2003): 1898–1903.

Klinghammer, Erich. "Imprinting and Early Experience: How to Avoid Problems with Tame Animals." *Ethology Series* 8. Battle Ground, Indiana: North American Wildlife Park Foundation, 1994.

Klinghammer, Erich, and Patricia Ann Goodman. "Socialization and Management of Wolves in Captivity." *Man and Wolf,* edited by H. Frank Dordrecht (The Netherlands: Dr. W. Junk Publishers, 1987).

Kobobel, Darlene. Colorado Wolf & Wildlife Center. Interview by Ceiridwen Terrill. August 5, 2007.

Kohane, M. J., and P. A. Parsons. "Domestication: Evolutionary Change Under Stress." *Evolutionary Biology* 23 (1988): 31–48.

Koler-Matznick, J., et al. "The New Guinea Singing Dog: A Living Primitive Dog." In *Dogs Through Time: An Archaeological Perspective*, BAR International Series 889, edited by S. J. Crockford (Oxford: Archaeopress, 2001), 239–247.

———. "An Updated Description of the New Guinea Singing Dog (*Canis hallstromi,* Troughton 1957)." *Journal of Zoology* 261 (2003): 109–118.

Koler-Matznick, Janice. "The Origin of the Dog Revisited." *Anthrozoös* 15, no. 2 (2002): 98–118.

———. Interview by Ceiridwen Terrill. June 1, 2007.

Kramek, Barbara J. "The Hybrids Howl: Legislators Listen—These Animals Aren't Crying Wolf." *Rutgers Law Journal* (1992). http://members.tripod.com/~Methos_5000/wolfleg.html (accessed April 15, 2010).

Kreeger, Terry J. "The Internal Wolf: Physiology, Pathology, and Pharmacology." In *Wolves: Behavior, Ecology, and Conservation*, edited by L. David Mech and Luigi Boitani (Chicago: University of Chicago Press, 2003), 192–217.

Krushinsky, Leonid V. "A Study of the Phenogenetics of Behaviour Characters in Dogs." *Biological Journal* 7, no. 4 (1938): 869–891.

Kubinyi, Eniko, Zsofia Viranyi, and Ádám Miklósi. "Comparative Social Cognition: From Wolf and Dog to Humans." *Comparative Cognition & Behavior Reviews* 2 (2007): 26–46.

Kukekova, Anna V. "Backcrossed F_1 to Tame Parents." E-mail to the author. May 11, 2009.

Kukekova, Anna V., et al. "The Genetics of Domesticated Behavior in Canids: What Can Dogs and Silver Foxes Tell Us about Each Other?" In *The Dog and Its Genome*, edited by Elaine A. Ostrander, Urs Giger, and Kerstin Lindblad-Toh (New York: Cold Spring Harbor Laboratory, 2006), 515–537.

———. "A Marker Set for Construction of a Genetic Map of the Silver Fox (*Vulpes vulpes*)." *Journal of Heredity* 95, no. 3 (2004): 185–194.

———. "Measurement of Segregating Behaviors in Experimental Silver Fox Pedigrees." *Behavioral Genetics* 38 (2008): 185–194.

———. "A Meiotic Linkage Map of the Silver Fox, Aligned and Compared to the Canine Genome." *Genome Research* 17 (2007): 387–399.

Kunert, Charles. Interview by Ceiridwen Terrill. December 18, 2009.

LaBat, Sherrie, and Charlie LaBat. Howling Acres Wolf Sanctuary. Interview by Ceiridwen Terrill. July 7, 2005.

"Lacey Act Amendments of 1981." *Federal Wildlife Laws Handbook,* November 16, 1981. http://wildlifelaw.unm.edu/fedbook/laceyame.html (accessed March 3, 2009).

Leonard, Jennifer. "Wolfdog Hybrids." E-mail to the author. August 3, 2007.

———. "Wolf Hybrids' Gene Expression Patterns." E-mail to the author. April 28, 2008.

Leonard, Jennifer A., and Robert K. Wayne. "From Wild Wolf to Domestic Dog." In *The Dog and Its Genome,* edited by Elaine A. Ostrander, Urs Giger, and Kerstin Lindblad-Toh (New York: Cold Spring Harbor Laboratory, 2006), 95–117.

Leonard, Jennifer, et al. "Ancient DNA Evidence for Old World Origin of New World Dogs." *Science* 298 (2002): 1613–1616.

———. "Megafaunal Extinctions and the Disappearance of a Specialized Wolf Ecomorph." *Current Biology* 17 (2007): 1146–1150.

Lindberg, Julia, et al. "Selection for Tameness Has Changed Brain Gene Expression in Silver Foxes." *Current Biology* 15, no. 22 (2005): R915–916.

———. "Selection for Tameness Modulates the Expression of Heme-Related Genes in Silver Foxes." *Behavioral and Brain Functions* 3, no. 18 (2007). http://www.behavioralandbrainfunctions.com/content/3/1/18 (accessed April 4, 2008).

Lindblad-Toh, Kerstin. "Genetics." E-mail to the author. May 28, 2008.

Lindblad-Toh, Kerstin, et al. "Genome Sequence, Comparative Analysis and Haplotype Structure of the Domestic Dog." *Nature* 438 (2005): 803–819.

Lindsay, Steven R. *Handbook of Applied Dog Behavior and Training,* Vol. 1 (Iowa: Iowa State Universtiy Press, 2000).

Linnell, J. D. C., et al. *The Fear of Wolves: A Review of Wolf Attacks on Humans.* NINA Report: Large Carnivore Initiative for Europe, Ministry of the Environment, 2002.

Lockwood, Randall. "Shelter Agrees to $425,000 Settlement in Fatal Attack by Wolf-dog Hybrid." *Shelter Sense* 14, no. 2 (1991): 7–9.

———. "Wolf Hybrids: Some Facts About a Growing Problem." *Shelter Sense* 15, no. 4 (1992): 9–12.

Loftus, Mace. "Wolf-Hybrids." *The PAWlitically Incorrect Dog Symposium.* DVD. Novato, CA: Tawzer Dog Videos, February 24–25, 2002.

Lonsdale, Steven H. "Attitudes Towards Animals in Ancient Greece." *Greece & Rome,* 2nd ser. 26 Cambridge: Cambridge University Press, no. 2 (1979): 146–159.

Lopez, Barry. *Of Wolves and Men.* 1978. A special twenty-fifth anniversary edition with a new afterword by the author (New York: Scribner, 2004).

Lute, Jill. Zoo Supervisor. Folsom City Zoo Sanctuary. Interview by Ceiridwen Terrill. July 6, 2008.

———. "Rabies Vaccinations." E-mail to the author. January 26, 2009.

MacKay, Barry Kent. "Captive Breeding: To What Purpose?" *Animal Issues* 30 (1999): 1.

"Man Fined for Releasing Wolves." *Wolf News* 9, no. 3 (1991): 8.

Manwell, C., and C. M. A. Baker. "Origin of the Dog: From Wolf or Wild *Canis Familiaris?*" *Speculations in Science and Technology* 6 (1983): 213–224.

Masson, Jeffrey Moussaieff. *The Dog Who Couldn't Stop Loving* (New York: Harper, 2010).

McCain, Joel. *Dog Logic: Companion Obedience, Rapport-Based Training* (New York: Howell Book House, 1992).

McNay, Mark E. "A Review of Evidence and Findings Related to the Death of Kenton Carnegie on November 8, 2005, Near Points North, Saskatchewan." Alaska Department of Fish and Game, Fairbanks, Alaska. May 25, 2007. http://wolfcrossing.org/blog/wp-content/uploads/2007/11/mcnay-conclusions-carnegie-case-edited.pdf (accessed February 4, 2009).

Mech, L. David. "Alpha Status, Dominance and Division of Labor in Wolf Packs." *Canadian Journal of Zoology* 77 (1999): 1196–1203.

———. "Alpha Wolf." E-mail to the author. August 14, 2007.

———. "Diet: Vegetable Matter." E-mail to the author. March 14, 2008.

———. Resolution pertaining to wolfdog hybrids. IUCN Wolf Specialist Group. April 24, 1990.

———. "Whatever Happened to the Term 'Alpha Wolf'?" *International Wolf* 18, no. 4 (2008): 4–8.

———. *The Wolf: The Ecology and Behavior of an Endangered Species* (New York: Natural History Press, 1970).

Mech, L. David, and Luigi Boitani. "Wolf Social Ecology." In *Wolves: Behavior, Ecology, and Conservation,* edited by L. David Mech and Luigi Boitani (Chicago: University of Chicago Press, 2003), 1–34.

Meltzer, Erica. "Wolf-dog Ordinance Would Limit Breeding." *Arizona Daily Star,* August 21, 2006, B1.

Metallinos, D. L. "Canine Molecular Genetic Testing." *The Veterinary Clinics of North America: Small Animal Practice* 31, no. 2 (2001): 421–429.

Miklósi, Ádám. *Dog: Behavior, Evolution, and Cognition* (Oxford: Oxford University Press, 2007).

———. "Human-Animal Interactions and Social Cognition in Dogs." In *The Behavioural Biology of Dogs*, edited by P. Jensen (Wallingford, UK: CABI, 2007), 207–222.

———. "Wolf-dog Hybrids." E-mail to the author. October 19, 2008.

Miklósi, Ádám, and K. Soporoni. "A Comparative Analysis of Animals' Understanding of the Human Pointing Gesture." *Animal Cognition* 9 (2006): 81–93.

Miklósi, Ádám, et al. "A Simple Reason for a Big Difference: Wolves Do Not Look Back at Humans, but Dogs Do." *Current Biology* 13 (2003): 763–766.

———. "Use of Experimenter-Given Cues in Dogs." *Animal Cognition* 1 (1998): 113–121.

Miles, Kim. "Of Wolves & Dogs: Dispelling the Myths." *Florida Lupine News* 2, no. 3 (Fall 2000): 1, 4–5.

Milstein, Michael. "Carcass Could Be That of a Wolf." *The Oregonian*, October 20, 2000.

———. "Genetic Tests Show Animal Shot Dead in Eastern Oregon was a Wild Wolf." *The Oregonian*, February 3, 2001.

———. "Idaho Wolf Spotted in Northeast Oregon." *The Oregonian,* January 25, 2008.

Monks of New Skete. *How to Be Your Dog's Best Friend.* 1978. Completely revised and updated second edition (New York: Little, Brown and Company, 2002).

Moore, Jill, and Monty Sloan. "On Selection, Traits and Inheritance." March 7, 2007. www.wolfpark.org.

Morell, Virginia. "Minds of Their Own: Animals Are Smarter Than You Think." *National Geographic* 231, no. 3 (2008): 36–61.

———. "The Origin of Dogs: Running with the Wolves." *Science* 276, no. 5319 (1997): 1647–1648.

Moskowitz, Clara. "Wolves Beat Dogs on Logic Test." LiveScience. September 3, 2009. www.livescience.com (accessed October 9, 2009).

Motter, Gale. Wolf Park. "Rabies Vaccinations." E-mail to the author. January 29, 2009.

Myers, Steve. "Just a Memory: Michael Landers, 4, Probably Won't Suffer Lasting Effects from Attack by Wolf-dog." *Mail Tribune,* June 16, 1982.

———. "Tests Determine Wolf-dog Not Rabid." *Mail Tribune*, April 2, 1982.

———. "Wolf-dog Destroyed; Tests Set." *Mail Tribune*, March 31, 1982.

———. "Wolf-dog Suspected of Attack on EP Child." *Mail Tribune*, March 29, 1982.

———. "Wolf-dog That Bit Boy to Be Destroyed." *Mail Tribune*, March 30, 1982.

"Mystery Beast Ravages Flocks of Montana Sheep," *USA Today*, May 22, 2006, A3.

National Animal Control Association. "Wolf Dog Hybrids: Breeders vs. Behaviorists." *National Animal Control Association News* 4, no. 5 (1991): 4–7.

National Association of State Public Health Veterinarians, Inc. "Compendium of Animal Rabies Prevention and Control," 2001.

———. (NASPHV). "Compendium of Animal Rabies Prevention and Control," 2005.

National Wolfdog Alliance. "Current State Regulations as They Pertain to Wolves and Wolfdogs." 2002. http://wolfdogalliance.org/legislation/statelaws.html (accessed February 12, 2007).

"New Wolf-Dog Rules Not Based on Attack," *Milwaukee Sentinel*, January 19, 1995.

"November 18th Necropsy Report on One of the Wolves." *Canadian Cooperative Wildlife Health Center*. http://www.cbc.ca/sask/features/wolves/images/wolves1-2.pdf (accessed February 4, 2009).

Nowak, Ronald M. "Wolf Evolution and Taxonomy." In *Wolves: Behavior, Ecology, and Conservation*, edited by L. David and Luigi Boitani (Chicago: University of Chicago Press, 2003), 239–258.

Olsen, Stanley J. "Early Domestic Dogs in North American and Their Origins." *Journal of Field Archaeology* 1, no. 3/4 (1974): 343–345.

———. *Origins of the Domestic Dog: The Fossil Record* (Tucson, AZ: University of Arizona Press, 1985).

Oregon Department of Fish and Wildlife. "Draft Updated Oregon Wolf Conservation and Management Plan." September 2010. http://www.dfw.state.or.us/agency/commission/minutes/10/10_oct/Exhibit%20E_Attachment%204_Draft%20Plan.pdf (accessed October 15, 2010).

Ostrander, Elaine. "Wolves and Dogs." E-mail to the author. January 3, 2007.

Ostrander, Elaine A., Urs Giger, and Kerstin Lindblad-Toh, eds. *The Dog and Its Genome* (New York: Cold Spring Harbor Laboratory Press, 2006).

Packard, Jane. "Wolf Behavior: Reproductive, Social, and Intelligent." In *Wolves: Behavior, Ecology, and Conservation*, edited by L. David Mech and Luigi Boitani (Chicago: University of Chicago Press, 2003), 35–65.

Pang, Jun-Feng, et al. "mtDNA Data Indicate a Single Origin for Dogs South of the Yangtze River, Less Than 16,300 Years Ago, from Numerous Wolves." *Molecular Biology and Evolution* 26, no. 12 (2009): 2849–2864.

Parker, Heidi, and Elaine Ostrander. "Canine Genomics and Genetics: Running with the Pack." *Genetics* 1, no. 5 (2005): 507–513.

Parker, Heidi, et al. "Genetic Structure of the Purebred Domestic Dog." *Science* 304, no. 5674 (2004): 1160–1164.

Pesce, Carolyn. "Hybrid Wolves: Dangerous Breed; Fatalities Spur Call for Tougher Laws on Canines," *USA Today*, May 4, 1990.

Peterson, Rolf O., and Paolo Ciucci. "The Wolf as a Carnivore." In *Wolves:*

BIBLIOGRAPHY

Behavior, Ecology, and Conservation, edited by L. David Mech and Luigi Boitani (Chicago: University of Chicago Press, 2003), 104–130.

Peterson, Rolf O., Amy K. Jacobs, Thomas D. Drummer, L. David Mech, and Douglas W. Smith. "Leadership Behavior in Relation to Dominance and Reproductive Status in Gray Wolves, *Canis lupus*." *Canadian Journal of Zoology* 80 (2002): 1405–1412.

Pierotti, Ray. "Dogs & Wolves." *The PAWlitically Incorrect Dog Symposium.* DVD. Novato, CA: Tawzer Dog Videos, February 24–25, 2002.

Popova, N. K. "The Role of Brain Serotonin in the Expression of Genetically Determined Defensive Behavior." *Russian Journal of Genetics* 40, no. 6 (2004): 624–630.

Popova, N. K., et al. "Evidence for the Involvement of Central Serotonin in Mechanism of Domestication of Silver Foxes." *Pharmacology Biochemistry & Behavior* 40 (1991): 751–756.

Prendergast, Dorothy, ed. *Above Reproach: A Guide for Wolf Hybrid Owners* (Gallup, New Mexico: Rudelhaus Enterprises, 1996).

———. *The Wolf Hybrid* (Gallup, New Mexico: Rudelhaus Enterprises, 1984).

Price, E. O. "Behavioral Development in Animals Undergoing Domestication." *Applied Animal Behaviour Science* 65 (1999): 245–271.

Pryor, Karen. *Don't Shoot the Dog! The New Art of Teaching and Training* (New York: Bantam Books, 1984, 1999).

Purdy, Chris. "Wolves Drawn to Mine's Landfill." *Star Phoenix.* October 31, 2007. http://www.canada.com/saskatoonstarphoenix/news/third_page/story.html?id=053f0ab8-3a19-46f6-9100-8d37a7cf0cb4 (accessed February 4, 2009).

Reed, Patricia, and Kelly Reed. Eagle Tail Mountain Wolf Sanctuary. Interview by Ceiridwen Terrill. April 23, 2007.

Renee, Stormy. "Wolfdogs." E-mail to the author. January 14, 2009.

Robbins, Jim. "Livestock Predator Still a Mystery, Two Months After Its Death," *New York Times,* December 30, 2006, A16.

Sacks, J. J., et al. "Breeds of Dogs Involved in Fatal Human Attacks in the United States, 1979–1998. *Journal of the American Medical Association* 217 (2000): 836–840.

———. "Dog Bite-Related Fatalities from 1979–1988." *Journal of the American Medical Association* 262, no. 11 (1989): 1489–92.

———. "Fatal Dog Attacks, 1989–1994." *Pediatrics* 97 (1996): 891–895.

Saetre, Peter, et al. "The Genetic Contribution to Canine Personality." *Genes, Brain and Behavior* 5 (2006): 240–248.

———. "From Wild Wolf to Domestic Dog: Gene Expression Changes in the Brain." *Molecular Brain Research* 126 (2004): 198–206.

Savolainen, Peter. "mtDNA Studies of the Origin of Dogs." In *The Dog and Its Genome,* edited by Elaine A. Ostrander, Urs Giger, and Kerstin Lindblad-Toh (New York: Cold Spring Harbor Laboratory, 2006), 119–140.

Savolainen, Peter, et al. "Genetic Evidence for an East Asian Origin of the Domestic Dog." *Science* 298 (2002): 1610–1613.

Schenkel, Rudolph. "Submission: It's Features and Function in the Wolf and Dog." *American Zoologist* 7 (1967): 319–329.

Schmidt, Lori. Wolf Curator. International Wolf Center. "Captive Grays." E-mail to the author. February 13, 2009.

———. "Rabies Vaccinations." E-mail to the author. January 26, 2009.

———. "Wolfdogs." E-mail to the author. December 2, 2006.

———. "Wolf Pups." E-mail to the author. July 14, 2008.

Scholfield, Dan. Technical Information Specialist. U.S. Department of Agriculture, ARS, NAL, Animal Welfare Information Center. "Number of Wolfdog Hybrids in U.S." E-mail to the author. January 12, 2009.

Scott, John Paul, and John L. Fuller. *Genetics and the Social Behavior of the Dog* (Chicago: University of Chicago Press, 1965).

Sharma, Dinesha K., et al. "Ancient Wolf Lineages in India." *Proceedings of the Royal Society of London* B (Suppl.) 271 (2004): S1–S4.

Shireman, Michelle. Oregon Zoo. "Rabies Vaccinations." E-mail to the author. January 28, 2009.

Siino, Betsy. "Crossing the Line." American Society for the Prevention of Cruelty to Animals. *Animal Watch* (2000): 22–29.

———. "Wolf-dog Hybrids: The New Fad." American Humane Association. *Advocate.* Spring 1991.

Sime, Carolyn. Wolf Coordinator for Montana Fish, Wildlife and Parks. Interview by Ceiridwen Terrill. April 8, 2008.

Simpson, Dora. Cottonwood Kennel. Interview by Ceiridwen Terrill. June 9, 2009.

———. "More of Our Dogs." E-mail to author. January 20, 2009.

———. "So, You Want to Become a Wolfdog Breeder." www.cottonwoodz .com (accessed October 16, 2008).

———. Telephone interview by Ceiridwen Terrill. October 18, 2008.

Sims, Margaret "Cookie." Interview by Ceiridwen Terrill. June 1, 2007.

Singh, M., and H. N. Kumara. "Distribution, Status and Conservation of Indian Gray Wolf (*Canis lupus pallipes*) in Karnataka, India." *Journal of Zoology* 270 (2006): 164–169.

Sloan, Monty. Wolf Park. "Rabies Vaccinations." E-mail to the author. January 30, 2009.

———. Interview by Ceiridwen Terrill. October 4, 2008.

Soproni, Krisztina, Ádám Miklósi, and József Topál. "Comprehension of Human Communicative Signs in Pet Dogs (*Canis familiaris*)." *Journal of Comparative Psychology* 115, no. 2 (2001): 122–126.

Spencer, Wendy. Wolf Haven International. "Captive Breeding." E-mail to the author. February 14, 2009.

———. "Rabies Vaccinations." E-mail to the author. January 29, 2009.

———. Interview by Ceiridwen Terrill. June 8, 2007.

Stark, Mike. "Tests Show Vexing Predator was Domestic Wolf." *Billings Gazette,* March 1, 2007.

Straughan, Dyan. Telephone Interview by Ceiridwen Terrill. February 19, 2008.

———. Interview by Ceiridwen Terrill. June 2, 2007.

Svartberg, Kenth. "Individual Differences in Behaviour—Dog Personality." In *Behavioural Biology of Dogs*, edited by P. Jensen (Wallingford, UK: CABI, 2007), 182–206.

Sykes, Wally. Interview by Ceiridwen Terrill. March 7, 2007.

———. Interview by Ceiridwen Terrill. April 8, 2008.

Thomas, Elizabeth Marshall. *The Hidden Life of Dogs* (New York: Simon & Schuster, 1993).

Thompson, Courtenay. "Wolf Tests Oregon's Welcome." *The Oregonian,* June 3, 1999.

Thompson, Courtenay, and Richard Cockle. "Wild Wolf Found Dead Near Baker City." *The Oregonian,* June 2, 2000.

Tomasello, Michael, and Juliane Kaminski. "Like Infant, Like Dog." *Science* 4 (2009): 1213–1214.

Topál, József, et al. "Attachment to Humans: A Comparative Study on Hand-reared Wolves and Differently Socialized Dog Puppies." *Animal Behaviour* 70 (2005): 1367–1375.

———. "Differential Sensitivity to Human Communication in Dogs, Wolves, and Human Infants." *Science* 4 (2009): 1269–1272.

Trut, L. N., et al. "Change in the Pituitary-Adrenal Function of Silver Foxes During Selection According to Behavior." *Genetika* 8 (1974): 585–591.

———. "An Experiment on Fox Domestication and Debatable Issues of Evolution of the Dog." *Genetika* 40 (2004): 794–807.

Trut, Lyudmila. "Early Canid Domestication: The Farm-Fox Experiment." *American Scientist* 87 (1999): 160–169.

———. "Experimental Studies of Early Canid Domestication." In *The Genetics of the Dog*, edited by A. Ruvinsky and J. Sampson (Wallingford, UK: CABI, 2001), 15–43.

———. "Fox Experiments." E-mail to the author. May 25, 2008.

———. Interviews by Ceiridwen Terrill. September 7–12, 2009.

Trut, Lyudmila, Irina Oskina, and Anastāsiya Kharlamova. "Animal Evolution During Domestication: The Domesticated Fox as a Model." *BioEssays* 31, no. 3 (2009): 349–360.

Tucker, Pat, and Bruce Weide. *Can You Turn a Wolf into a Dog?: Commonly Asked Questions about Wolves and Hybrids in Captivity.* Booklet (Hamilton, Montana: Wild Sentry, 1998).

Tulleners, Lois. White Wolf Sanctuary. Interview by Ceiridwen Terrill. June 24, 2005.

Udell, Monique A. R., et al. "Wolves Outperform Dogs in Following Human Social Cues." *Animal Behavior* 76 (2008): 1767–1773.

United States American Wolfdog Association. "Standard of the American Wolfdog." October 1996. http://www.canineworld.com/usawa/ BreedStandard.htm (accessed September 30, 2007).

United States Department of Agriculture. Animal and Plant Health Inspection Service. "Licensing and Registration Under the Animal Welfare Act: Guidelines for Dealers, Exhibitors, Transporters, and Researchers." 1992. http://www.nal.usda.gov/awic/pubs/IACUC/law.htm (accessed March 3, 2009).

———. "Questions and Answers on Animal Care's Regulation of Commercial Animal Dealers." April 2008. www.aphis.usda.gov/animal-welfare (accessed March 3, 2009).

———. Virus-Serum-Toxin Act http://www.aphis.usda.gov/vs/cvb/PDFs/vsta .pdf (accessed March 23, 2009).

United States Environmental Protection Agency. "Regulations to Implement the Captive Wildlife Safety Act." *Federal Register* 72, no. 158 (2007): 45938–45947.

U.S. Fish and Wildlife Service. "Gray Wolf Population and Range in the United States." September 2010. http://www.fws.gov/midwest/wolf/ aboutwolves/popandrange.htm (accessed October 10, 2010).

U.S. Fish and Wildlife Service. Office of Law Enforcement. *Captive Wildlife Safety Act.* December 19, 2003. http://www.fws.gov/le/pdffiles/ PL108-191_CWSA.pdf (accessed March 3, 2009).

Vas, Judit, et al. "A Friend or an Enemy? Dogs' Reaction to an Unfamiliar Person Showing Behavioural Cues of Threat and Friendliness at Different Times." *Applied Animal Behaviour Science* 94 (2005): 99–115.

Verardi, A., V. Lucchini, and E. Randi. "Detecting Introgressive Hybridization Between Free-Ranging Domestic Dogs and Wild Wolves (*Canis lupus*) by Admixture Linkage Disequilibrum Analysis." *Molecular Ecology* 15 (2006): 2845–2855.

Verginelli, F., et al. "Mitochondrial DNA from Prehistoric Canids Highlights Relationships Between Dogs and South-East European Wolves." *Molecular Biology and Evolution* 22.12 (2005): 2541–2551.

———. "The Origins of Dogs: Archaeozoology, Genetics, and Ancient DNA." *Medicina nei Secoli* 18, no. 3 (2006): 741–54.

"Vermont Toddler Attacked by Wolf-Hybrid Dies." *Boston Globe*, December 11, 1993, 16.

Vilà, Carles, and Jennifer Leonard. "Origin of Dog Breed Diversity." In *Behavioural Biology of Dogs*, edited by P. Jensen (Wallingford, UK: CABI, 2007), 38–58.

Vilà, Carles, J. Maldonado, and R. K. Wayne. "Phylogenetic Relationships,

Evolution, and Genetic Diversity of the Domestic Dog." *Journal of Heredity* 90 (1999): 71–77.

Vilà, Carles, and Robert K. Wayne. "Hybridization Between Wolves and Dogs." *Conservation Biology* 13 (1999): 195–198.

Vilà, Carles, et al. "Combined Use of Maternal, Paternal and Bi-Parental Genetic Markers for the Identification of Wolf-Dog Hybrids." *Heredity* 90 (2003): 17–24.

———. "Mitochondrial DNA Phylogeography and Population History of the Grey Wolf *Canis lupus*." *Molecular Ecology* 8 (1999): 2089–2103.

———. "Multiple and Ancient Origins of the Domestic Dog." *Science* 276 (1997): 1687–1689.

Virányi, Z., et al. "Comprehension of Human Pointing Gestures in Young Human-Reared Wolves (*Canis lupus*) and Dogs (*Canis familiaris*)." *Animal Cognition* 11 (2008): 373–387.

———. "Dogs Respond Appropriately to Cues of Humans' Attentional Focus." *Behaviorial Processes* 66 (2004): 161–172.

vonHoldt, Bridgett. Interview by Ceiridwen Terrill. April 25, 2007.

———. "Wolves and Dogs." E-mail to the author. July 17, 2007.

———. "Wolves and Dogs." E-mail to the author. October 6, 2007.

vonHoldt, Bridgett, et al. "Genome-Wide SNP and Haplotype Analyses Reveal a Rich History Underlying Dog Domestication." *Nature,* advance online publication March 17, 2010. doi:10.1038/nature08837.

Wadler, Joyce. "My Monkey, My Self." *New York Times*, February 25, 2009.

Washoe County Animal Ordinances. Washoe County Regional Animal Services. February 9, 2008. http://www.co.washoe.nv.us/repository/files/44/chapter_55_with_ord_1269.pdf.

Watson, Paula. Wolfwood. Interview by Ceiridwen Terrill. August 8, 2007.

Wayne, Robert K. "Cranial Morphology of Domestic and Wild Canids: The Influence of Development on Morphological Change." *Journal of Morphology* 187 (1986): 301–319.

———. "Molecular Evolution of the Dog Family." *Trends in Genetics* 9, no. 6 (1993): 218–224.

———. "Wolves and Dogs." E-mail to the author. June 13, 2007.

Wayne, R. K., and S. J. O'Brien. "Allozyme Divergence Within the Canidae." *Systematic Zoology* 36 (1987): 339–355.

Wayne, R. K., B. Van Valkenburgh, and S. J. O'Brien. "Molecular Distance and Divergence Time in Carnivores and Primates." *Molecular & Biological Evolution* 8, no. 3 (1991): 297–319.

Wayne, R. K., et al. "Mitochondrial DNA Variability of the Gray Wolf: Genetic Consequences of Population Decline and Habitat Fragmentation." *Conservation Biology* 6 (1992): 559–569.

Wayne, Robert K., and Elaine A. Ostrander. "Origin, Genetic Diversity, and

Genome Structure of the Domestic Dog." *BioEssays* 21 (1999): 247–257.

Weber, Kent. Mission: Wolf. Interview by Ceiridwen Terrill. August 7, 2007.

West, Captain John D. Division of Law Enforcement. Florida Fish & Wildlife Conservation Commission. "Mock Case." E-mail to the author. June 9, 2009.

Whitford, Gail. "Wolfdogs." E-mail to the author. October 14, 2008.

Wilde, Nicole. *Living with Wolfdogs: An Everyday Guide to a Lifetime Companionship* (Santa Clarita, CA: Phantom Publishing, 1998).

———. *Wolfdogs A–Z: Behavior, Training & More* (Santa Clarita, CA: Phantom Publishing, 2000).

Willems, Robert A., DVM. "The Wolf-Dog Hybrid: An Overview of a Controversial Animal." Animal Welfare Information Center Newsletter 5, no. 4 (1994/1995). http://www.nal.usda.gov/awic/newsletters/v5n4/5n4wille.htm (accessed June 18, 2005).

Wilson, D. E., and D. M. Reeder, eds. *Mammal Species of the World: A Taxonomic and Geographic Reference*, 2nd ed. (Washington, D.C.: Smithsonian Institution Press, 1993).

"Wolfdogs Arouse Fear—and Affection." *Toronto Star,* August 10, 1991, F6.

Woolpy, J. H., and B. E. Ginsburg. "Wolf Socialization: A Study of Temperament in a Wild Social Species." *American Zoologist* 7, no. 2 (1967): 357–363.

Yin, S. "Dominance Versus Leadership in Dog Training." *Compendium Continuing Education for the Practicing Veterinarian* 29 (2007): 414–32.

———. "Dominance vs. Unruly Behavior." *Low Stress Handling, Restraint and Behavior Modification of Dogs and Cats* (Davis, CA: CattleDog Publishing, 2009), 52–73.

Yordi, Rob. "Training Gray Wolves (*Canis lupus*) as Conservation Ambassadors at Busch Gardens Williamsburg." 19th Annual North American Wolf Conference, Flagstaff, Arizona. April 25, 2007.

Zawistowski, Stephen. Executive Vice President, National Programs and Science Advisor, ASPCA. "Wolfdog Hybrids." E-mail to the author. May 5, 2008.

———. "Wolfdogs." E-mail to the author. June 4, 2007.

About the Author

Ceiridwen Terrill is an associate professor at Concordia University in Portland, Oregon, where she teaches environmental journalism and science writing. When she's not writing and teaching, she's sailing the San Juan Islands, jumping horses, topping out on Mount Hood, free-climbing through the narrow slot canyons of Utah, or backpacking with Argos, her 100% pure American street dog. To see photos and video from *Part Wild* and to learn more about Ceiridwen Terrill's work, visit www.myurbanwild.com. Follow Ceiridwen on Twitter @myurbanwild.